W9-DDO-580

COLUMBIA UNIVERSITY STUDIES IN ENGLISH AND COMPARATIVE LITERATURE

THE BACKGROUND OF GRAY'S "ELEGY"

THE BACKGROUND OF GRAY'S ELEGY

A STUDY IN THE TASTE FOR MELANCHOLY POETRY

1700-1751

By
AMY LOUISE REED, Ph.D.
PROFESSOR OF ENGLISH, VASSAR COLLEGE

NEW YORK
RUSSELL & RUSSELL · INC
1962

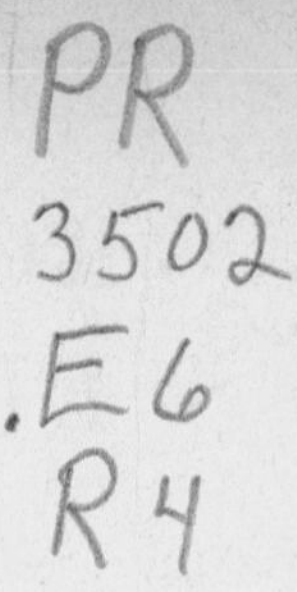

REISSUED, 1962, BY RUSSELL & RUSSELL, INC.
L. C. CATALOG CARD NO: 62—13846

PRINTED IN THE UNITED STATES OF AMERICA

PREFACE

This book is the belated consequence of a slight study of eighteenth century melancholy undertaken some years ago at Yale in a class of Professor Tinker's, but I owe to Professor E. H. Wright of Columbia the suggestion that the subject would prove fruitful for further investigation. In fact, the poetry of melancholy in English is so abundant, the varieties of it which I have been obliged to neglect are so many and so fascinating, I am now aware that it offers material not for one volume but for several. The news is, therefore, welcome that at least one such is now under way, a study of romantic melancholy.[1]

In my own work, I was at first simply looking for the earliest manifestations of romantic melancholy. I found to my surprise that the more closely I inspected " romantic beginnings " such as, for instance, Parnell's *Night Piece on Death,* the more readily they resolved themselves into elements thoroughly familiar to readers of the preceding century, or even earlier, and the less they seemed to presage a new literary era. I came at last to the conclusion that up to the middle of the eighteenth century, the literature of melancholy included nothing which could be accurately described as romantic in the modern sense of that adjective, however influential such poems as Young's *Night Thoughts,* Blair's *Grave* and Gray's *Elegy* were later to become in the romantic movement.

[1] By H. H. Clark, Harvard. See *Mod. Lang. Notes* for March and April, 1924.

This conclusion — which now seems to me quite natural rather than surprising — is, I know, merely an opinion, not capable of actual proof, and there may be many students to differ with me. The following pages collect and describe the evidence on which that opinion is based. There is much more material of the same character; almost any collection of miscellaneous seventeenth and eighteenth century pamphlets will yield several melancholy poems or prose pieces. But there is a point beyond which it seemed useless to confirm my statements further by quoting or listing publications of feeble literary quality. Except in a few cases, I have thought it unnecessary to the argument to seek out first editions.

Unfortunately for me, this book was completed in practically its present shape almost a year before the appearance of Professor R. D. Havens's illuminating study of *The Influence of Milton.* I am painfully conscious that in the light of such work as his, my numerous references to Milton's influence must seem lamentably superficial. But I have thought best to let them stand as they were written, without peppering my pages with footnote references to his monumental volume, which must be already familiar to anyone likely to be interested in my subject. I regret that a few of my sentences which resemble his in idea and phrasing are not evidence of any debt to him, for could I have read his book before beginning mine, I could have worked faster and to better purpose.

My chief indebtedness is to Professor W. P. Trent of Columbia University, who first, many years ago, introduced me to the delights of the eighteenth century, and under whose advice this study has been prepared for the press. With great patience and kindness, Professor Trent has read my manuscript at two different stages, the entire galley and part of the page proof, and has placed at my service the resources of his scholarship. To Professor E. H. Wright I am also very grateful for reading manuscript and proof and for criticism of much acumen. My friend, Professor Laura J. Wylie of Vassar College, has done me the favor to read the manuscript and to point out lacunae in the treatment, not all of which I have been able to fill satisfactorily. But none of my critics should be held responsible for mistakes, blindnesses, or inadequate statements still to be found in the work.

I wish, finally, to express my appreciation of the many courtesies extended to me as a reader by the New York Public Library and the libraries of Columbia, Yale, and Harvard Universities and of Vassar College.

A. L. R.

VASSAR COLLEGE
Poughkeepsie, New York.

CONTENTS

THE BACKGROUND OF GRAY'S "ELEGY"

CHAPTER I

THE SEVENTEENTH CENTURY DEFINITION OF MELANCHOLY

SADNESS is so characteristically the mood of the greatest English lyrists, from the days of *The Wanderer* and *The Seafarer* to *August 1914*, that any historic study of English poetry must necessarily involve some recognition of the habitual melancholy of the English poets, its causes and its chosen means of expression. Such attention has been very fully given in the case of certain individual poets such as Byron or Cowper, and of some literary periods such as the Old English or that of the Romantic Movement. The phenomenon has been somewhat neglected on the other hand in the case of such an interesting period as the English Renaissance, while in the literary history of the early eighteenth century it has invariably received only cursory treatment as a harbinger of romanticism. A more detailed study of the melancholy of that half century will, I believe, show that it had a special character of its own, very curious and interesting and different in many respects from "romantic melancholy."

As a contribution to such a detailed study, these pages endeavor to explain the *furore* created by Gray's *Elegy* in 1751 on the theory that the poem came before its public not as a presentation of novel thought but as the perfectly adequate expression of a widespread popular feeling, the "melancholy" of the first half of the eighteenth century. This mood, I hope to make clear, was partly an implication in the classic and in the English literary tradition, partly the result of the political and religious upheavals of the seventeenth century, and partly the by-product of contemporary philosophic and scientific thought. It was a sentiment widely diffused among everyday, average people, and had been repeatedly the subject of poetical effusions by authors who had found the largest popular audience. Against such a background of melancholy literature, Gray's skilful synthesis of the mood and thought of the moment stood out with peculiar effectiveness, and was therefore destined both to find instant popularity and to become a new center of influence radiating melancholy lyricism throughout the second half of the century.

Wide as is the appeal of the *Elegy* today, we miss its full meaning because we are more or less unaware of the connotations of the word "melancholy" in 1751. Gray himself, always a fastidious artist in diction, must have been conscious, as he wrote the line,

> And Melancholy mark'd him for her own,

that he was using a term whose import had been the center of battles medical, literary, philosophic, and ethical, within his own lifetime. In fact, the entire poem is, as this book attempts to explain, a sort of challenge to opposing parties and a defense of melancholy. To understand Gray's position, we must go back to the year 1700 and even farther, back to the seventeenth century meaning of the word.

In the search for a definition, the lack of dictionaries is more than made up for by the encyclopedic character of Burton's *Anatomy of Melancholy*, first published in 1621. Not only do all contemporary uses of the word merely confirm and illustrate Burton's analysis, but also we find that his work continued to be issued in new editions until the last quarter of the century, an indication that its opinions were still well received.[1]

Before reaching a definition, Burton, in a preliminary essay, explains the importance of the subject and his own point of view. The existence of melancholy is, he tells us, a phenomenon to be taken seriously, for it is a disease, "a common infirmity of body and soul," dangerous to individuals and to states. (Vol. I, p. 52.) He writes of it as a divine, not as a physician, but, as he remarks, "who knows not what an agreement there is betwixt these two professions?" His purpose is twofold, to relieve his own dark mood and to show others the way out of gloom. "I write of melancholy, by being busy to avoid melancholy. . . . (Vol. I, p. 32.) Something I can speak out of experience. . . . I would help others out of a fellow feeling." (Vol. I, p. 34.) There is great need for such a work, he says, because of "the generality of the disease, the necessity of the cure, and the . . . common good that will arise to all men by the knowledge of it. . . . And I doubt not but that in the end you will say with me, that to anatomize this humour aright . . . is as great a task, as to . . . find out the quadrature of a circle and . . . as great trouble as to perfect the motion of Mars and Mercury . . . or to rectify the Gregorian *Kalendar*." (Vol. I, pp. 53, 54.)

Using the name of Democritus Junior, he explains his choice of pseudonym and describes his special qualifications for his task, which are those of a scientific observer, a scholar, and a philosopher. The Democritus whose name

[1] The British Museum has 2d ed. 1624, 3d 1628, 4th 1632, 5th 1638, 6th 1652, 7th 1660, 8th 1676, all at Oxford. Then no more until the 9th ed. corr. 1800, 2 vols. My quotations are from *The Anatomy of Melancholy* . . . by Democritus Junior. New ed. by Democritus Minor. Boston, 1859. 3 vols.

he has borrowed was, he tells us, "a little wearish old man, very melancholy by nature, averse from company in his latter days," when "*hortulo sibi cellulam seligens, ibique seipsum includens, vixit solitarius.*" He was "a famous philosopher in his age, *coævus* with Socrates . . . wrote many excellent works, a great divine . . . an expert physician, a politician, an excellent mathematician." He draws a parallel with his own way of life as a fellow of Oxford and holder of certain ecclesiastical positions in the neighborhood. "I have lived a silent, sedentary, solitary, private life, *mihi et musis* in the University"—for there is poetry in the *Anatomy,* both translated and original—"to learn wisdom . . . penned up most part in my study. . . . For thirty years I have continued a scholar. . . ." But he had also a great desire "not to be a slave of one science . . . as most do, but to rove abroad . . . to have an oar in every man's boat, to taste of every dish, and sip of every cup." To such a nature, travel, except on a map, is unnecessary. Therefore, writes Democritus Junior, "Though I live still a college student, as Democritus in his garden, and lead a monastic life *ipse mihi theatrum,* sequestered from those tumults and troubles of the world, *et, tanquam in specula positus* . . . in some high place above you all . . . I hear and see what is done abroad . . . as a mere spectator of other men's fortunes and adventures." Nevertheless he did occasionally walk abroad himself for his recreation, and make some little observation of life at first hand "with mingled mirth and spleen." As the ancient Democritus had written a book on "melancholy and madness," which was subsequently lost, it occurred to this intellectual inheritor of his tastes and temper to "revive, continue, and finish" the same subject. (Vol. I, pp. 26–31.)

If the reader doubt the need of such a work, Democritus Junior will "desire him to make a brief survey of the world. . . . Thou shalt soon perceive that all the world is mad, that it is melancholy, dotes," which he proceeds to prove by illustration, in language distantly parallel to Shakespeare's *Sonnet 66,* and sometimes quoting directly from *Ecclesiastes.* " Never so much cause of laughter as now, never so many fools and madmen." What would the ancient Democritus have said, cries this pessimist, had he been alive to see " our religious madness," of which the one extreme is Romanism, the other, Protestant schism, " so many bloody battles for no real cause, such homage paid to rank and wealth, so many saints in poverty and neglect! so many lawyers, so little justice! such hypocrisy! And yet men know not that they are mad. . . . Also kingdoms, provinces, families are melancholy as well as private men." Hereupon he arraigns the general state of civilization in contemporary England, and ends his preface with a sort of Utopian sketch of the nation as it might be, if only it could rid itself of melancholy.

He sets aside, as not the true melancholy, all merely transitory sadness or depression such as comes to every man in sickness, fear, grief, or passion, for " melancholy in this sense is the character of mortality." Even such events as the death of friends, the loss of fortune, the shock of terror, or the misfortune of imprisonment, he calls merely " adventitious causes," for the effect of them passes away, they bring on not the settled melancholy, the abnormal, diseased state, but only temporary, natural sorrow. On the contrary, " this melancholy of which we are to treat is a habit, a settled humor." (Vol. I, pp. 191–195.) Its physical cause is an excess of black choler, but this physical cause may have, as we shall presently see, some antecedent, non-physical cause, and its symptoms are certain effects upon the disposition.

Here, at last, we reach his definition. (Vol. I, p. 225.) In common parlance, melancholy is defined, says Burton, as "a kind of dotage without a fever, having for [its] ordinary companions, fear and sadness, without any apparent occasion." The last four words are the essence of the matter; melancholy is a general depression of spirits apparently causeless, or else out of proportion to its immediate cause. Burton notes that it always deranges "some one principal faculty of the mind, as imagination, or reason"; also, that to some of its victims it is not painful but "most pleasant." The modern word most nearly corresponding is "melancholia," but this is for us a distinctly medical term, while in Burton's time the word was so freely used by "the common sort" as to have lost its technical character. It was applied as noun or adjective to describe a disease apparently as familiar as influenza nowadays,[2] and as varied in its outcome.

About two thirds of the *Anatomy* is occupied with a discussion of the causes, symptoms, and cures of this disease. So far as these are physiological, they are no longer of interest to us, partly because of the enormous change in the science of medicine in the past two hundred years, partly because these aspects of melancholy appeared but little in poetry. Certain other portions of the discussion, however, we must repeat at some length, because they reappear so often in the general literature of the next hundred and fifty years.

[2] For further definitions and illustrations, see Murray's *New Eng. Dict.*, Johnson's *Dictionary*, 1755, with their examples, and Bartlett's *Concordance to Shakespeare*, 1894, under "melancholy."

Burton distinguishes three varieties of melancholy: head melancholy, or madness, melancholy of the whole body, and hypochondriacal melancholy, which, from the description, I take to be synonymous with that digestive disorder which is today called jaundice. But the classification which he thus sets up is, as he himself observes (vol. I, p. 234), confusing rather than helpful, because patients so often had all three kinds together. Only the second kind, general melancholy, need concern us, for the other varieties did not prove attractive as subjects for poetry.

The causes of melancholy, says Burton, may lie within or without ourselves. And very far without indeed, for God may send it as a direct punishment for sin. In such a case, there is no cure save by a second act of divine intervention. Sometimes, however, it is not God, but the devil who afflicts the victim with melancholy, and he may do this either by directly affecting the imagination, or indirectly working upon it through the physical man, for "the devil, being a slender incomprehensible spirit, can easily insinuate and wind himself into human bodies, and cunningly couched in our bowels vitiate our healths, terrify our souls with fearful dreams, and shake our mind with furies." (Vol. I, p. 265.) Here we remember *Hamlet*, act II, sc. 2, 627:

> The spirit that I have seen
> May be the devil: and the devil hath power
> To assume a pleasing shape; yea, and perhaps
> Out of my weakness and my melancholy,
> As he is very potent with such spirits,
> Abuses me to damn me. . . .

According to Burton, the devil does this by God's permission and, with the same divine consent, witches and magicians may deliver the soul over to melancholy. The stars at nativity also influence the matter. Or we may inherit the disease from our parents, or acquire it as the natural concomitant of old age. All these causes lie beyond the control of the individual.

Within our own control, and therefore important to be studied and regulated, are matters of diet, digestion, air, exercise, social intercourse, and physical or mental occupation. Here two details have bearing on the poetry of the period, the association of melancholy with certain times, seasons, and places, and its association with solitude.

In discussing the effects of good and bad air, Burton notes especially that bad weather, tempestuous seasons, and night air are bad for melancholy persons. "The night and darkness makes men sad, the like do all subterranean vaults; dark houses in caves and rocks, desert places cause melancholy in an instant." (Vol. I, p. 320.) As frontispiece of the original edition appears a border of ten small symbolic pictures surrounding the title. One of these, called *Solitudo*, shows certain animals:

> Buck and Doe,
> Hares, Conies in the desart go:
> Bats, Owls the shady bowers over,
> In melancholy darkness hover. . . .

and we shall hear a great deal of some of these creatures later.

As for solitude, he declares that too much of it is both a cause and a symptom of melancholy; that is, if the solitary way of life is of one's own choosing, and not enforced as it is in the case of country gentlemen or prisoners.

> Voluntary solitariness is that which is familiar with melancholy, and gently brings on like a siren, or a shoeing horn, or some Sphinx [Burton's powers of collocation are wonderful!] to this irrevocable gulf. . . . Most pleasant it is at first, to such as are melancholy given, to lie in bed whole days, and keep their chambers, to walk alone in some solitary grove, betwixt wood and water, by a brook side, to meditate upon some delightsome and pleasant subject which shall affect them most; . . . a most incomparable delight it is to melancholize, and build castles in the air. . . . So delightsome are these toys at first, they could spend whole days and nights without sleep, even whole years alone in such contemplations and fantastical meditations. . . . They run earnestly on in this labyrinth of anxious and solicitous melancholy meditations . . . still pleasing their humours, until at last the scene is turned upon a sudden, by some bad object, and they being now habituated to such vain meditations and solitary places, can endure no company, can ruminate of nothing but harsh and distasteful subjects. Fear, sorrow, suspicion, *subrusticus pudor,* discontent, cares, and weariness of life surprise them in a moment, and they can think of nothing else. . . . They may not be rid of it, they cannot resist.

But there is, of course, "some profitable meditation, contemplation, and kind of solitariness to be embraced, which the fathers so highly commended." Here he mentions Jerome, Chrysostom, Augustine, and the recommendations to solitary musing of Petrarch, Erasmus, Democritus, Cicero, and others. (Vol. I, pp. 327–331.) [3]

Other causes which are, or ought to be, within our control, are all passions and perturbations of the mind, such as sorrow, fear, shame, and disgrace; envy, malice, hatred; emulation, desire of revenge; anger, lusts, desires, ambition; covetousness; love of gaming and dissipation generally; self-love and pride; and finally, general discontent, or a too great sense of the cares and evils of life, for which our term today would be pessimism, or perhaps *Weltschmerz*. Over this last point, Burton pauses, describing in a long passage the unavoidable miseries of human existence, which, he says, are a general, ever present cause, an accident inseparable from life itself. Here Burton's thought is often parallel with philosophical passages in *Hamlet*, *Lear*, *Macbeth*, and the historical plays of Shakespeare.[4]

[3] Jerome's *Lives of the Fathers of the Desert* and Augustine's *De Opere Monachum* are described in Montalembert, *Monks of the West*, bk. III, and Chrysostom's *Adversus Oppugnatores Vitae Monasticae* in bk. II. Erasmus, *De Contemptu Mundi*, in praise of the monastic life, written about 1486 when he was scarcely twenty, was not published till 1521, when he added a chapter neutralizing the preceding rhetoric by severe criticism of the habitual condition of the monasteries of the time. Petrarch's *De Vita Solitaria* was published about 1485. Cicero, *De Officiis* III, attributes to Scipio Africanus the saying continually quoted by lovers of solitude, *Nunquam minus solus, quam cum solus; nunquam minus otiosus, quam cum . . . otiosus.*

[4] The resemblance is never close enough to make it certain that Burton actually has Shakespeare in mind. For instance, compare Burton, vol. I, pp. 362–3, "Or what so secure and pleasing a morning have we seen, that hath not been overcast before evening?" with Shakespeare's *Sonnet 33*, "Full many a glorious

Pliny, Seneca, Lucretius, *Job,* and *Ecclesiastes* are skilfully combined with many others into a wonderful pattern of quotation and allusion, descriptive of the futility of life, the uncertainty of human activity.

In his section on the mental symptoms of melancholy, he has another memorable passage, with quotations from Seneca, on that *taedium vitae* [5] which so often tempts the melancholy man to suicide, and again he emphasizes, as an index of the state of the victim's mind, the love of solitude and the marked inability to "do that which concerns him," a phrase which reminds us anew of Hamlet, especially of his self-accusation in the soliloquy of act II, scene 2. Once more he describes with fulness the pleasures of the earlier stages of the love of solitude, the horrors of its extreme. After dwelling on the physical symptoms of general melancholy "abounding in the whole body," he again calls attention, in a transferred quotation from Apuleius, to the hallucinations caused by such a physical state:

> Dead men's bones, hobgoblins, ghosts are ever in their minds, and meet them still in every turn; all the bugbears of the night, and terrors, fairy-babes of tombs, and graves are before their eyes and in their thoughts . . . if they be in the dark alone. If they hear, or read, or see any tragical object, it sticks by them, they are afraid of death, and yet weary of their lives, in their discontented humours they quarrel with all the world, bitterly inveigh, tax satirically, and because they cannot otherwise vent their passions, or redress what is amiss, as they mean, they will by violent death at last be revenged on themselves (vol. II, p. 45). . . .

---

morning have I seen." And is the reference to Timon's abandoning the world (*ibid.* p. 372) a reference to Shakespeare's *Timon of Athens?*

[5] Burton uses this expression often, as though it were familiar in his day. It is not used at all by Caesar or Cicero, and is not frequent in Latin until after Augustus. In Tacitus the phrase occurs usually in connection with suicide.

for all the forms of melancholy lead to madness or suicide.

Burton gives but little space to the discussion of bad dreams and sleeplessness, but seems to take for granted that these are recognized symptoms of melancholy. (Vol. I, p. 331; vol. II, p. 403.)

The Third Part of the *Anatomy* takes up certain special aspects of the subject hitherto passed over, that is, Love-Melancholy and Religious Melancholy. The first has two forms, physical passion and jealousy. Among numerous remedies, we find Burton urging men to cultivate charity, which is a general love of all mankind and the lack of which is the ultimate cause of all our discontent and melancholy.[6]

He classifies religious melancholy as a variety of love-melancholy. "That there is such a distinct species of love-melancholy, no man hath ever yet doubted . . . [but] no physician hath as yet distinctly written of it." It arises from worshiping God in a wrong way. At the one extreme we have the "superstitious idolators, ethnics, Mahometans, Jews, heretics, enthusiasts, divinators, prophets, sectaries and schismatics," who all have too little religion. At the other extreme are "impious epicures, libertines, atheists, hypocrites, infidels, worldly, secure, impenitent, unthankful, and carnal-minded men, that attribute all to natural causes, that will acknowledge no supreme power." Of the strict Puritans he observes, "They are certainly far gone with melancholy, if not quite mad, and have more need of physic than many a man that keeps his bed, more need of hellebore than those that

[6] This "cure" reminds us of the later deistic insistence on benevolence as a cure for pessimism. Burton is somewhat like the deists also, presumably because of his similar fondness for Platonic ideas, in his suggestion that "beauty is the object of all love," but that materialists forget the beauty of God in their absorption in the beauty of his creatures. (Vol. III, p. 455.)

are in Bedlam." Religious melancholy, like the other varieties, leads to despair, and the melancholy man is assisted along the downward path sometimes by the devil, sometimes by physical causes, sometimes by his own guilty conscience, and very often by the denunciations of "thundering ministers." The cure offered for religious despair is put in the form of a long and eloquent argument urging the mercy and goodness of God. (Vol. III, pp. 473–501.)

The conclusion of the entire work may be summed up in ten words. "Be not solitary, be not idle."

Sperate, Miseri:
Cavete, Felices.

We have already noticed Burton's frequent resemblance to Shakespeare. That he should not acknowledge his indebtedness would be only natural on the part of an author who had such contempt for the vernacular.[7] Whether or not Shakespeare is a source of Burton's thought, all of his seventy-odd uses of the noun and adjective fit into Burton's exposition, and a number of his characters are but Melancholy incarnate. It is true that the treatment is often light or humorous in cases such as we should call sentimental, which Burton leaves out of his more serious consideration, giving them only a passing glance in a single chapter. (Vol. I, pp. 191–195.) Nevertheless Shakespeare often recognizes melancholy not as a mere mood, but as an abnormal state on the verge of madness, and he then coincides with Burton in the physical and mental causes to which he ascribes it. He also agrees that "melancholy is the nurse of phrenzy" (*Taming of the*

[7] "It was not mine intent to prostitute my muse in English . . . but to have exposed this more contract in Latin, if I could have got it printed. Any scurrile pamphlet is welcome to our mercenary stationers in English; they print all. . . . But in Latin they will not deal. (Vol. I, p. 44.)

Shrew, Ind., sc. 2, 135), and may lead to suicide, and he suggests many of the same cures.

In his earlier plays, he is evidently much amused at the affectation of melancholy, or melancholy humor, assumed by persons who, because of foreign travel, or much city experience, or a superior education, pretend to refinement. Don Armado in *Love's Labour's Lost* is such a person, and Jaques in *As You Like It,* whose sophisticated affectation is elaborately burlesqued by Touchstone. In *Twelfth Night,* three cases of love-melancholy — we should call it sentimentality — are satirized, the Duke's, Olivia's, and Viola's, though only the Duke's melancholy is quite without cause, and all three figures remain charming rather than ridiculous. The epithet, "melancholy," is not applied to Malvolio, but it is plain that the other characters think him Puritanic, that is to say, tending towards religious mania. In playing their trick on him, the jesters expect to make a "contemplative idiot" of him (act II, sc. 5, 23), and are a little afraid that he may really go mad (*ibid.* 213), as would be quite natural on the part of one who already has "religion in excess." They have only to turn his religious mania into love-mania. Biron and Benedick are recognized to be in love by their showing symptoms of melancholy. The death of the princess's sister in *Love's Labour's Lost* and of Viola's in *Twelfth Night* are ascribed to love-melancholy.

More seriously presented is the melancholy of Don John, bastard and villain, in *Much Ado,* and it makes serious trouble for others, though we are left uncertain of his own fate. Timon of Athens goes gradually mad from general melancholy and his malady is called melancholy by others in the play (act IV, sc. 3, 203, 402). He writes his own epitaph, rears his own tomb, and commits suicide.

It is in the seventeenth century sense that Hamlet is melancholy. He seems so to himself (act II, sc. 2, 630) and to the King (act III, sc. 1, 173). Other signs of it are: his bad dreams; walking much by himself, incessant reading, and dislike of interruption; satirical generalizations about the nature of men and women, complaint that the time is out of joint; hesitation between different courses of conduct; preoccupation with the idea of death, graves, physical decay; thoughts of suicide; presentiment of approaching calamity. Polonius in his talk with Ophelia (act II, sc. 1) believes he has diagnosed the case as love-melancholy, already in the stage of madness, and so reports to the King and Queen in scene 2. The diagnosis is put to the test by the King (act III, sc. 1) and judged incorrect, although Hamlet is still considered as dangerously melancholy.

> Love! his affections do not that way tend;
> Nor what he spake, though it lack'd form a little,
> Was not like madness. There's something in his soul,
> O'er which his melancholy sits on brood;
> And I do doubt the hatch and the disclose
> Will be some danger. . . .

But to say that Hamlet's state of mind throughout the play is melancholy in the old sense, is not to accuse him of being morbid in the modern sense or to detract from his heroic character,[8] for to present him as "melancholy" would but make him the more interesting to Shakespeare's audiences. His assumption of madness is also made easier and more natural thereby.[9]

[8] An interpretation of Hamlet as afflicted with melancholia is presented by A. C. Bradley in his *Shakespearean Tragedy*, pp. 120–128. This view is combated by E. E. Stoll in his *Hamlet: an Historical and Comparative Study*.

[9] In Ben Jonson's comedies, melancholy is only one of the "humours," the display of which is the purpose of his characteristic plot. In *Everyman in his Humour* (c. 1606), Stephen, the country gull, affects pride and melancholy because they are gentlemanlike," and the love-melancholy of Kitely, caused by jealousy and amounting to temporary insanity, is accorded comic treatment.

The life — and the death — of the poet, John Donne, Dean of St. Paul's from 1621 to 1631, furnishes another illustration of differences between modern and seventeenth century applications of the word "melancholy." Most of Donne's modern critics insist that melancholy was a fundamental trait in his character. Miss Spearing speaks of the "morbidness of fancy" which plays continually on the note, "When I am dead."[10] Professor Grierson finds melancholy in his sermons, his verse, and his letters to noble ladies, and emphasizes the *contemptus mundi* of the *Anniversaries*.[11] Mr. Pearsall Smith believes that Donne's mind was "essentially mediaeval, and in no way more so than in his mediaeval sense of death's horror," and calls his love of ugliness "almost morbid."[12] Mr. Gosse also terms him melancholy, regarding his fantastic preparation for death during his last illness as illustrative in the highest degree of the morbid character of his genius. But Mr. Gosse[13] is at some pains to explain that the whole elaborate and long-drawn performance has a peculiarly renaissance, not a mediaeval quality. And, indeed, when we gaze on a reproduction of the *macabre* statue in St. Paul's Cathedral, for the sketch of which, as Walton tells us, Donne crawled out of his dying bed to pose, wrapped in his shroud; when we read his last sermon, published under the appropriate title, *Death's Duel*, or those other sermons which picture the world as a churchyard, this life on earth as one long burden-bearing in a prison, and man himself as "less than a worm," sermons which describe with such gusto the relentless onward march of death, the putrefaction of

[10] *Modern Language Review*, vol. VIII, p. 49. Jan. 1912.

[11] *Poems of John Donne*, ed . . . Grierson, vol. II, Introduction, pp. X, XV, VII, XX, XXVIII.

[12] *Donne's Sermons: Selected Passages*, ed. L. P. Smith, p. XXVI.

[13] Gosse, *Life and Letters of John Donne*, vol. II, pp. 280–291.

corpses, and the "splendid terrors" of the Judgment—we are disposed to agree with the critics that Donne is morbid, or even to say that he has melancholia in the modern sense.[14]

But we must realize that he did not seem melancholy to the seventeenth century, for that disease was believed to arise from an excess of melancholy humor, while to the men of his time Donne's character presented an admirable balance. Says Walton:

> The melancholy and pleasant humour were in him so contempered, that each gave advantage to the other, and made his company one of the delights of mankind.

It is true that he had "occasional melancholy," due to special, adequate causes. His wife's death produced "my lone devout melancholy," as he calls it, out of which grew the series of devotional sonnets, *La Corona*.[15] Before that event, too, during his terrible struggle with sickness and abject poverty, he had written (1608) a prose defense of suicide, *Biathanatos*, which, however, remained unpublished till after his death.[16] Also, in 1623 during an acute attack of his chronic ailment (which Mr. Gosse conjectures to have been gastritis), he suffered a dreadful dejection. On complaining to his physician, he was told that it was "my melancholy, the vapours," but he found the explanation unsatisfactory. He wrote out an account of his state of mind, apparently with the intention of dispelling the mood by a critical analysis. In these *Devotions . . . and severall Steps in my Sickness*, he sometimes thinks so closely with Burton that Mr. Gosse conjectures he may have seen the newly published *Anatomy*.[17]

[14] *Donne's Sermons*, pp. 239, 69, 196, 91; 3, 10; 195, 197, 202.

[15] Written 1617. Gosse, *Life and Letters of John Donne*, vol. II, p. 104.

[16] *Ibid.* vol. I, pp. 258–63.

[17] *Ibid.* vol. II, pp. 181–186.

But Donne's melancholy is not habitual, and it is quite without the two accompanying symptoms noted by Burton, "fear and sadness." He believes melancholy to be irreligious. Shall any sad soul, he reasons, come into a Church to gather arguments from the preaching in favor of its own condemnation?

> Wilt thou force God to second thy irreligious *melancholy*, and to condemne thee at last, because thou hadst precondemned thy selfe, and renounced his mercy? [18]

He denounces "the sick soul." [19] Let no man, he says,

> present his complexion to God for an excuse, and say . . . My Melancholy enclined me to sadnesse, and so to Desperation, as though thy sins were medicinall sins, sins to vent humours.[20]

In his *Funeral Sermon on Magdalen Herbert, Lady Danvers,* he is careful to clear her from the imputation of melancholy.

He was in fact sociable and friendly, not given to solitude, which, he thinks, "is a torment . . . not threatened in hell itself." [21] He is even a little suspicious of the religious contemplation recommended by the Fathers.

> [It] is not in the body of his Testaments, but interlined and postscribed by others, that the way to the communion of saints should be by such a solitude as excludes all doing of good here.[22]

So, too, his preoccupation with death, its paraphernalia and consequences, is without fear although grim and gruesome enough. Fear is "a stifling spirit, a spirit of suffocation,[23] unworthy of a Christian. While he holds his own mind and the attention of his congregations steadily on the thought of our latter end, he rises almost unfailingly to the mood of joy in salvation, welcome to Death the

[18] *Donne's Sermons,* p. 133.
[19] *Ibid.* p. 194.
[20] *Ibid.* p. 177.
[21] Donne, *Devotions,* p. 23.
[22] *Ibid.* p. 24.
[23] *Ibid.* p. 30.

Deliverer, and ecstasy in the thought of perfect communion with God in the future life. *Death's Duel* is really less characteristic than the often quoted "Death of Ecstasy."[24] Of the death of the body, it is true

. . . I know I must die that death, what care I? . . . but I will finde out another death, *mortem raptus,* a death of rapture, and of extasie, that death which *S. Paul* died more than once, The death which S. Gregory speaks of, *Divina contemplatio quoddam sepulchrum animae,* The contemplation of God, and heaven, is a kinde of buriall, and Sepulchre, and rest of the soule; and in this death of rapture, and extasie, in this death of the Contemplation of my interest in my Saviour, I shall finde my self, and all my sins enterred, and entombed in his wounds, and like a Lily in Paradise, out of red earth, I shall see my soule rise out of his blade, in a candor and in an innocence, contracted there, acceptable in the sight of his Father.

In the imaginative realization, then, of Donne's actual character as of Hamlet's fictitious one, the reader must constantly bear in mind the seventeenth century meaning of the word "melancholy." So far as I have been able to observe, no writer in that century, except John Milton, gives the word any wider application than Burton. He, however, took the term as Burton left it and provided it with an original set of connotations, molding it, as a great poet may, to a new use.

The probable indebtedness of Milton, both in idea and in rhythm, to the little poem called *The Author's Abstract of Melancholy,* which is in the form of a Dialogus prefixed to the *Anatomy,* has long been recognized, having been first mentioned by Warton in his edition of Milton's *Poems on Several Occasions* . . . London, 1785.[25] Milton

[24] *Donne's Sermons,* pp. 202–3. Quoted at length and with admiring comment by Professor Grierson in his edition of the *Poems,* vol. II, p. LIV. See also Miss Ramsay's, *Les Doctrines Médiévales chez Donne,* p. 260 f.

[25] Warton's long note, pp. 93–94, quotes Burton's poem in full

had most probably read Burton, but he does not follow him in describing alternately the pleasures and pains of melancholy. To Milton, the solitary life is all pleasure. It is, perhaps, not an accident that *L'Allegro* is placed first of the two companion poems, for the progress of the idea from the first to the second is logical. In the opening stanza, Burton's view of melancholy — the usual view, I take it — is adopted. She is the hated child of Hades and Midnight. She is hideous. Let her be banished to her proper haunts, a dark cave in a desert. But the rest of the poem describes the positively jocund pleasures of the man who, though he may walk alone, is yet a sympathetic observer of his fellow men. In *Il Penseroso* Milton seems to react against Burton's conception altogether, and while keeping the word melancholy to describe the thoughtful mood of the man who loves to be alone by night, indoors or out, reading or simply musing by himself, or who by day courts the brown shadows in the close coverts of a wood by the brook, he deliberately rejects all the associations of the word with disease, madness, suicide and fear. Deliberately also, he sets up a new set of connotations, with saintliness, with wisdom, with beauty, with leisure, with poetry, philosophy, and music, with lovely outdoor scenes, and with a widening experience maturing with age.

Milton's title, *Il Penseroso,* puts into Italian form a word already in use as a synonym for the adjective "melancholy." By its derivation from the French "pensive" ought to mean merely "thoughtful." But John-

---

and points out other resemblances between the two authors. There is no external evidence that Milton had read Burton, but Masson takes it for granted (*Poetical Works of John Milton . . .* ed. Masson, 2d ed. London, 1890, vol. I, p. 135). So, apparently, does Burton's latest interpreter, Professor Edward Bensley, in *Camb. Hist. of Eng. Lit.,* vol. IV, ch. XIII. Indeed, the internal evidence is convincing.

son's *Dictionary* (1755), defining it as "sorrowfully thoughtful, melancholy," supports the definition by quotations from Spenser, Shakespeare, and Hooker as well as from Herbert, Prior, and Pope. "Pensive" is not in Blount's *Glossographia* (1670), but one of Blount's meanings for "melancholy" is "pensiveness." When, about 1740, *Il Penseroso* attained the height of its popularity as the great poem of melancholy, it helped to fix for nearly a century in the minds of English readers of poetry the connection between reflection, solitude, delight in nature, and melancholy.

But this pleasanter meaning attributed to melancholy did not immediately do away with its use in a derogatory sense. It must be remembered that these poems of Milton, first published in 1645, were not overwhelmingly popular, until, as Dr. Good has established in his *Studies in the Milton Tradition*,[26] they were set to music by Händel in 1740 and sung into fame as part of his *Samson Oratorio*. They cannot, therefore, be regarded as affecting in the popular mind the meaning of the word "melancholy" in the seventeenth century. Throughout that century and

[26] P. 169. While I believe that Dr. Good successfully proves his general point, namely, that before about 1740 it was Milton's epic that was known and admired, rather than the minor poems, he seems to me to neglect some evidence of the popularity of the two companion pieces. He does not, for instance, mention John Philips's parody, *The Splendid Shilling*, 1701, which, though in blank verse, follows in idea the plan of the companion pieces and which had a great vogue. Nor does he refer to Lady Winchilsea's imitations, some of them before 1700, and all before 1713, Watts's *True Riches*, 1706, Parnell's *Hymn to Contentment*, and *Night-Piece on Death*, 1713 (?), Dyer's *Country Walk*, and *Grongar Hill*, 1726, and a passage in Thomson's *Winter*, 1726, line 253–300. All these distinctly show the influence of *L'Allegro* and *Il Penseroso*. Dr. Havens, in his *Influence of Milton on English Poetry*, lists a greater number of poems significantly influenced by the minor poems, but confirms Dr. Good's general conclusion.

considerably later its meaning remains essentially that so fully expounded by Burton, "a disease recognizable by its effect on the mind and temper," manifesting itself as chronic depression, often accompanied by fear, and all without any apparent or immediate cause.[27] This description fits the state of mind which we today call melancholia, and which many of us would consider a disease, though we do not associate it with an excess of black bile, or "melancholy humor." Nor does the adjective "melancholy" readily come to our lips nowadays in describing a man who simply likes to be alone, or loves the night and a storm, or is given to quiet reflection; or who cannot shut his eyes to the miseries of the world; or is fanatically religious, or atheistic, or a materialist in the scientific sense. But in discussing the poetry of the late seventeenth and early eighteenth century, we must remember that a poem voicing any of these moods or beliefs would have been termed by its readers "melancholy."

[27] These fears might take a grossly superstitious form, witness the "Accidents of John Aubrey," wherein he views his whole life as a series of dangerous accidents which befell him in fulfilment of his horoscope and which just missed being fatalities. Aubrey's portrait, *aetat.* 40, shows an apparently hale and hearty man, but he had had "a terrible fit of the spleen" . . . within the year, and he was evidently chronically melancholy in Burton's sense. When he left Oxford in 1643 because of an epidemic of smallpox there, he led "a sad life in the country for three years." During his visit in 1695 at Lavington, the estate of his patron, the Earl of Abingdon, he declares that he enjoyed "the contentment of solitude." Yet the fruit of that leisure, *Miscellanies upon Various Subjects* (1696), was a collection of prodigious fatalities, omens, dreams, apparitions, visions, and other hobgoblins of the mind, an interest in which Burton would have regarded as a sure sign of the true melancholiac. There could scarcely be a greater contrast in the literature of melancholy than that furnished by Aubrey's little book and Milton's *Il Penseroso.* See Aubrey's *Brief Lives* under "Aubrey, John" and his *Miscellanies,* Library of Old Authors ed.

Such connotations of the word " melancholy " should not be regarded as in themselves evidences of the dawn of romanticism, but as survivals of seventeenth century usage, the nature and reason of which will be more fully explained in the following chapter.

The reading of Burton helps us also to understand the relation of *Il Penseroso* to its other chief source, the song, *Melancholy,* in Fletcher's play, *The Nice Valour.* The song, it will be remembered, is sung by the " passionate madman " at the height of his folly. The " delights " which he spurns are not the joys of life in general, but the pleasures of wanton passion. Now in Burton's conception, and doubtless also in Milton's, sensual passion was " love-melancholy," as dangerous as any other form of insanity. The madman, in invoking solitude and " lovely melancholy " as a charm against Cupid is merely alternating between two extremes of madness. It may have occurred to Milton, in hearing or reading the song,[28] that the " melancholy " which is the true refuge from passion should not be regarded as another form of self-indulgence but rather as the highest sanity and self-control. In endeavoring to express more seriously and adequately the mood of the thoughtful man who rejects the follies of love, he retained Fletcher's idea and some of his phrasing as a sort of text for his poetical sermon, but in general he paralleled, or rather summarized, as Warton noted (*op. cit.* p. 94), Burton's course of thought in his chapter, *Exercise rectified both by Body and Minde.*[29]

[28] *The Nice Valour* was not published until 1647 but was acted long before, and the song almost certainly known before *Il Penseroso* was written. Trent's ed. of *L'Allegro, Il Penseroso, Comus, and Lycidas,* N. Y., [c] 1895.

[29] Cf. Burton, vol. II, pp. 174–189.

" To walk amongst orchards, gardens, bowers, mounts, and arbours, artificial wildernesses, green thickets, arches, groves, lawns,

Of the readiness with which the word was applied to states of mind or body, and the eagerness with which cures were sought, we get several illustrations in Richard Baxter's *Reliquiae Baxterianae.*[30] He gave us a lamentable history of his bodily infirmities in his childhood, and of his sufferings under the wrong diagnosis, until, at about the age of eighteen, "divers eminent physicians agreed that my disease was the hypochondriacal melancholy and not the scurvy." Nevertheless

I was never overwhelm'd with real Melancholy. My Distemper never went so far as to possess me with any inordinate fancies,

---

rivulets, fountains, and such like pleasant places . . . brooks, pools, fish-ponds, between wood and water, in a fair meadow, by a river side . . . to disport in some pleasant plain, park, run up a steep hill sometimes, or sit in a shady seat, must needs be a delectable recreation. . . . What so pleasant as to see some pageant or sight go by, as at coronations, weddings, and such like solemnities, to see an ambassador or a prince met, received, entertained with masks, shows, fireworks, etc. To see two kings fight in a single combat, as Porus and Alexander. . . . The very reading of feasts, triumphs, interviews . . . is most acceptable and pleasant.

"The country hath his recreations, the city his several gymnics and exercises, May games, feasts, wakes, and merrymeetings, to solace themselves; the very being in the country; that life itself is a sufficient recreation to some men.

"Every palace, every city almost hath his peculiar walks, cloisters, terraces, groves, theatres. . . . All seasons almost, all places have their several pastimes; some in summer, some in winter, some abroad, some within; some of the body, some of the mind; and diverse men have diverse recreations and exercises.

"But amongst those exercises, or recreations of the mind within doors, there is none so general, so aptly to be applied to all sorts of men, so fit and proper to expel idleness and melancholy, as that of study."

30 *Reliquiae Baxterianae: or, Mr. Richard Baxter's Narrative of The Most Memorable Passages of his Life and Times.* Faithfully Publish'd from his own Original Manuscript by Matthew Sylvester . . . London . . . 1696.

or damp me with sinking sadness, although the physicians call'd it the hypochondriacal melancholy. I had at several times the advice of no less than six and thirty physicians, by whose order I us'd drugs without number almost, which God thought not fit to make successful for a cure; and indeed, all authors that I read, acquainted me that my disease was incurable; whereupon I at last forsook the doctors for the most part, except when the urgency of a symptom or pain, constrained me to seek some present ease.

Having thus discovered for himself the way to ease melancholy, by simply disregarding it, he writes in 1671,

I was troubled this year with multitudes of melancholy persons, from several parts of the land, some of high quality some of low, some very exquisitely learned, some unlearned. I know not how it came to pass, but if men feel melancholy, I must hear from them or see them, (more than any physician I know). Which I mention only for these three uses to the reader. 1. That we must very much take heed lest we ascribe melancholy phantasms and passions to God's spirit: for they are strange apprehensions that melancholy can cause. . . . 2. I would warn all young persons to live modestly, and keep at a sufficient distance from objects that tempt them to carnal lusts. . . . 3. I advise all men to take heed of placing religion too much in fears, and tears, and scruples. . . . And that tears and grief be not commended inordinately for themselves, nor as mere signs of a converted person. *Reader,* I do but transcribe these three counsels for thee, from a multitude of melancholy persons and experiences. (Pt. III, p. 86.)

Baxter reports two cases of cures of religious melancholy. In one case the cure was effected by prayer after the patient had been quite mad for ten or twelve years. The other was that of a good man who "had fallen into deep melancholy, feeding it daily with the thoughts of the number that will be damned, and tempted by it to constant blasphemy against the goodness of God, who could save them, and would not, but decreed their damnation." This man was cured by reading Baxter's tract called *The Vindication of God's Goodness.*

Of these five authors, then, all but Milton agree in regarding melancholy as a disease, or at least as an abnormal state, curable in its early stages partly by medicine, partly by intelligent self-treatment, but after a time probably incurable and likely to result in madness and death, very probably by suicide. Towards the end of the century there is some tendency to reserve "melancholy" for use in the more general sense of "sadness," and to employ the word "spleen" as a technical term for the physical disease and for the mental state which we now call melancholia, though the words were still used interchangeably. "Spleen" is not defined in Blount's dictionary in 1670, but by 1730 it is so much the fashionable ailment of the moment that Bailey's dictionary not only gives definitions of the noun, and of the adjective "spleenful," but also of seven derivatives. In the eighteenth century, as dictionary definitions show, medical theory as to the cause and cure of the disease was changing, and, as we shall see later, the melancholy mood was affirmed to be within the individual's own control. Controversy arose, based on opposed ethical and social theories, between those who condemned and those who approved indulgence in melancholy and its frank, personal expression in literature — between the followers of Pope and Johnson, and the followers of Milton, Thomson, and Gray.

In an effort to bring my subject within the limits of industry, I have excluded from the following pages any consideration of love-melancholy as such, and of elegiac poetry as such, remembering that Burton himself considers the death of friends among the merely adventitious causes of melancholy. Each of these subjects would require a book in itself. My purpose is rather to describe the growth to perfect expression of that mood of sorrow which is apparently without adequate specific cause in the poet's own experience. I have excluded satiric poetry also, although much of seventeenth and eighteenth century satire may well be regarded as the poetry of despair. Nevertheless, since a sense of superiority is an essential element in the satiric spirit,[31] the satirist never feels himself actually engulfed by the weltering waters of melancholy. He may be a castaway, but he is still riding the waves on the plank of intellect. Nor does he give direct expression to his feeling of depression, but conceals it by an attack on the folly or wickedness of other men, or of the world in general. Satiric poetry is therefore in a class by itself. But I have not found it possible to discuss the melancholy poetry of the eighteenth century without reference to that religious melancholy which Burton claims to have been the first to treat fully, for the literary taste of the early eighteenth century was very largely determined by the religious struggles of the seventeenth.

Because of these exclusions, the succeeding chapters do not furnish anything like a complete analysis of melancholy literature even in the chosen period, but only a chronological study of the various "melancholy" elements which successively emerged into popular favor and which in 1751 were combined by the artistry of Gray into an enduring lyric whole.

[31] Tucker, *Verse Satire in England,* p. 8.

CHAPTER II

THE TASTE FOR MELANCHOLY IN 1700

To determine just what the people of England were reading in a given year is a task which, if not wholly impossible, would at least require the combined effort of a goodly number of students working in several fields. Nevertheless, some sense of the widespread fondness for melancholy subjects in literature about the year 1700 may be gathered from an examination of the titles of books published and reprinted during, let us say, the ten years just before that date. At the same time we must bear in mind that attention given wholly to a single phase of literature necessarily exaggerates its importance, and we must do what we can to correct our impressions by reference to general studies of the literature of the period.

Such studies, we notice, invariably emphasize the prosaic character of the literary output and especially the dearth of true lyric poetry at the end of the seventeenth century. This temporary disappearance of the *genre* which had been one of the great glories of the Elizabethan age was a not unnatural consequence of the immense social changes of the seventeenth century. It seems to have been due to the exhaustion of certain springs of feeling which usually underlie and give rise to lyric expression. Political, religious, and social dissension had deprived poets of one powerful source of inspiration, the sense of national unity. The disillusion and cynicism which inevitably follow wars were unfavorable to the expresson of joyous or ideal moods, while they encouraged the production of satire. Taste for the classics, fostered by the imitation of French models, happened to direct attention rather to epic and dramatic forms of poetry than to lyric.[1] In the lyric *genre* itself, the interest in Cowley and his example fostered the grandiose Pindaric rather than the simpler lyric forms. Generally speaking, in the literary effort of the time, real enthusiasm was for science, philosophy, and history, rather than for poetry.

However, there was no counting on any homogeneous feeling in this reading public, or any specially developed literary taste. Nor did the lack of unity in readers imply a tolerance or liberality of spirit such as might have encouraged a widely varied literature and authors of marked individuality.[2] The effect of warring tastes was merely destructive. The cleavage between Protestant and Catholic, churchman and non-conformist, Whig and Tory, middle class and noble, town and country, was relatively more disastrous for literature than such differences are today, simply because the actual number of educated readers was so much smaller. At the same time, the reaction against Restoration excesses was making for a narrow didacticism in almost all writing.

It had been true, even of the Age of Restoration, that the largest number of readers were serious-minded, books of religion constituting the largest class in the publishers' lists, with books of science next, and history third. The output of plays, which usually looms so large in the mind of the student of Restoration literature, was not two per cent of the total English books of the time (1660–1688)

[1] In the types of literature translated from the Greek in the last half of the seventeenth century, Philosophy, Fable, Epic, and History were far more numerous than the translations of lyric poetry. See Dr. F. M. K. Foster's *English Translations from the Greek.*

[2] Beljame, *Le Public et les Hommes de Lettres en Angleterre,* pp. 143, 206–7, 338.

either in printed bulk or in price.[3] At the end of the century this seriousness seems to have been on the increase, for in the year 1700 books of " Divinity " formed fifty per cent of all the books listed in the *Term Catalogues*, (not counting reprints) as compared with thirty-four per cent in 1690, and forty-four per cent in 1696. Of reprinted books in any given term between 1690 and 1700, they constituted from ten to twenty-five per cent. The class, " Divinity," included, of course, technical discussions of theological or ecclesiastical questions, and it must be remembered that all such matters in the seventeenth century had chiefly a political bearing.[4] But setting aside all works of interest only to religious or political partisans, there still remain a large number which were hortatory or devotional, or which, though partly controversial, nevertheless appealed to thoughtful readers of any faith.

Thus the truly popular authors between 1690 and 1700, to judge from the frequency with which they were reprinted, were Jeremy Collier, Bishop Taylor, Archbishop Tillotson, John Bunyan, Richard Baxter, and George Herbert. The favorite subjects were " the four last things," i.e., death, judgment, heaven, and hell — life in this world, if it was treated at all, being regarded chiefly as a preparation for death. We find Taylor's *Holy Living and Holy Dying* in its fifteenth edition in 1690, and its eighteenth in 1700; Sherlock's *Practical Discourse Concerning Death,*

[3] Arber, *Term Catalogues*, vol. 1, pp. XV–XVI; vol. III, p. VII. These publishers' lists, though not complete, may fairly be taken as representative.

[4] Just as books of the class, Sociology, have today. Of English book production in the year 1921, Fiction, the largest class, forms about 17½%, Sociology, the next in size, nearly 7½%, Religion, third, 7+%, Poetry and Drama 5½+%. In American book production, Fiction makes about 11½%, Science, 8%, Sociology 7%, and Poetry and Drama 6%. (Percentages calculated from figures in the *Publishers' Weekly*.)

first published in 1689, reaches a tenth edition in 1699,[5] and his *Practical Discourse Concerning a Future Judgment*, a fifth edition in the same year. *The Great Concern . . . Recommended as Proper to be Given at Funerals* has a nineteenth edition in 1697 and is reprinted in 1698 and 1699. *The Midnight Cry, A Sermon Preached on the Parable of the Ten Virgins,* has two editions in 1691 and another in 1692. Other popular titles are Drelincourt's *The Christian's Defense against the Fear of Death,* fourth edition, 1700,[6] John Shower's *Serious Reflections on Time and Eternity,* third edition, 1696, Bunyan's *The Pilgrim's Progress,* first part, fourteenth edition, 1699, and *Sighs from Hell,* ninth edition, 1692.[7]

[5] And Prior writes a poem on it, *To Dr. Sherlock on His Practical Discourse concerning Death.*

[6] Defoe's pamphlet, *A True Relation of the Apparition of One Veal,* 1706, may be taken as evidence of the popularity of Drelincourt's work, since, according to the latest research, it is not an advertising hoax, but a piece of realistic reporting. The apparition, an honest ghost whose actuality is authenticated by the wearing of a gown of "scowered silk," reminds her friend Mrs. Bargrave, of former days—"what books they read, and what comfort in particular, they received from Drelincourt's Book of Death, which was the best, she said, on that subject ever written. She also mentioned Dr. Sherlock . . . and several others. But Drelincourt, she said, had the clearest notions of death, and of the future state, of any who had handled that subject. The notions we have of heaven now, are nothing like what it is, as Drelincourt says." Note that the two ladies, one of whom is poor, the other well-to-do, are unmistakably of the lower middle class. The pamphlet may, of course, have done something in its turn to stimulate the reading of Drelincourt's book, which had a new (5th?) edition early in 1707. New editions in French were published in Amsterdam in 1714 and 1724, and in Leyden, 1760. In English it was reissued together with Defoe's tract in 1719, 1732, 1751, 1776, 1810. See Trent, *Daniel Defoe,* p. 65. But William Lee, in his *Mrs. Daniel Defoe,* vol. 1, pp. 127–8, disputes the opinion that Defoe had any effect on Drelincourt's popularity.

[7] Titles and dates from Arber's *Term Catalogues.*

At the same time, the change in the social life of the court at the accession of William and Mary, together with the increased wealth, power, and social prominence of the bourgeois and the country gentry meant also an increased demand for decency in literature.[8] Coarseness and filth, while still tolerated in the satiric poems which had proved such effective political weapons, were becoming unfashionable in the epic, lyric, and dramatic *genres*. Erotic and sensual songs, though they doubtless continued to circulate surreptitiously,[9] as such verse will in any age, were openly disapproved of.

To this increased taste for seriousness and decency, the poets of this decade catered by serving up " divine and moral " poems, in great number.[10] Between 1690 and 1700

[8] A full account of this change in taste with reference to comedy will be found in a forthcoming Columbia University dissertation by Joseph Wood Krutch, entitled *Comedy and Conscience*. Professor Krutch's discussion of the Societies for the Reformation of Manners, which began to be of importance in the 1690's, brings to light much new material and has special bearing on the entire period covered by my study. See also the more generalized treatment of Beljame, *op. cit.*, pp. 198–205, 244–259.

Burnet, *History of his Own Time,* vol. IV, pp. 181, 239, 529, emphasizes the reforming influence of the new court of William and Mary.

If, as Sir Walter Besant says, *The Athenian Mercury* (1690–96) is a true index of the manners and ideas of the English bourgeois at the end of the seventeenth, or the beginning of the eighteenth century, there can be no doubt of the insistent demand of the middle classes for at least an external decency. See his " Prefatory Letter " to *The Athenian Oracle; a selection,* ed. John Underhill, London, n. d.

[9] The Earl of Rochester's *Poems,* for instance, containing much indecent stuff not by him, as well as some of his own authorship, found new editions in 1691 and 1696.

[10] Such a movement was, of course, only one step in the never ending crusade to restore poetry to an imagined former state of power and purity, a brief review of which from the Renaissance to 1700 may be found in Paul, *John Dennis,* pp. 120–122. But

there were, for example, four attempts at an epic of the life of Christ, and Blackmore had produced his exemplary *Prince Arthur* (1696) and *King Arthur* (1697) in the hope of furnishing "harmless Entertainment" for "the young gentlemen and Ladys who are delighted with Poetry," as his two Prefaces explain.[11] The book of *Ecclesiastes* was twice versified in 1691 and 1692, by anonymous authors. Nahum Tate, who in his poem *On the Present Corrupted State of Poetry* (1684) had accused poetry of "Flatt'ring in Court, and Rev'lling on the Stage," of satirizing virtue, uttering blasphemy and atheism, and inciting to sensual vices, was in 1691 using poetry as a vehicle for his *Characters of Virtue and Vice . . . Attempted in Verse from a Treatise of the Reverend Joseph Hall.* Atheism was discussed in poetry, and religion was proved to be the only happiness.[12] The secular *Miscellanies* were paralleled by Tate's *Miscellanea Sacra* (vol. I, 1693). Sir John Davies's *Nosce Te Ipsum* was reprinted and rechristened *The Original, Nature, and Immortality of the Soul,* a title designed to draw attention to its applicability in the current controversy. There were, finally, a number of volumes, during these ten years, of odes and "elegies" on divine and moral subjects, many devotional poems, and several versions of the *Psalms* for use in churches and non-conformist assemblies. Poets of ineffable dulness found publishers and readers merely because they

---

the crusaders seem to have been especially active at the end of the seventeenth century, and peculiarly successful, not in producing great poetry on noble lines, but in silencing opposition and securing followers.

[11] He attributes the success of Congreve's *Mourning Bride* (1697) to the fact that in it, with "some few exceptions . . . all things are Chast, Just, and Decent." Preface to *King Arthur.*

[12] *An Anatomy of Atheism,* by a person of Quality, 1693. *Religion the Only Happiness,* 1694.

were serious and moral, for it must be confessed that the new audience was less keen witted than the courtly circles of Charles II.[13]

Even Dryden, though still acknowledged to be without rival as a poet, felt obliged in 1700 to make a " retraction " as complete as Chaucer's. In his *Preface to the Fables* he pleads guilty to Collier's accusation of obscenity, profaneness, and immorality, withdraws all offending thoughts or expressions, protests that he is not conscious of any such in his present work, asks pardon if, by chance, " a thought too wanton " be found therein, and closes with the exemplary resolution: "But I will no more offend against good manners: I am sensible as I ought to be of the scandal I have given by my loose writings; and make what reparation I am able, by this public acknowledgment." [14]

These apologies, we note, occur in the preface to a volume not of original composition but of free translation or paraphrase of other men's work. Indeed, for poets who, like Dryden, judged the quality of poetry not by its subject only but by its style, and who delighted in the free play of mind over the whole range of human life, there was for the moment no refuge from divinity and morality except in translation or imitation. It will be recalled that

[13] See John Dennis's complaint (in 1702) that a large part of the theatrical audiences of the day were not qualified by nature or education to appreciate comedy. He observes that, by contrast with the reign of Charles II, the present is a reign of politics and business, when most people are lacking in leisure, serenity, and disinterestedness. " The Court of England at present has other things to mind than to take care of Comedy. 'Tis true, there may be several Gentlemen in it who are capable of setting others right, but neither have they leisure to do it, nor have others time to attend to them." *A Large Account of the Taste in Poetry,* in Durham, *Critical Essays of the Eighteenth Century, 1700–1725,* pp. 113–142.

[14] *Essays of John Dryden,* ed. Ker, vol. II, pp. 250–251, 272.

Dryden had begun to be "troubled with the disease of translation" about 1685, according to his own account,[15] and that the bulk of his work after the loss of his laureateship in 1688 consisted of translations from Juvenal and Persius, Virgil, Ovid, and finally, Chaucer and Boccaccio. The four volumes of *Miscellany Poems* edited by him between 1684 and 1694 also consist largely of translations by his own and "other hands," for instance those of Sedley, Mulgrave, Roscommon, Rochester, Otway, Rymer, Tate, Duke, Creech, in the First Miscellany (1684) and Mulgrave, Prior, Congreve, Granville, Henry Cromwell, and Yalden in the Third Miscellany (1693).

There were special reasons at this time why translation from the classics, a fascinating pursuit ever since the Renaissance, should be more than ever practised. The translator of the classics, especially of Latin,[16] was sure in those uncertain times, of a large audience of cultured people, for the culture of antiquity was the foundation of all education, whether for clerical or secular professions, and was beloved alike by saints and sinners.[17] The trans-

[15] Dryden, Preface to *Sylvae* (the Second Miscellany) in his *Poems*, Cambridge ed., p. 175.

[16] Dr. Foster's study of *English Translations from the Greek* (see n. 1) shows in the chart on p. XII that while the number of translations (both original and reprinted) was mounting, it had only just reached in 1680, after a period of depression, the high water mark of 1640. In 1690 it was only a very little beyond that point. There seem to be no references directly to Greek originals by the poets of this decade. Greek influence on melancholy lyricism is practically negligible up to the time of Pope, Collins, and Gray, except as it is indirectly exerted through the reading of Latin imitations.

[17] Watts in his note-books commended the good teaching he received in the classics at the dissenting academy at Stoke-Newington (*Dict. of Nat. Biog.*, *Watts*), and though he afterwards found it necessary for his soul's good to burn parts of Ovid and Martial, he continued to place "the moral odes of Horace" on

lator was safe from accusations of immorality, indecency, atheism, or libel, against all of which he could comfortably set up the very ancient defence that he was not speaking in his own person.[18] Furthermore, the late seventeenth century was aware of the analogy between certain political and social conditions and states of mind of their own England and those of Rome at the end of the Republic and during the Empire. Accordingly both poets and readers seized with avidity upon an older literature expressing their own moods with a skill and felicity which both incited to imitation and perpetually defied it.[19] Besides a con-

---

a level with "the Psalms of David and the holy Transports interspers'd in the other sacred writings," in their power "to diffuse Vertue and allure Souls to God." (Watts, Preface to *Horae Lyricae,* 3rd ed. 1715, p. XXI). Richard Baxter admired Seneca. (Baxter, *The Epistle to the Reader,* dated 1681, in his *Poetical Fragments. . . .* 3rd ed. 1699.) Anthony Ashley Cooper, afterwards third Earl of Shaftesbury, put the case strikingly in a letter to his father in 1689 giving advice about his younger brother's education. "And for Latin, besides the accomplishment of gentlemen, it is absolutely necessary to every considerable station and almost every office (except within the camp) as well in the pulpit, as on the Bench. This one single, easy, pleasant language has been the stumbling block in my brother's fortunes, and this must be got over by my brother Maurice, or he must do as my brother John, and apply either to sea-serving or to merchant's affairs." (In his *Life, Unpublished Letters,* ed. Rand, p. 283.)

[18] Thus Dryden in the Preface to *Sylvae.* "I am only the translator, not the inventor; so that the heaviest part of the censure falls upon Lucretius, before it reaches me." (*Essays of John Dryden,* ed. Ker, p. 263.)

[19] As Samuel Johnson says (in 1780), "In the reign of Charles the Second began that adaptation which has since been very frequent of ancient poetry to present times." *Lives of the English Poets,* ed. Hill, vol. I, p. 224. In the Renaissance, for the most part, the difference between ancient and modern times was not distinctly realized, and it was supposed that sixteenth century Englishmen could even under different conditions easily imitate the

tinued interest in the favorite Latin authors of the Renaissance, there was a special satisfaction at the end of the seventeenth century in Lucretius's *De Rerum Natura* and in Virgil's *Georgics,* which took a place in popular liking by the side of those universal and perennial favorites, Horace and Ovid.

---

conduct and culture of antique heroes, as, for instance, Ascham recommends in *The Scholemaster.* From the nineteenth century onwards, our sense of separation from former ages has been increasing, and the endeavor of the student of history has been to realize imaginatively but with scientific accuracy the exact character of a past which seems to us ever more strange and remote. But in the seventeenth and eighteenth centuries, by the average reader at least, the satires of Persius, Juvenal, Horace; the comedies of Plautus and Terence; the histories of Sallust, Livy, Tacitus; the *Lives* of Plutarch and Suetonius; the doctrines of Cicero and Seneca; the epigrams of Martial — were all considered applicable to contemporary society with little more than a change of names and external details. See Tucker, *Foreign Debt of English Literature,* ch. I, II. On the beginnings in France of the adaptation of the classics to contemporary taste by paraphrase instead of exact translation, and the transfer of that method to England by Cowley and Denham, see Spingarn in *Camb. Hist. of Eng. Lit.* vol. VII, pp. 298–299.

The essential resemblance between the general mood of thoughtful Englishmen at the end of the seventeenth century and of many Romans at the close of the Republic was, however, not fanciful. Cf. Sellar, *Roman Poets of the Republic,* 3d ed., especially pp. 270–9. Sellar emphasizes the political unsettlement of the times which drove men of sensitive and refined natures into seclusion. The solitary way of life was a symptom of the despair over the welfare of the state, and the result was the diversion of thought to the affairs of the individual. The dissolution of religious belief awoke a deeper interest in ultimate questions of existence, the nature of the gods, and the destiny of the human soul. At the same time men discovered, in the poetry of Lucretius, a new delight open to the human spirit through sympathy with nature and the deepening of a fellow feeling uniting them not only with humanity but with all sentient existence.

The very great vogue of Lucretius in the second half of the century is partly to be explained by his novelty to English readers,[20] and partly by the timeliness and variety of his appeal. He had the sanction of the great French philosopher, Gassendi. The scientific character of his subject, " the nature of things," interested the members of the Royal Society, such as Evelyn, Sprat, and Dryden,[21] who made translations of parts of the work, and Creech, who printed a complete translation in 1664, and an edition with notes of a popular nature in 1695. His philosophy, an enlightened Epicureanism, offered to vigorous thinkers a possible solution of the almost impossible problems of conduct in the chaotic Age of Restoration, when neither the Church nor the State could command the complete loyalty of the nation. His denial of the immortality of the soul, his attack on superstition, his picture of the gods as remote from any interest in human affairs, his arguments against the fear of death, and his inference of the existence of a divine power from the evidence of the natural world, were all felt to be powerful and pertinent in the three-sided controversies of deists, atheists, and orthodox churchmen. Allusions to his ideas, imitations of his descriptive metaphors and similes, became imbedded in the philosophical

[20] Cf. Sandys, *History of Classical Scholarship*, vol. II, pp. 355–6.

[21] Evelyn's prose translation of the first book appeared in 1656, the other five remaining unpublished. Sprat's translation of *The Plague of Athens* (Lucretius, *De Rerum Natura*, VI, 1138–1286), first printed in 1659, was widely read after the London plague of 1665 and was kept in mind for over a century by dread of the return of the pest. (New ed. 1665, 1676, 1683, 1688, 1703, and in 1716 ed. of Dryden's *Miscellany Poems*.) Dryden's translations in *Sylvae* (1685) include the invocation of Venus (*De Rerum Natura*, I, 1–40), the description of the simple life (II, 1–60), the passage against the fear of death (III, 830–1094), and that on the nature of love (IV, 1052–1286). Flatman, Rochester, and Howard also translated a few lines each.

prose and the reflective poetry of the seventeenth and eighteenth centuries, and are distinctly traceable for a long time in the work of individual poets.[22]

Dryden regarded the descriptions and the moral philosophy of Lucretius as the poetical sugar coating which hid and sweetened the real, scientific subject, the nature and constitution of the material universe. He considered that Virgil in his *Georgics* had successfully borrowed and applied the same method, conveying much information and practical advice on farming in four poems which, in Dryden's opinion, "are more perfect than even his divine Aeneids."[23]

Now in these Latin classics, so well-known in the original, so widespread in translation by Dryden and others, certain themes recur which have a perennial appeal and which, moreover, were specially congenial to the general mood of the late seventeenth century. I have called these, for convenience of reference, the Complaint of Life, the Retirement theme, and the Death theme. They occur, singly or in combination, very frequently and strikingly in the poetry of Lucretius, Virgil, Horace, Martial, Seneca, and other poets of antiquity.

The Retirement theme is the expression of the poet's preference for the life of the country over that of the city, for solitude as opposed to society, for moderate means as opposed to wealth, for obscurity as opposed to ambitious prominence. It is a favorite Epicurean doctrine, enun-

[22] Creech's translation of Lucretius, 2nd ed. revised by "another hand," 1714, 2 vols., lists in the footnotes a number of parallels between passages in the *De Rerum Natura* and lines by Cowley, Milton, Butler, Dryden, Otway, and Lee. I suspect that a study of the influence of Lucretius in English literature would show him to be almost as much of a "poet's poet" as Spenser, Shakespeare, or Milton He was very evidently a source of power in the early work of Shelley and of Tennyson.

[23] Dryden, Preface to *Sylvae*, 1685.

ciated by Lucretius and repeated in Virgil, and is a characteristic note in Horace.

The beginning of the second book of Lucretius condemns self-indulgent luxury, and describes the simple " Epicurean picnic " thus:

> O wretched man! in what a mist of life,
> Inclos'd with dangers and with noisy strife,
> He spends his little span, and overfeeds
> His cramm'd desires with more than nature needs!
> For nature wisely stints our appetite,
> And craves no more than undisturb'd delight:
> Which minds, unmix'd with cares and fears obtain;
> A soul serene, a body void of pain.
>
> . . . .
>
> If golden sconces hang not on the walls,
> To light the costly suppers and the balls;
> If the proud palace shines not with the state
> Of burnish'd bowls, and of reflected plate;
> If well-tun'd harps, nor the more pleasing sound,
> Of voices, from the vaulted roofs rebound;
> Yet on the grass, beneath a poplar shade,
> By the cool stream our careless limbs are laid;
> With cheaper pleasures innocently blest,
> When the warm spring with gaudy flow'rs is dress'd.
> Nor will the raging fever's fire abate
> With golden canopies and beds of state;
> But the poor patient will as soon be sound
> On the hard mattress, or the mother ground.
>
> (Tr. Dryden.)

A similar thought at the end of Virgil's second *Georgic* (458) develops into a description of the happy life of the tiller of the soil. This is almost exactly paralleled in thought by Horace's *Epistles* I,10, and again, in Horace's *Odes* II,16, the happy life is declared to be life on a country estate of moderate size. This ode appears in the Third Part of *Miscellany Poems,* 1693.

Happy the man with little blest,
Of what his Father left possest;
No base desires corrupt his Head,
No fears disturb him in his Bed.
. . . .
Thy portion is a wealthy stock,
A fertile Glebe, a fruitful Flock,
. . . .
For me a little Cell I chuse,
Fit for my Mind, fit for my Muse,
Which soft content does best adorn,
Shunning the Knaves and Fools I scorn.
(Tr. Otway.)

Martial's version of the same idea (47) is included in Tate's *Poems by Several Hands*, 1685.

What makes a happy Life? O what?
A Fortune by Descent, not got;
An answ'ring Farm, still smoaking home;
Dependence seldom, Law-suits none:
A Mind compos'd, a lively Soul,
An active Body, round and whole;
An open Plainness, but discreet,
Friendships agreeable and fit;
No over-curious Bill of Fare,
No drunken Nights, yet void of care;
A merry Wife, and only yours,
A sleep that never tells the Hours;
Contented with thy Destiny,
And neither wish nor fear to dye.
(Tr. Wilson.)

Now the passage just referred to at the end of Virgil's second *Georgic*, 458–548, contains three motifs or themes, each one of which might furnish material, as the seventeenth century poets perceived, for a short lyric. Lines 458–474 might be called *The Happy Husbandmen*, lines 475–489, *On Contemplation*, and lines 490–540, *On Contentment*, or perhaps *Of Obscurity*. Each section presents one aspect of the Retirement theme. Poems under any of these titles, or under the more general name *Retirement,* are numerous in this century and the next, and in most cases it is safe to assume that they are either directly or indirectly inspired by Virgil.

In all these Latin poets, but especially in Horace, the image is frequently presented of the poet lying at full length under a large tree, upon soft grass, and usually beside a gently flowing stream.[24] But in reading all such descriptions, we must remember that the reclining figure is not supposed to have chosen mere ease or inactivity, but rather a very simple, inexpensive, healthful, and harmless form of pleasure.

In Stoic doctrine, the purpose of seclusion is slightly different. Cicero (*De Officiis,* I, 20–21 and III, 1) praises retirement, it is true, because it is easier and safer than public life, but demands that it shall also be philosophically productive. The solitary life is not to be entirely devoted to pleasure, however harmless, but to thought and study, pursuits which demand leisure and calmness of mind unattainable in the press of affairs. Similar reflections *On the Philosopher's Seclusion, On the Reasons for Withdrawing from the World, On Worldliness and Retirement, On Quiet and Study* are to be found in Seneca's *Ad Lucilium Epistulae Morales,* 8, 14, 19, 36, and (humorously put) 56. The Stoic version of the safety of obscurity is sung by the chorus in Seneca's *Thyestes,* at the end of act II, beginning "*Stet quicumque volet*":

> Upon the slippery tops of humane State,
> The gilded Pinnacles of Fate,
> Let others proudly stand, and for a while
> The giddy danger to beguile,

[24] Cf. Virgil, *Georgics* II, 488–9; Horace, *Odes* I, 1; II, 3; *Epodes* 2; Lucretius, II, 28–29; Tibullus, I, 1, 27–28. In Burton and Milton, this pastime is one of the pleasures of melancholy.

With Joy, and with disdain look down on all,
Till their Heads turn, and down they fall.
Me, O ye Gods, on Earth, or else so near
That I no Fall to Earth may fear,
And, O ye Gods, at a good distance seat
From the long Ruines of the Great.
Here wrapt in th' Arms of Quiet let me ly;
Quiet, Companion of Obscurity.
(Tr. Cowley, in his *Essays in Prose and Verse.*)

The Death theme is found in its most impressive form in the third book of Lucretius in a passage usually called *Against the Fear of Death*, a passage which fascinated Dryden though he felt obliged to protest against its leading idea, that there is no individual consciousness after death. "The thought of being nothing after Death," he wrote in the Preface to *Sylvae,* is "a burden unsupportable to a virtuous Man, even though a Heathen" His translation begins vigorously:

What has this Bugbear Death to frighten Man,
If Souls can die, as well as Bodies can?

The poet argues that we shall be no more conscious after death than we were before birth. It is unreasonable for a man to have fears as to the disposal of his corpse, or to dread separation by his own death from his wife and children, for when that time comes, he, being dead, will care not at all. The voice of "the nature of things" rebukes us for this self-pity. If life has been pleasant, why not retire like one satisfied? If unpleasant, why repine to leave it? As for the old, they ought to be glad to make room for future generations. Punishment after death is a myth, or rather an allegory of the miseries of this life. Great, wise, and good men have perished before us; why should we, whose lives are so much less worth while, hesitate to follow them? Our restless attempt to get the most out of life, by rushing from one place to another, would cease, if we turned our minds to the study of science, which alone has eternal value. The craving for life is futile, for the end is inevitable, and even if it were not so, to prolong life would be only to prolong boredom, without affecting one's state after death.

When once the Fates have cut the mortal Thred,
The Man as much to all intents is dead,
Who dyes today, and will as long be so,
As he who dy'd a thousand years ago.[25]

It will be noticed that while the purpose of the argument is to remove the dread of death, Lucretius actually so stresses the universality, inevitability, and finality of death, and the misery and boredom of living, that the total effect of the passage is pessimistic. Christian poets, therefore, promptly attacked the arguments with "anti-Lucretian" poems asserting personal immortality, and deists and optimistic freethinkers a little later began the agitation in favor of the doctrine, Whatever is, is right.[26]

In Horace, these same ideas about death are present,

[25] Here Dryden's phrasing recalls not Lucretius but Drummond, *A Cypresse Grove,* though Drummond's idea is essentially the same as that of Lucretius:

"If thou dost complain that there shall be a time in the which thou shalt not be, why dost thou not too grieve that there was a time in the which thou wast not? . . . For, not to have been a thousand years before this moment, is as much to be deplored, as not to be a thousand after it, the effect of them both being one: that will be after us which long long ere we were was. . . . The violets have their time, though they empurple not the winter, and the roses keep their season, though they discover not their beauty in the spring." *Poems of William Drummond . . .* ed. Ward, vol. II, p. 245. But the roses and violets smell not of Lucretius nor of the late seventeenth century. They belong to the Melancholy of the Renaissance. See *post,* pp. 48–53.

[26] See *post,* ch. III.

but are not elaborated. He has only one or two entire poems about death, such as *Odes,* I, 28, but here and there throughout his poetry a few words, a pungent phrase, are sprinkled like salt to bring out the flavor of life itself. For instance, in *Odes* I, 4 and IV, 7, the thought of death immediately follows a description of the coming of spring. In *Odes* II, 3, 14, 18, the thought of the certainty of death is used partly as an argument against the accumulation of riches, partly as a warning to enjoy the life of the moment. The beauty of Horace's phrasing tantalized the seventeenth century poets into translating the same poems again and again, and his very condensed expression often caused his sayings about death to be dissociated from their context and used as "mottoes" for meditative poems upon death itself.

In Virgil's *Georgics* III, 66–68, are just two lines in similar tone, but in certain descriptions both in the *Aeneid* and the *Georgics,* he strikes the note of horror of the supernatural, or superstitious dread of some undefined evil. Such "horror" passages as the description of the birdless place in *Aeneid* VI, 237–42, the dim halls of Dis in *Aeneid* VI, 268–81, portents and specters, *Georgics* I, 466–83, trees of ill omen, *Georgics* II, 257–58, the figures of Tisiphone and Hydra, *Aeneid* VI, 555–77, and the ghastly details of the cattle plague,[27] *Georgics* III, 551–567, are recognizable as the sources of many gruesome descriptions in English odes, elegies, and pastorals on the death of famous persons in the latter half of the century.

Cicero's *Tusculan Disputations,* Book I, *On the Contempt of Death,* conducts in prose the same arguments against the fear of death. In Seneca's *Troades,* the Chorus at the end of act II is evidently founded on Lucretius.

[27] The description of the cattle plague is, of course, inspired by Lucretius's description of the plague at Athens, at the end of his sixth book.

After death nothing is, and nothing death,
The utmost limits of a gasp of breath.
Let the ambitious zealot lay aside
His hope of Heaven, (whose faith is but his pride):
Let slavish souls lay by their fear,
Nor be concern'd which way, or where,
After this life they shall be hurl'd:
Dead, we become the lumber of the world,
And to that mass of matter shall be swept,
Where things destroy'd with things unborn are kept;
Devouring Time swallows us whole,
Impartial Death confounds body and soul.
For Hell, and the foul fiend that rules
The everlasting fiery goals,
Devis'd by rogues, dreaded by fools,
With his grim grisly dog that keeps the door,
Are senseless stories, idle tales,
Dreams, whimsies, and no more.
(Rochester's paraphrase.)

Other lines from this chorus, omitted in Rochester's paraphrase, contribute the images which liken the "fleeting breath" of the spirit to the vanishing smoke from burning fires, or clouds scattered by the wind. The song ends impressively, "Dost ask where thou shalt lie when death has claimed thee? Where they lie who were never born."

We have seen that Lucretius, in his attempt to do away with the fear of death, had used as one argument that life was in itself either wretched or tedious. With this theme, the Complaint of Life, as I have called it, Dryden was especially pleased. He found that Lucretius had "pathetically urged" and "beautifully expressed" the reasons why men should not be too much in love with life. "Such as are the natural Satiety, proceeding from a perpetual enjoyment of the same things; the inconveniences of old age . . . the decay of understanding and memory."[28] Other reasons alleged by Lucretius are the cares of life,

[28] Preface to *Sylvae*.

the uncertainty of fortune and of public honor, and the natural restlessness of men. This passage Dryden imitated in *Aurengzebe,* act IV, sc. 1:

> When I consider life, 'tis all a cheat;
> Yet, fooled with hope, men favor the deceit;
> Trust on, and think tomorrow will repay;
> Tomorrow's falser than the former day;
> Lies worse, and, while it says, we shall be blest
> With some new joys, cuts off what we possest.
> Strange cozenage! None would live past years again,
> Yet all hope pleasure in what yet remain;
> And, from the dregs of life, think to receive,
> What the first sprightly running could not give.

Two out of these three themes were also familiar scriptural themes, and had often been the subjects of religious, non-classical poems. The "penitential psalms," *Ecclesiastes,* and *Job* set forth the vanity of life, the insignificance of man, and the finality of death. Favorite passages in *Job* were the third chapter, beginning, "Let the day perish when I was born," the tenth, beginning, "My soul is weary of my life" and closing with the description of the state beyond the grave as "the land of darkness and the shadow of death," and the fourteenth, "Man that is born of woman is of few days and full of trouble." Sundry verses in *Job* and the *Psalms* often furnished to poetry the metaphors which figure the life of man as a weaver's shuttle, a wind, a cloud (*Job* VII, 6–10), a flower cut down, a shadow (*Job* XIV, 2; *Psalm* CII, 11; CXLIV, 4), a tale that is told (*Psalm* XC, 9), a sleep (*Psalm* XC, 5), or grass (*Psalm* XC, 5, 6; CII, 11; CIII, 15, 16). Job's complaints of sleeplessness and evil dreams (*Job* VII, 4, 13, 14) paralleled the classical passages expressing the longing for sleep as a relief from care.[29] The descriptions of the last judgment in *Matthew* XXV, 31–46; *Revelations*

[29] As in Horace, *Odes* III, 1; Statius, *Silvae* V, 4, *Ad Somnum.*

VI, 12–17; XX, 11–15, were considered by the reformers of poetry as better poetic material than those of the classical Hades [30] and had long ago found moving poetic expression in the Latin hymn, *Dies Irae*. While the Retirement theme had no exact scriptural counterpart, the practice of solitary meditation had long been a part of Christian discipline, as Burton noted (*ante* p. 9).[31]

These three themes then, existed as common elements in both the classical and the Biblical literary tradition, and offered to any poet who could give them a new turn the possibility of appealing to many classes of readers at once. For the common ground between the court and the middle class, Whig and Tory, non-conformist and churchman, atheist and believer, was precisely their common disgust with life, disillusionment, skepticism. While it was politically and scientifically a very active age, many people seemed to feel uncertain of the purpose of that activity, and to lack confidence in the outcome. Reflection on the spectacle of public affairs was likely to be gloomy, emerging in the expression of one or more of these themes. All three fall within the seventeenth century definition of melancholy. The complaint of life was one of its symptoms, retirement was its chosen way of living, death was its obsession. Accordingly, almost all the meditative or the would-be lyrical poems of the time, so far as they were not merely official or occasional, were on such subjects as Retirement, Contemplation, Meditation, Midnight Thoughts, Solitude, Obscurity, Grief, Melancholy, the Vanity of Life, the Littleness of Man, Sleep, Death, or the Last Day. Melancholy was the dominant mood. The same thoughts appeared again and again, in language reminiscent now of the classics, now of the Bible, and now of both at once.

[30] Cf. Watts, Preface to *Horae Lyricae*, 1706.

[31] Cf. Montalembert, *Monks of the West*, Introduction, ch. III, V.

In the English literary tradition also, there were perhaps a score of poems and some prose which, though written before 1650, may have been influential at the end of the century for certain special reasons, and which would have strengthened this combination of classical and religious melancholy.

I have already explained that the attitude of Donne would have been classified in his own time as non-melancholy. It is rather a striking fact that, in spite of his importance in the literature of the early half of the seventeenth century, neither Donne's poetry nor his sermons are to be reckoned among the survivals in popular interest in the last decade of the century. Though Dryden and Cowley, Herbert, Crashaw, Vaughan and other poets read him and borrowed from him many a didactic turn, piece of "metaphysical wit," or transcendental idea, it was not his poetry but theirs which was in circulation at the time of which we are speaking. His versification and his use of English had seemed out of date to Dryden in 1693.[32] There was no edition of his poetry in that century after 1669, nor of his other work after 1661. So far as his manner of thought affects the taste for melancholy, it is indirectly exerted through his friends, Bishop Henry King and Sir Henry Wotton, or his disciple Cowley, and Cowley's followers, Flatman and Tate.[33]

Of Donne's contemporaries who had written poems expressive of melancholy, we find that Raleigh, Wotton, Shirley, Beaumont, and Webster had still a certain importance about the year 1700.

[32] *Essays of John Dryden,* ed. Ker, vol. II, p. 19, 102.

[33] Repeated editions of Walton's *Lives* probably kept the public mindful of Donne's elaborate, long-drawn-out, and public preparations for death. But Mr. Gosse is of the opinion that even in 1631 such a death was "old-fashioned." Gosse, *Life and Letters of John Donne,* vol. II, p. 286.

Interest in the life and death of Sir Walter Raleigh had persisted throughout this century of civil struggle. His name became so much the synonym for a victim of royal ingratitude that the life of Clarendon was published under the title *Raleigh Redivivus.* Sir Walter's *Remains,* reprinted at frequent intervals, contained those grim criticisms of life, *The Lie* and *His Pilgrimage.* The works now attributed to his friend Sir Henry Wotton, whose poem, *The Happy Life,* is essentially a Retirement poem, also reappeared four times between 1651 and 1685. Besides these, we have ascribed to the one or the other author, though often falsely,[34] sundry satiric complaints and mortuary musings. *A Farewell to the Vanities of the World*[35] (author uncertain) is a plea for obscurity, since

> Fame, honour, beauty, state, train, blood, and birth
> Are but the fading blossoms of the earth.
> . . . .
> Welcome, pure thoughts! welcome, ye silent groves!
> These guests, these courts, my soul most dearly loves.
> . . . .
> Then here I'll sit and sigh my hot love's folly,
> And learn to affect an holy melancholy.

A Description of the Country's Recreations[35] (in *Rel. Wotton.* but author uncertain) has a first stanza rather suggestive of Milton's *Il Penseroso* and Fletcher's *Melancholy,* but ends in pastoral description. In *De Morte*[35] (*Rel. Wotton.*),

> Man's life's a tragedy: his mother's womb,
> From which he enters, is the tiring room.

[34] For identifications, I have depended on the Aldine edition of the *Poems of Sir Walter Raleigh; Collected and Authenticated with Those of Sir Henry Wotton and Other Courtly Poets, 1540–1650,* ed. J. Hannah.

[35] To be found in *The Book of Elizabethan Verse,* ed. Braithwaite.

Five acts are described as a progress in folly and vice, until

> diseases clog
> And trouble him; then death's his epilogue.[36]

The revival of the theaters during the Restoration probably put the late seventeenth century in mind of the lyrics of late Elizabethan playwrights, such as Shirley's *Death's Emissaries,*[35] and his magnificent *Death the Leveller.*[35]

> The glories of our blood and state
> Are shadows, not substantial things;
> There is no armour against Fate;
> Death lays his icy hand on kings;
> Sceptre and Crown
> Must tumble down,
> And in the dust be equal made
> With the poor crooked scythe and spade.
> . . . .
> Your heads must come
> To the cold tomb:
> Only the actions of the just
> Smell sweet and blossom in their dust.

Probably also Beaumont's *On the Tombs in Westminster Abbey*[35] Webster's *Vanitas Vanitatum,*[35] *Land Dirge,*[35] and *The Shrouding of the Duchess of Malfi,*[35] were known to play-goers and the recollection of them may have crossed the minds of any who loved to "melancholize." The absence of explicit reference to originals and the growing communism of matter and manner among poets at the

[36] Cf. *The English Poems of Henry King,* ed. Mason, *The Dirge,* in which life is compared to a storm, a flower, a dream, a sun-dial,

> a weary enterlude
> Which doth short joyes, long woes include.
> The World the Stage, the Prologue tears,
> The Acts vain hope, and vary'd fears;
> The Scene shuts up with loss of breath,
> And leaves no Epilogue but Death.

end of the century make it almost impossible to determine what memory of these authors then survived.

But if these are the models, the late seventeenth century copies are badly distorted. In the latter poetic intensity is gone, the Complaints of Life lack pungency and brevity, the thought of death is confronted hopelessly and drearily, not exultantly, or grimly, or adventurously. This earlier group are belated Elizabethans like Donne, still writing in the Renaissance spirit, which loved to wear melancholy as a decoration, to play with it as a toy, or toss it aside as a faded flower. The temper of the end of the century is quite different.

One may see the change in process of becoming in the work of William Drummond, Laird of Hawthornden, friend of Drayton and host of Ben Jonson. His earlier poems have the right Renaissance ring, and a Greek feeling for beauty. But after fire and famine in Edinburgh and a long illness, he wrote a whole series of religious musings called *Flowers of Sion* and *A Cypresse Grove*, which is a prose meditation on Death. Because of seventeenth century interest in Scottish affairs, Drummond's *History of Scotland* was republished in 1681 and 1682 (and again in 1711), and the edition included each time his poems and this piece of prose. His little poem,

> This Life, which seems so fair
> Is like a bubble blown up in the air
> By sporting children's breath [37]

[37] In Henry King's version, life is compared to the falling of a star, the flight of eagles, the hue of spring, drops of morning dew, a wind, or bubbles.

> "The Wind blowes out; the Bubble dies;
> The Spring entomb'd in Autumn lies;
> The Dew dries up; the Starre is shot;
> The Flight is past; and Man forgot."

Dr. Mason (*op. cit.* p. 208) refers to fifteen other stanzas like King's and conjectures that the source is in " some classical author;

may have sent that particular metaphor floating down the poetic ages, whither we shall chase it in succeeding chapters. More pessimistic is the tone of *The World a Game.*

> This world a hunting is,
> The prey poor man, the Nimrod fierce is Death;
> His speedy greyhounds are
> Lust, sickness, envy, care,
> Strife that ne'er falls amiss,
> With all those ills which haunt us while we breathe.
> Now, if by chance we fly
> Of these the eager chase,
> Old age with stealing pace
> Casts up his nets, and there we panting die.

The Shadow of the Judgment, conceived on too large a scale, remains an ineffective fragment, but *A Cypresse Grove* is a finely executed whole.

Two thirds of it utters much the same thought and in the same dispassionate tone as Lucretius's considerations against the fear of death. Drummond first confronts fairly the dreadful thought of death as the end of being, the wreck "of such a wonderful masterpiece as the body." But he finds consolation in the thought that the same fate is common to all, and that the law of nature is continual change. "This is the highway of mortality, our general home: behold, what millions have trod it before thee! . . . Thy death is a piece of the order of this All, a part of the life of this world; for while the world is the world, some creatures must die, and others take life . . . the taking away of what is old being the making way for what is young." Again, like Lucretius and Job, he finds death not really an evil, because life itself is a series of painful,

---

e.g., cf. Seneca's *Troades,* 378–399; *Oedipus,* 131, 132; *Phaedra* 764–772." But none of these uses the figure of the bubble.

yet trivial experiences. Nor is the last moment to be feared, for it is but cessation of pain, and it is moreover but an instant. Nor does it matter whether a man dies young or old, for "Days are not to be esteemed after the number of them, but after the goodness." As for the desire to live in men's memory, the earth is but a point in space and earthly reputation less than the merest nothing. At this juncture, however, Drummond ceases to contemplate death in its earthly aspects, and devotes himself to proving that, after death, soul and body will be reunited and both absorbed into the Universal Intelligence. The piece ends with a rhapsodic description of this happy state, strongly tinged with Platonic philosophy.[38]

To modern readers the greatest melancholy lyric of the seventeenth century is *Il Penseroso* and we should naturally infer that it was also popular and influential in its own time. Historical criticism, however, seems to have proved that before 1730 the minor poems of Milton were much less popular than *Paradise Lost,* and their influence on the work of the other poets almost negligible.[39] The vogue of *Paradise Lost,* however, begins to be noticeable as early as 1690. Very naturally, therefore, we shall find poets of the next century drawing on his magnificent descriptions of Sin, Death, and Hell as freely as on the Virgilian passages already noticed (*ante* p. 44) as models for "horror machinery." In the particular decade we are

[38] *The Poems of William Drummond of Hawthornden,* ed. Ward, vol. II, Appendix II.

[39] Dr. Good's argument in his *Studies in the Milton Tradition,* ch. V is to the effect that before 1730, "in England, his Minor Poetry was little noticed, his Prose was little liked, while his Epic was, perhaps, the most noticed, most read, most criticized, and finally the most exalted Poem in the English Tongue." Cf. the usual view (not documented) in Elton, *The Augustan Ages,* p. 208. Dr. Havens, in his *Influence of Milton,* Part III, grants more interest in the minor poems than does Dr. Good.

considering, however, the Companion Poems were not fully appreciated.

The average reader of that day would have been far more likely to satisfy a taste for melancholy by turning to the poetry of Abraham Cowley, whose *Works,* edited by Sprat in 1668, the year after Cowley's death, reached a sixth edition in 1680–81, and a ninth in 1700.

Cowley was, in fact, the conspicuous example in the seventeenth century of pleasure in Retirement. He had been called from the academic life to serve as a secretary of kings, and at the Restoration had experienced the proverbial ingratitude of kings. He thereupon wrote *The Complaint.*

In a deep Vision's intellectual scene,
Beneath a Bow'r for sorrow made,
Th' uncomfortable shade,
Of the black Yew's unlucky green,
Mixt with the mourning Willow's careful gray,
Where Reverend *Cham* cuts out his famous way,
The Melancholy *Cowley* lay.

The Muse of Pindar appears to him, reproaches him with having wasted his life in courts and cities, and taunts him with having received none of the royal manna. The melancholy Cowley retorts that it is she, the Muse, who has spoiled him for all gainful occupation. The king may yet send him some reward, but to the Muse the poet says:

However, of all Princes thou
Shouldst not reproach Rewards for being small or slow;
Thou who rewardest but with popular breath,
And that too after death.

Living first at Barn-Elms and then at Chertsey, he emphasizes again and again in his *Several Discourses by way of Essays in Verse and Prose,*[40] the use and pleasures of the retired life, supporting his own opinions by a wealth of classic allusion and translation.

The titles of these little essays show their range and point of view; *Of Liberty, Of Solitude, Of Obscurity* (already quoted, *ante*, p. 41), *Of Agriculture, The Garden,* (dedicated to John Evelyn, and usually prefixed to Evelyn's *Sylva*), *Of Greatness, Of Avarice, The Dangers of an Honest Man in Much Company, The Shortness of Life and Uncertainty of Riches, The Danger of Procrastination, Of Myself*. They largely concern themselves, in fact, with the unsatisfactoriness of public life, and the praise of Stoic simplicity, and to them all is appended a Latin epitaph for himself, asserting that he had remained

> *Non* Indecora pauperie *Nitens,*
> *Et Non* inerti *nobilis* otio.

Of Solitude makes the general point (so often disputed in the eighteenth century attack on melancholy) that intelligence and virtue are necessary prerequisites of the solitary life, and that solitude, in its turn, fosters these qualities. He quotes Scipio's saying (Cicero, *De Officiis* III, 1), *Nunquam minus solus, quam cum solus,*[41] but, complains that most men nowadays, when they are without company, are " like a becalmed Ship, they never move but by the wind of other men's breath, and have no Oars of their own to steer withal." The solitary man must constantly have recourse to study and to books, for " Cogitation is the thing which distinguishes the Solitude

[40] First published in the *Works* of 1668. My quotations are from the critical edition of Cowley's *Essays, Plays, and Sundry Verses*, by Waller.

[41] " Every Man and almost every Boy for these seventeen hundred years, has had it in his mouth." Cowley, *Essays*, p. 392.

of a God from a wild Beast." The poem that follows is introduced by a " motto " from Virgil's *Georgics* II, 488:

> *. . . O quis me gelidis sub montibus Æmi*
> *Sistat, et ingenti ramorum protegat umbra?* [42]

Cowley's poem begins with a salutation to the trees on his estate:

> Hail, old Patrician Trees, so great and good!
> Hail, ye *Plebeian* under wood!
> Where the Poetique Birds rejoyce,
> And for their quiet Nests and plenteous Food
> Pay with their grateful voice.
>
> Hail, the poor Muses richest Manor Seat!
> Ye Countrey Houses, and Retreat,
> Which all the happy Gods so Love,
> That for you oft they quit their Bright and Great
> Metropolis above.
>
> . . . .
>
> Here let me, careless and unthoughtful lying
> Hear the soft winds above me flying,
>
> . . . .
>
> A Silver stream shall roul his waters neer.

Here it is Nature who builds the house. A wretched man is he who loves not his own company. Solitude is sacred, for it was the estate of God before the one became the many. Solitude, like a burning glass, brings together and intensifies the faint beams of reason and thus creates " noble fires."

> Whilst this hard Truth I teach, methinks, I see
> The monster *London* laugh at me,
> I Should at thee too, foolish City,
> If it were fit to laugh at Misery,
> But thy Estate I pity.

[42] These two lines, of course, are the original of Cowper's felicitous

> " O for a lodge in some vast wilderness,
> Some boundless contiguity of shade."
> (*Task* II, 1–2)

If all the wicked left London, it would dwindle to a village smaller than Islington, and would itself become almost a solitude.

The third essay, *Of Obscurity*, quotes Horace, *Epistles* I, 18, 103 and versifies the chorus of Seneca's *Thyestes*, already quoted (*ante* p. 41). The sixth, *Of Greatness*, likewise emphasizes the inconveniences of Grandeur.

I confess, I love Littleness almost in all things. A little convenient Estate, a little chearful House, a little Company, and a very little Feast; and, if I were ever to fall in love again (which is a great Passion, and therefore, I hope, I have done with it) it would be, I think, with Prettiness, rather than with Majestical Beauty.

The poem imitates Horace's *Odes* III, 1. It has one good stanza which, along with Shakespeare's famous lines, may have suggested to many later poets, such as Young, the complaint of inability to sleep.

Sleep is a God too proud to wait in Palaces;
And yet so humble too as not to scorn
    The meanest Country Cottages;
" His Poppy grows among the Corn."

The essays entitled *Of Avarice, The Shortness of Life, and Uncertainty of Riches*, and *The Dangers of an Honest Man in Much Company*, all evidently based upon classical sources, are essentially Complaints of Life. The essay on *The Garden* compares Cowley's own garden to the Garden of Eden, and makes the Epicurean point that the owner of such an estate is not occupied in ignoble pursuits.

The last essay, *Of Myself*, is most interesting from our point of view because of its subjectivity. It is an autobiographical account of the author's own tastes in youth, before he became interested in public affairs to his undoing. It is a rather early example of self-analysis, apparently a sincere expression of personal feeling. The poet pictures himself as a lover of books and of seclusion:

> As far as my Memory can return back into my past Life, before I knew, or was capable of guessing what the world, or glories, or business of it were, the natural affections of my soul gave me a secret bent of aversion from them, as some Plants are said to turn away from others, by an Antipathy imperceptible to themselves, and inscrutable to man's understanding. Even when I was a very young Boy at School, instead of running about on Holydaies and playing with my fellows; I was wont to steal from them and walk into the fields, either alone with a Book, or with some one Companion, if I could find one of the same temper. . . .
>
> With these affections of mind, and my heart wholly set upon Letters, I went to the University; But was soon torn from thence by that violent Publick storm which would suffer nothing to stand where it did, but rooted up every Plant, even from the Princely Cedars to Me, the Hyssop. Yet I had as good fortune as could have befallen me in such a Tempest; for I was cast by it into the Family of one of the best Persons, and into the Court of one of the best Princesses of the World. . . .
>
> I saw plainly all the Paint of that kind of life, the nearer I came to it; and that Beauty which I did not fall in Love with, when, for ought I knew, it was reall, was not like to bewitch, or intice me, when I saw that it was Adulterate. I met with several great Persons, whom I liked very well, but could not perceive that any part of their Greatness was to be liked or desired, no more then I would be glad, or content to be in a Storm, though I saw many Ships which rid safely and bravely in it: . . . Though I was in a croud of as good company as could be found any where, though I was in business of great and honourable trust, though I eate at the best Table, and enjoyed the best conveniences for present subsistance that ought to be desired by a man of my condition in banishment and publick distresses; yet I could not abstain from renewing my old School-boys Wish in a Copy of Verses to the same effect.
>
> Well then; I now do plainly see
> This busie World and I shall ne're agree, etc.
>
> And I never then proposed to myself any other advantage from His Majesties Happy Restoration, but the getting into some moderately convenient Retreat in the Country. . . .

Anticipating Young's *Ocean* and Gray's *Elegy,* the essay ends with an epitaph, already quoted (*ante,* p. 55).

Next to Cowley, probably, in general popularity, stand those two complete contrasts, John Wilmot, Earl of Rochester, the reprobate, and Wentworth Dillion, Earl of Roscommon, the exemplary, whose poems in later editions often appeared together.

Roscommon has an *Ode Upon Solitude,* the first lines of which are reminiscent of the beginning of the second book of Lucretius:

> Hail, sacred Solitude! from this calm bay,
> I view the world's tempestuous sea,
> . . . .
> With pity mov'd for others, cast away
> On rocks of hopes and fears, I see them toss'd
> On rocks of folly and of vice, I see them lost.

The later stanzas, though not closely resembling Lucretius in phrasing, nevertheless contain the characteristic Epicurean idea of " cheap and virtuous luxury ":

> Hail, sacred Solitude! soul of my soul,
> It is by thee I truly live,
> Thou dost a better life and nobler vigour give;
> . . . .
> Here in a full and constant tide doth flow
> All blessings man can hope to know;
> Here in a deep recess of thought we find
> Pleasures which entertain, and which exalt the mind,
> Pleasures which do from friendship and from knowledge rise,
> Which make us happy as they make us wise:
> Here may I always on this downy grass,
> Unknown, unseen, my easy minutes pass:
> Till with a gentle force victorious Death
> My solitude invade,
> And, stopping for a while my breath,
> With ease convey me to a better shade.

Among Roscommon's poems are also to be found a translation of Horace's *Odes* III, 6, the subject of which is " the corruption of the times" and one stanza of which describes the patriots of former days:

Rough, hardy, season'd, manly, bold,
Either they dug the stubborn Ground,
Or through hewn Woods their weighty strokes did sound.
And after the declining Sun
Had chang'd the shadows, and their Task was done,
Home with their weary Team they took their way,[43]
And drown'd in friendly Bowls the labour of the day.
Time sensibly all things impairs,
Our Fathers have been worse than theirs,
And we than Ours; next Age will see
A race more profligate than we
(With all the pains we take) have skill enough to be.[44]

Roscommon's poem, *The Grove,* was enormously popular, appearing first in a play, and afterwards being continually reprinted in various collections of Miscellany Poems.[45] It is a translation of part of the fifth scene of the second act of Guarini's *Pastor Fido,* and is in praise of the life of solitude, and of pure love between lovers in moderate circumstances. The same poet's *The Day of Judgment* is a free and vigorous translation of the *Dies Irae.* His *Prospect of Death* remained in manuscript until 1704.

Rochester is usually too cynical to be melancholy, but in his famous *Satire Against Mankind* he belittles human intelligence in a vein deeply pessimistic.

[43] Cf. Gray's *Elegy,*
"The ploughman homeward plods his weary way."

[44] This is Horace's form of the classic idea of the degeneration of the world from its golden age. In Lucretius, V, 925–1165, the emphasis is on the strength and fearlessness of primitive man, and the greater fertility of the earth in the primitive age, as compared with the present. In Virgil, *Georgics* II, 492–512, the happy life of the husbandman is contrasted with the restlessness and destructiveness of worldly ambition, and the poet concludes, "Such was the life golden Saturn lived on earth."

[45] See Dryden's *Miscellany Poems,* 3rd ed. 1702, p. 392.

In the case of these two men, the melancholy tone is evidently only an occasional variation from their usual strain, a piece of virtuosity.[46] But it is the characteristic vein of Thomas Flatman (1637–1688), the miniature painter. As his friend Tate wrote,

> But he the mournful Song so sweetly sings,
> That more of Pleasure than Regret it brings.[47]

The Retirement, Pindaric Ode Made In The Time of The Great Sickness, 1665, is a deliberate indulgence in melancholy for the pleasure thereof:

> I thought on every pensive thing,
> That might my passion strongly move,
> That might the sweetest sadness bring;
> Oft did I think on death, and oft on Love,
> The triumphs of the *little God,* and that same *ghastly King;*
> The *ghastly King* what has he done,
> How his pail Territories spread!
> Strait scantlings now of consecrated ground
> His swelling Empire cannot bound,
> But every day new *Colonies* of dead
> Enhance his Conquests, and advance his Throne.

The poet longs to see again the mighty City of London whose buildings are too much like the pyramids of Egypt —

> Eternal Monuments of Pride and Sin,
> Magnificent and tall without, but Dead men's bones within.

Since Flatman has not been reprinted since the fourth edition, 1686, it may be well to quote him rather fully here in order to indicate where Young may have caught suggestions for some of his most admired effects in the *Night Thoughts.* Flatman's poem *The Fatigue* begins:

[46] The poems cited of Rochester and Roscommon may be found in Chalmers, *English Poets,* vol. VIII.

[47] *To Mr. Flatman, On his Excellent Poems,* in Flatman, *Poems,* 1684, p. 12.

From thee, false world, my deadly Foe,
Into some Desert let me go;
Some gloomy melancholy Cave,
Dark and Silent as the Grave,
Let me withdraw . . . .
Kind *Philomel* would teach me there
My sorrows pleasantly to bear.

In *Death, A Song,* the poet sees in imagination the day of his own death, when friends shall stand about his couch, pitying his dying groans and struggles. In *A Dooms-Day Thought,* the reader is urged to

Go to the dull Church-yard, and see
Those Hillocks of Mortalitie,
Where proudest Man is one'ly found
By a small swelling in the Ground;
What crouds of Carcasses are made
Slave to the pickax and the spade!
Digg but a foot, or two, to make
A Cold Bed, for thy dead friend's sake,
'T is odds but in that scantling roome
Thou robb'st another of his Tombe,
Or in thy delving smit'st upon
A shinbone, or a Cranion:
When th' Prison's full, what next can be
But the grand Jayl Deliverie?
The great *Assise,* when the pale Clay
Shall gape, and render up its Prey. . .

Then the souls shall endeavor to hide themselves, but in vain.

What shall we do? we cannot run
For Refuge, or the strict Judge shun.
'T is too late *then* to think what course to take,
While we live here, we must Provision make.

Job is a paraphrase of *Job* XIV, 1, beginning

Few be the days, that feeble man must breathe.

Nudus Redibo is also a paraphrase of *Job:*

Naked I came when I began to be
A man among the sons of miserie.

. . . .

Naked I shall return, and nothing have,
Nothing wherewith to bribe my hungry grave.
Then what's the proudest Monarch's glittering Robe
Or what's he more, than I, that rul'd the Globe?
Since we must all without distinction die,
And slumber both stark naked, He and I.

Other melancholy poems are *The Desperate Lover* (a suicide poem), *Lucretius Paraphrased* (the lines of self-pity at the thought of death, in Lucretius, III, 896), and a long Pindaric ode *On the Death of My Dear Brother, Mr. Richard Flatman,* in which sorrow, though evidently genuine, is completely overlaid with the ghastly paraphernalia of death and the grave.

The prompt success of John Oldham (1653–83) as a political and social satirist was doubtless due in part to the timeliness and in part to the mere sensationalism of his four *Satyrs upon the Jesuits* (written upon the occasion of the Popish plot), *Satyr upon a Woman,* and *Satyr against Vertue.* But Dryden in his verses *To the Memory of Mr. Oldham* was quick to acknowledge his genuine power as a poet and publicly mourned his loss to literature:

For sure our souls were near allied, and thine
Cast in the same poetic mould as mine.

There were repeated issues of his *Works and Remains* at the end of the century. Some stanzas in the satires have the tone of Complaints of Life, especially these lines at the close of the *Drunkard's Speech in a Masque:*

Beset with Link-boys, we'll in triumph go,
A Troop of stagg'ring Ghosts, down to the Shades below:
Drunk we'll march off, and reel into the Tomb,
Nature's convenient, dark, Retiring Room:
And there, from Noise remov'd, and all tumultuous Strife,
Sleep out the dull Fatigue, and long Debauch of Life.

His non-satiric poetry consists chiefly of lamentations, wherein, unlike Flatman, he seems to be trying to inflict pain rather than to produce pleasure. Yet even when he is most tortured and unnatural, he always has vigor and the ring of sincerity. The very long poem, *To the Memory of my Dear Friend, Mr. Charles Morwent,* his school and college mate who died in 1674, is chiefly eulogistic but has some stanzas minutely descriptive of the transformation of the body by disease into a repulsive carcass. He translates Bion's lament for Adonis, and the lament of Moschus for Bion, applying the latter to the death of the Earl of Rochester. He turns David's mourning over Saul and Jonathan into a Cowleian ode:

> Oh Death! how vast an Harvest hast thou reap'd of late!
> . . . .
> Upon the fatal Mountain's Head,
> Lo! how the mighty Chiefs lie dead:
> . . . .
> They're all to the dark Grave, and Silence fled,
> And never now, in Story, shall be read,
> And never now shall take their Date,
> Snatcht hence by the preventing Hand of envious Fate.

In his paraphrase of the one hundred and thirty-seventh *Psalm,* he heightens at the end the expression of longing for revenge:

> Blest, yea thrice blessed be that barbarous Hand
> . . . .
> Who tears out Infants from their Mother's Womb,
> And hurls them, yet unborn, into their Tomb:
> . . . .
> Who with thy Skulls, and Bones, shall pave thy Streets all o'er,
> And fill thy glutted Channels with their scatter'd Brains and Gore.

His little prose essay, *A Sunday Thought in Sickness,* has the tone of a seventeenth century sermon. It begins: "Lord, how dreadful is the Prospect of Death! . . . All the Jolity of my Humor and Conversation is turn'd on a sudden into Chagrin and Melancholy black as Despair, and dark as the Grave;" argues that "there is a Hell, and damned Fiends, and a never-dying Worm;" but ends with a short poem expressing confidence in God's mercy.

The Reverend John Norris (1657–1711) is today seldom mentioned in histories of literature, and then only as one of the Cambridge Platonists opposed to the philosophy of Locke. But his poetry, first published in 1687, reached a fifth edition in 1705, and was warmly commended by Watts in the Preface to *Horae Lyricae* (1706). Norris's preface *To the Reader*, dated All-Souls' College, June 1, 1678, says that "poetry is of late mightily fall'n from the Beauty of its Idea, and from its ancient Majesty and Grandeur, as well as Credit and Reputation." Like music, it has become mere "light, frothy stuff." His own is to be, by contrast, the expression of "substantial massy Sense." Thereupon, we have, in perfectly conventional and entirely unpoetic language all the usual melancholy themes: *The Third Chapter of Job Paraphras'd; The Retirement; The Choice* (a paraphrase, probably in emulation of Cowley, of Seneca's *Stet quicumque volet*); *The Meditation,* on the approach of death; *The Refusal,* to emerge from retirement; *A Hymn to Darkness; The Invitation,* which is a Retirement poem based on the *Song of Solomon* VII, 11; *Sitting in an Arbour* (another Retirement poem); *The Prospect,* which is a vision of the writer's own death. *The Complaint* [48] begins:

Well, 't is a dull perpetual *Round*
Which here we silly Mortals *tread;*
Here's nought I'll swear *worth living* to be found,
I wonder how 'tis with the *Dead.*
Better, I hope, or else, ye Powers divine,
Unmake me, I my immortality *resign.*

[48] Quotations from Norris, *A Collection of Miscellanies,* 1687.

A poem *To Melancholy* declares

> No *Pain* is like *thy* Pain, no *Pleasure* too like *thine*.

And among the prose essays is one *On Solitude* in which the course of thought is like Cowley's, but without Cowley's richness of allusion and stately diction.

Nahum Tate, certainly of no importance today, must be regarded as influential at the end of the century, because of his public position as laureate after Shadwell, and because the miscellaneous character of his literary activities brought him into contact with so many other writers. His early poems, which appeared in 1677 (second edition 1684), are in the lugubrious manner of Flatman. Of his poem *On the Present Corrupted State of Poetry* I have already spoken (*ante*, p. 32). Among the great mass of his productions, we observe sundry instances of melancholy themes.

The Vision, written in a dangerous Fit of Sickness, is another name for the usual *Prospect of Death*. In a dream, the poet is borne to "Death's sad Courts" where

> dead men's Bones in Heaps were round me laid,
> And Skulls of largest size the Pavement made.
> The Sun to this dark Mansion darts no Ray,
> But glim'ring Lamps make all the feeble Day.

He is summoned to hear his own indictment before Death, who is attended by Disease. Asked whether he has anything to say for himself, he pleads for indulgence for his youth. But Death orders the demons to bear him to "Regions of Despair."

> In Liquid Flames of Sulphur let him roul
> In sharpest Torments of a Hell-wreckt Soul.
> Thus let him howl Eternity away,
> Ever in Flames, yet never more see Day.

At this instant appears his guardian angel, who tells him this doom is in compassion revoked, and he is to be borne to heaven, but first he must leave his body behind. He gladly does so, but once freed from the flesh, his soul is surprised at the loathsomeness of the body.

> Bless me (said I) what ghastly thing lies there?
> Was this the Mansion where so many a Year
> I lingered 'twixt successive Hope and Fear?
> Was this the thing I took such Care t' improve?
> Taught it to cringe, and in just measures move?
> The thing that lately did in Business sweat,
> That talkt so much of being Rich and great!

What woman now would deign to kiss the ghastly face?

> Why is the Corps so long detain'd from ground;
> 'Tis more than time those Hands and Feet were
>   bound.
> Haste, let the Fun'ral Peal be rung aloud,
> In Winding-Sheets th' offensive Carkass shroud
> And in some Nook the useless Lumber crowd.

Just as Heaven is in view, he wakes and the dream has fled. We notice that Tate's poem *Melancholy* is not an expression of pleasure in that mood, like Milton's *Il Penseroso,* but a description of the disease and its effect on the mind.

> Malignant Humour, Poyson to my Blood!
> Bane of those Spirits that were wont to glide
>   And sport within the Circling Tide;
> As Fish expire in an infected Flood.
> When all th' Horizon of my soul is clear,
>   Streight like a suddain Storm I find
>   Thy black Fumes gath'ring in my Mind,
> Transforming All to Egyptian Darkness there;
>   Darkness where nothing comes in sight
>   But Flashes more amazing than the Night,
> And fiery Spectres through the troubled Air.

The victim finds no relief in sleep, but only troubled dreams.

> Through Charnel Houses then I'm led,
> Those gloomy Mansions of the dead,
> Where pensive Ghosts by their lov'd Reliques stay,
> And curse the Breaking Day.

Or perhaps he is shipwrecked and sinking through the seas, or he is fighting some savage monster in the desert of Sahara, or is pinned beneath a mountain, like Typhon. Though his destiny may actually be a happy one, melancholy, by a sort of false astrology, makes him suffer all possible misfortunes in advance. Melancholy is the complete destruction of happiness. *The Male-Content* makes his complaint in the person of Thirsis, who retires to a cave in a wild cliff, longing to die. He begs the rock to fall on him and thus to become (by an arrangement particularly economical!) "at once my coffin, monument and grave." Other melancholy poems by Tate are *Amor Sepulchralis, The Mid-Night Thought, The Counter-Turn* (a sort of Hamlet-like meditation on the skull of a politician), *The Choice* (twelve lines on the happy life), *Recovering from a Fit of Sickness,* and *The Charnel House.* He also versifies the first three chapters of *Job.* The third chapter, beginning "Let the day perish, let it perish quite," is not without some flashes of power caught from the original.

The last word in dreariness is uttered by the saintly Richard Baxter in his most unpoetical *Poetical Fragments.*[49] *The Epistle to the Reader* defends "Holy Poetry," as he calls it, commends the works of Cowley, "Mr. Woodford's Paraphrases on the Psalms," the pieces of the "Lady (*sic*) Katherine Philips," "honest George

[49] *Poetical Fragments, Heart-Imployment with God and itself,* 1681.

Withers," Silvester on Du Bartas, " Sir Fulk Grevil," Lord " Brook," Sir John Davies's *Nosce Te Ipsum,* " Mr. George Herbert," and " Mr. George Sandys." Baxter's own poems contain many invectives against the vain world and vile man. *Man*[50] is full of grisly detail of the loathsomeness of the flesh.

> Vain Man! know'st thou no deeper than thy skin?
> Go see an open'd Corps, and that will shew
> What Garbage, Filth, and Dung are hid within,
> What thy vile Body is, thou there maist know.

It is refreshing to turn from Norris, Tate, and Baxter to the work of Anne, Countess of Winchilsea, known to her own circle as Ardelia. Those of her poems mentioned here, written between 1685 and 1702, must be regarded as symptomatic rather than influential, for they were, with few exceptions modestly passed about in manuscript volumes only, until the edition of 1713, and even then were received as of minor importance.[51] They are significant in this study because they show that one melancholy poet at least had discovered the consolation that lies in the love of the natural world, and had discovered it under the inspiration of Milton's minor poems; also because, though not intensely conceived or very skilfully written, they are so sincerely and simply expressed that they convince us of the genuineness of her enthusiasm for the life of retirement.

Lady Winchilsea's melancholy was greatest in her younger days, and for it there were two distinct and sufficient causes. In the first place, she suffered physically

[50] In *Additions to the Poetical Fragments,* 1700.

[51] Practically all I have to say about Lady Winchilsea is condensed or selected from the Introduction to *The Poems of Anne, Countess of Winchilsea, from the original edition of 1713 and from unpublished manuscripts,* ed. with int. and notes by Myra Reynolds.

from the disease called the spleen, realistically described in her poem of the same name.[52] The accuracy of the description was recognized by her friend, Dr. Stukely, the antiquary and physician, who republished the poem in his treatise on the spleen,[52] as supplementing his own account of the symptoms. She confirms Burton by her report of her experience of insomnia, bad dreams, and terrifying visions, and her struggle with an abnormal love of solitude, self-distrust, religious doubts, and a general depression of spirits. Her early poems, *On Grief*, *To Sleep*, and *To Melancholy* must be interpreted as growing out of this physical cause. *A Song on Griefe* represents Sorrow as an absolute monarch to whom she must submit.

> Thou, and cold fear, thy close Allie,
> Do not alone on life attend;
> Butt following mortalls to their end
> Do wrack the wretches, whilst they dye;
> And to eternal shades, too often with them flye.

Ardelia to Melancholy presents a similar thought. Ardelia has tried many interests, among them friendship and poetry, as charms against the power of her "old inveterate foe," but has obtained thereby only "encrease of pain." Now she surrenders.

> Thou, through my life, wilt with me goe,
> And make ye passage, sad, and slow.
> . . . .
> The Fort is thine, now ruin'd, all within,
> Whilst by decays without thy Conquest, too, is seen.

[52] *The Spleen* was first anonymously published in Gildon's *New Miscellany of Original Poems on Several Occasions. . . .* ed. by C. G. London, 1701. It had a "second" edition probably pirated, in *The Spleen, a Pindarique Ode*, by a Lady. Together with *A Prospect of Death; a Pindarique Essay*. London, 1709. (*British Museum Catalogue.*) Doctor William Stukeley's treatise is called *Of the Spleen, its Description and History, Uses and Diseases . . .* 2 pt. London, 1723. fol.

An Invocation to Sleep is the usual list of votive offerings intended to propitiate the reluctant god. The turn of thought at the end is that sleep intends to absent himself until she has put away all her cares.

> Thou 'llt stay, 'till kinder Death supplys thy place
> The surer Friend, tho' with the harsher face.

It seems probable that Lady Winchilsea suffered less from the spleen in her later years, and it is to be noted that these three poems were not published in the volume of 1713, but existed in manuscript only.

The second cause for Lady Winchilsea's melancholy was the fall of James II. She had been a maid of honor to Mary of Modena, and though she left that service on marrying Heneage Finch, her husband was still attached to the household of the king, to whom and to the queen she and her husband were personally devoted. They had thus suffered, in the revolution of 1688, " personal deprivations, frustrated ambitions, loss of faith in man, doubts of the providential ordering of human affairs." With this sad experience must be connected the loyalist poems, *The Petition for an Absolute Retreat, To Lady Worsley, The Change, The Losse, On the Death of King James.* Perhaps the *Enquiry after Peace* which remains a fragment of forty-one lines is the first draught of *The Petition for an Absolute Retreat.* Both are in the Miltonic verse form used through the greater part of *L'Allegro* and *Il Penseroso.*

The first strongly suggests Parnell's *Hymn to Contentment* (1713), and foreshadows also Dyer's *Grongar Hill* (1726), doubtless because all three have a common inspiration derived partly from Milton and partly from living in the country. It begins:

> Peace! where art thou to be found?
> Where, in all the spacious Round,

May thy Footsteps be pursu'd?
Where may thy calm Seats be view'd?
On some Mountain dost thou lie,
Serenely near the ambient Sky,
Smiling at the Clouds below,
Where rough Storms and Tempests grow?

All her experience of life has been such as to oppose peace — But here the fragment ends.

The Petition for an Absolute Retreat slightly suggests Cowley (*ante*, p. 56) in its longing for

A sweet, but absolute Retreat,
'Mongst Paths so lost and Trees so high,
That the world may ne'er invade,
Through such Windings and such Shade,
My unshaken Liberty.

Lady Winchilsea then passes to a half classical, half modern and realistic enumeration of the simple pleasures of the retired life — a plain table, set out with fruits, not truffles; plain and cheap garments, but new, "light and fresh as May"; no perfumes but the fragrance of flowers; also

A Partner suited to my Mind,
Solitary, pleas'd and kind. . . .

In this retreat, she desires to improve the moments by "Thoughts of Pleasure and of Use." The flowing river reminds her of the flowing of time into eternity. The pliant willows suggest the time of youth; the lonely, stubborn oak becomes the symbol of age. A low-lying helpless vine reminds her of her own former state, when she lay

Blasted by a Storm of Fate,
Felt, thro' all the *British* State. . . .

Then came to her the friendship of Arminda (Catherine, Countess of Thanet), who revived and consoled her as Jonathan did David. Friendship is, then, one of the pleasures of the retired life. She desires to be free from roving thoughts and absorption in material possessions, for the life of man consists not in the delight of the present only, but in high "Contemplations of the Mind." Let others enjoy "Courtship, Applause, Power," mirth, sensual pleasure,

> Whilst my Transports I employ
> On that more extensive Joy,
> When all Heaven shall be survey'd
> From those Windings and that Shade.

Without pausing over the other loyalist poems, which are, naturally, in the elegiac vein, we note that Lady Winchilsea also composed a number of scripture paraphrases, including the long Pindaric, *All Is Vanity,* and played her own quite orthodox variations on the Death theme in the poem, *To Death,* and on the Complaint of Life in a long poem called *Life's Progress.* These are quite in the usual seventeenth century manner.

But where Lady Winchilsea differs from other minor poets of that half century and strikes a new note, though still a note which her contemporaries and she herself would have called melancholy, is in her nature poems. The four little lyrics, *To the Eccho,* composed "in a clear night upon Astrop walks," *The Bird, The Tree* (all written before 1689), and *The Nightingale* (before 1702), as well as descriptive passages in other poems, are not remarkable for their power to create an image or paint a scéne, but rather for their power to convey a sense of life. In each case the author apostrophizes the bird, the tree, the wandering voice, and gives us its life history, its essential character, and in each case the reader feels that she is not simply indulging in a rhetorical device, but is moved by genuine sympathy to record an impression. While the first three again suggest by their meter that the author has been reading *Il Penseroso* and *L'Allegro,* and while the *Preface* to her folio distinctly implies that she had in mind certain literary predecessors, such as Beaumont, Denham, Tasso, we must agree with her latest critic and editor, Dr. Reynolds, that she is herself unusually sensitive in her response to nature, and unusually honest and accurate in her record.[53] The poems are free from any pathetic fallacy, and *The Bird* is in playful vein, but in the other three, sadness or pensiveness is the prevailing tone. Echo dwells in "a melancholy, sweet retreat." For the tree is foretold an end when

> [Thou] shalt, like ancient Heroes, burn,
> And some bright Hearth be made thy Urn.

The nightingale is compared to the poet.

> And still th' unhappy Poet's Breast,
> Like thine, when best he sings, is placed against a Thorn.

The Miscellanies of the period from 1684–1700, being compiled to suit all tastes, of course contained some admixture of melancholy. Dryden's *Miscellany Poems* consist for the most part of satires, gallant and occasional verse, prologues and epilogues, but pessimistic or pathetic musings

[53] I cannot feel, however, that she was "a heretic with romantic tastes," as Dr. Reynolds says (Int. p. XVII). At least, the purpose of the present study is to show that a good many other people had, or thought they had similar tastes, though they expressed them with less "delicate originality" than Ardelia. *The Nocturnal Reverie* belongs by its date (between 1702 and 1713) in the next chapter, and if that poem, or rather portions of it, had never been written, I doubt whether Wordsworth, Mr. Gosse, or Dr. Reynolds would have thought it worth while to "discover" her. Her poem, *The Nightingale,* for instance, shows no closer observation of nature or sympathy with bird life than Drummond's *To a Nightingale.*

occur sometimes in translations from Lucretius, Virgil, Horace, Ovid, and Statius.

In 1685, a year after Dryden issued his first *Miscellany Poems,* Tate also published a Miscellany, called *Poems of Several Hands and On Several Occasions.* It contains poems and translations by Cowley, Rochester, and Waller, with a few by Tate and lesser men, but the majority are anonymous. The translations are from Martial, Ovid, Horace, Tibullus, Anacreon, Statius, and Sannazaro. The collection is chiefly erotic, but in the midst of eroticism the melancholy note is several times sounded.

In *A Translation Out of Statius: To Sleep* (p. 53), the poet complains of sleeplessness:

> What horrid Crime did gentle Sleep displease?
> That he refuses me the common ease
> Of Bird and Beast? nay, ev'ry breeding Tree
> Seems but to nod with Sleep to waking me.
> Fierce Rivers softly glide, Seas faintly roar,
> And roul themselves asleep upon the Shore.

He has been sleepless for seven nights. He prays sleep to come to him.

> I will not ask him a whole night to stay,
> A happier Man must for that Blessing pray,
> Let him but call upon me in his way.

In *A Pastoral Reflection on Death* (p. 57), Damon and Strephon argue, somewhat didactically, for and against suicide. Damon desires to die.

> Did you but know how sweetly they repose
> On Beds of Earth that are lodg'd under ground!
> Unintercepted Rest they all enjoy,
> . . . .
> They but retreat to a far greater world.
> For how few tread the Surface of the Globe,
> Compar'd to crowding Colonies that Fate

Sends daily to the Bowels of the Earth,
That has been peopling ever since old time
Commenc'd! The subterranean Universe [54]
Still gapes to swallow down the upper World.[55]

When the body dies, God will turn death's black night to eternal day. Strephon tells Damon he must not precipitate his Fate, and begs him to live on.

A little poem called *Life* (p. 143) has more charm than most of the collection.

'Tis but a little space we have
Betwixt the Cradle and the Grave;
Yet are our Cares and Evils such,
That ev'n that little is too much.
Here's nothing real, we may seem
To live, but then that Life's a dream.
We talk as if we something were,
And whilst we talk we disappear.

When a friend dies,

With Praises we embalm his Name.
The Tomb-stone carries on the Cheat,
And falsely says, *Here lies the Great;*
When sordid Dust is there alone,
The Soul's to a strange somewhere gone.
It sees, and wonders why we thus
Bemoan his Loss who pities us.

On internal evidence alone I should say that the poem called *Secret Grief* (p. 149) is by the same hand, in which case we have by the same poet both a Complaint of Life and a Retirement poem. In the latter we note that there is evident pleasure in the free indulgence of melancholy.

[54] I have emended the punctuation.

[55] Cf. Flatman, [quoted] *ante* p. 62, for this idea that the number of the living is very small compared with the [immensely greater] number of the dead.

Farewel, fond Pleasures, I disdain
    Your nets of Roses, loose my chain,
And set my fetter'd Powers free
    (For you and I shall ne're agree)
Tempt me no more, 'tis all in vain.

The easie World with Charms assail,
Of Triumphs there you cannot fail,
    On those to whom the Cheat's unknown
You will infallibly prevail.
But let my Solitude and me alone.

Let the sad Cypress crown my Head,
The deadly Poppy on my Temples shed,
Through all my Veins its Juyce be spread.
Could I retrieve my former years,
I'd live them o're again in Tears.

In secret I'll enjoy my Grief,
Not tell the Cause, nor ask relief.
Though ne're so high the Streams should grow
Yet 'tis not fit the World should know
The Spring from whence my Sorrows flow.

The eighteenth century, then, inherited from the seventeenth, a decided taste for poems of melancholy, and a considerable body of poetry which satisfied that taste. In the popular passion for the reform of manners and of literature, there was a distinct tendency to estimate a poem as excellent in proportion to the gravity of its subject, the morality of its sentiments, and the decorousness of its expression, rather than to its originality of thought, its depth of feeling, or its rhythmic quality. If the poem, either by the wealth of its allusions or by its close imitation of the ideas of well-known classical literature, gave evidence of what in the popular mind was considered learning, it was even more highly valued. By these standards Cowley was the most admirable poet of the century, Milton being, for political reasons largely, neglected. Retirement poems and poems on Death or the Judgment Day were extremely popular. With Dryden dead, and Pope not yet beginning to write, the typical poem of the year 1700 is *The Choice,* by John Pomfret.

The poet expresses his preference for life on a small estate, with a little house, a little vault of the best wine, the company of two well-born friends, and the conversation of a fair neighbor, more reasonable than passionate. He desires to be spared the trouble of lawsuits, and of a wife. From such retirement he wishes not to emerge, unless it be "to oblige my country or to serve my king." The poem is, in fact, no more than a free rendering, rather more English than usual, of Martial's epigram on *The Happy Life.*

Why then was it, if we may believe Dr. Johnson, "the composition oftenest perused in the English language," reaching a tenth edition in 1736, and passing through four quarto editions within a year after publication?[56] Johnson's explanation is that it "exhibits a conception of life, adapted to common notions, and equal to common expectations, such a state as affords plenty of tranquillity, without exclusion of intellectual pleasures." In other words, it satisfied average taste.

Tranquillity of a not too stupid kind — that was the sincere desire of the average Englishman of the year 1700! Gone were the Elizabethan eagerness for experience, the Puritan faith and fervor, the Restoration delight in mere debauchery, the patriotic confidence in the State and the Church, mutually upheld and upholding. England was tired of strife within and inglorious wars without. She was familiar with disease and death, with plague, fire, earthquake, famine, persecution, massacre, and execution. She had seen corruption in high places, the fall of many illustrious men, the undeserved disgrace of many

[56] Johnson, *Lives of the English Poets,* ed. Hill, vol. 1, p. 302.

good men. The prevailing philosophies were materialistic, skeptical, pessimistic. The prevailing view of life presented it as a thing of little worth.

"When all is done," wrote Sir William Temple (in 1690) "Human Life is, at the greatest and best, but like a froward Child, that must be Play'd with and Humor'd a little to keep it quiet till it falls asleep, and then the Care is over."[57] "I know you loved me living," so runs John Locke's letter to Anthony Collins shortly before the former's death in 1704, "and will preserve my memory now I am dead. All the use to be made of it is that this life is a scene of vanity, that soon passes away, and affords no solid satisfaction but in the consciousness of doing well, and in hopes of another life. This is what I can say upon experience and what you will find when you come to make up the account."[58]

> Better thou mayest, but worse thou canst not be
> Than in this Vale of Tears, and Misery.

So Flatman puts it. And though Death had its terrors, it offered the one sure way of escape, for

> 'Tis all th' amends our wretched Fate can give
> That none can force a desperate Man to Live.[59]

[57] Temple, *Essays,* ed. Spingarn, p. 79.

[58] Quoted in Shaftesbury's letter, *To a Friend,* in his *Life,* ed. Rand, pp. 344–45.

[59] Flatman, *Poems and Songs,* 1674, p. 41.

CHAPTER III

THE REVOLT AGAINST MELANCHOLY

1700–1725

SEVENTEENTH century writers on melancholy themes continued to be read during the first quarter of the eighteenth. Pomfret, the favorite of the moment, produced in 1700 not only the pleasantly pagan *Choice,* but also a quite orthodox *Prospect of Death.* Charles Gildon's *New Miscellany,* issued in 1701, contained Lady Winchilsea's *The Spleen* and *Death.* Roscommon's *Prospect of Death,* previously known in manuscript only, was first published in 1704. Norris's *A Collection of Miscellanies* were in their fourth edition in 1706. Oldham was reprinted in 1722. Raleigh's *Remains* were reissued in 1702, and Drummond's *Works,* in a beautiful quarto edition, Edinburgh, 1711, brought to mind again *A Cypresse Grove.* Two elegies which had appeared on the death of Queen Mary in 1695 were still finding readers. One of these, reprinted in 1701 and pirated in 1709, *The Temple of Death,* by John Sheffield, Marquis of Normanby and Duke of Buckingham, has an opening stanza with a "horrid" description imitated from *Aeneid* VI, 237–42.

A dreadful Vale lies in a Desart Isle,
On which indulgent Heaven did never smile.
There a thick Grove of Aged Cypress Trees,
Which none without an awful horror sees,
Into its wither'd Arms, depriv'd of Leaves,
Whole Flocks of ill-presaging Birds receives.
Poisons are all the Plants the Soil will bear,
And Winter is the only Season there.

Millions of Graves cover the spacious Field,
And Springs of Blood a thousand Rivers yield:
Whose Streams opprest with Carcasses and Bones,
Instead of gentle Murmurs, pour forth Groans.[1]

The other, Congreve's *Mournful Muse of Alexis,* reappeared in 1713 in *A Select Collection of Modern Poems by Several Hands,* Dublin, 1713. Alexis and Menalcas are the speakers; the Queen is called Pastora, and there is a refrain dimly reminiscent of those in Greek pastorals:

I mourn Pastora dead, let Albion mourn,
And Sable clouds her chalky cliffs adorn.

Plants, birds, and beasts of ill omen are forbidden to approach Pastora's burial place:

There may no dismal Yew, nor Cypress grow,
Nor Holly-bush, nor bitter Elder's Bough;
Let each unlucky Bird far build his Nest,
And distant Dens receive each howling Beast;
Let Wolves be gone, and Ravens put to flight,
With hooting Owls, and Bats, that hate the Light,
And let the sighing Doves their Sorrows bring,
And Nightingales in sweet Complainings sing.[2]

The interest in Lucretius continued, so that Creech's translation had a second edition in 1714, with very full notes by another hand, and a third edition in 1722, while the passages Dryden had translated were republished in Tonson's reissue (1702–1709) of Dryden's *Miscellany Poems* with additions, in six volumes. Lucretius was also thoroughly advertised by Blackmore's attack in *Creation,* 1712.

The continued controversy over the immortality of the soul, which involved also the question of the right to commit suicide, may have caused the reprinting of John Donne's prose *Biathanatos: a Declaration of that Paradox*

[1] Chalmers, *English Poets,* vol. X. [2] *Ibid.*

or Thesis that self Homicide is not so naturally Sin, that it may never be otherwise.[3] A refutation of Donne's arguments by J. Adams, entitled *An Essay concerning Self-Murther*, was twice printed in 1700.

Lady Winchilsea was still writing. In 1703 she was moved to describe, in *The Hurricane*, a great storm [4] which wrought havoc on land and sea. As Dr. Reynolds observes,[5] this poem, in spite of the handicap of the Cowleian ode form, has passages of true description, conveying the author's feeling of delighted awe at the mighty massing of clouds and waters and the destructive power of the winds. The edition of her *Poems* in 1713 made public her best poem according to modern standards, *A Nocturnal Reverie.* While this descriptive piece is really an expression of joy in the sights and sounds and solitude of night, we must remember that, in her own time, this sort of pleasure would have been reckoned as evidence of a melancholy temperament.

The whole poem conveys perfectly the sense of stillness, and of a half transparent dusk. One feels rather than sees the animals happily bustling about, their presence revealed by sounds only. There are admirable realistic touches — the freshened grass straightening itself, the sounds of the grazing of a horse and the nibbling of sheep, the consciousness of odors unnoticed by day, the cry of the curlew, and the call of the partridge. Conventional, on the other hand, are the references to the zephyr, Philomel, the owl, the moon, the falling waters, the ancient ruin showing through the gloom, the compli-

[3] Written in 1608 during Donne's almost impossible struggle with illness and poverty, but not printed in his lifetime. First ed. 1644, 2d ed. 1700.

[4] Realistically and prosaically described by Defoe in his book, *The Storm,* 1704.

[5] Winchilsea, *op. cit.*, p. CXXIV.

ment to the Countess of Salisbury, and the turning of the mind to muse on

> Something too high for Syllables to speak.

Yet, as Dr. Reynolds notes, this is melancholy with a difference.[6] In her youth, her personal disappointments had found expression in melancholy poetry in the seventeenth century manner. In later life, her own natural goodness, the kindness of her friends and her husband, and the healing influence of nature brought about a sort of Miltonic calm, a mood pensive but by no means sad or gloomy.

The *Poems* of Lady Mary Chudleigh (Marissa), published in 1703,[7] though doubtless written and read in manuscript some years before that, are chiefly of the melancholy sort. In her Preface to *The Song of the Three Children Paraphrased* she shows much interest in the recently accepted theories of the origin and nature of the universe, combined with a lack of accurate knowledge to which she is, as a mere woman, serenely resigned. The poem is a long (and tiresome) nature rhapsody, including a description of the Day of Judgment. Many of her shorter poems, however, have the charm of personal revelation.

In her Pindaric ode *On the Vanities of this Life,* she wonders why anyone desires "the trifle Life," since it is only a succession of miseries. She describes the many futile ways of pursuing happiness, which, she believes, consists in obedience to virtue and serenity of mind, and can therefore be perfectly attained only in Heaven.

> Such as a lasting Happiness would have,
> Must seek it in the peaceful Grave,
> Where free from Wrongs the Dead remain:

[6] *Ibid.* p. CXXXIV.

[7] 2d ed. 1713. 3rd ed. 1722. (*British Museum Catalogue.*) My quotations are from the third edition.

Life is a long continu'd Pain,
A lingering slow Disease,
Which Remedies a while may ease,
But cannot work a perfect Cure:
Musick with its enchanting Lays,
May for a while our Spirits raise;
Honour and Wealth may charm the Sense,
And by their pour'ful Influence
May gently lull our Cares asleep;
But when we think ourselves secure,
And fondly hope we shall no future Ills endure,
Our griefs awake again,
And with redoubl'd Rage augment our Pain.

She remarks with great common sense that the exercise of reason will not dispel real grief.

The most that Reason can, is to persuade the Mind
Its Troubles decently to bear,
And not permit a Murmur or a Tear,
To tell th' inquiring World that any such are there.

Books, too, are unsatisfactory, because there is always so much more to know than one can possibly get at by reading. In short,

The *Phoenix* Truth wrapt up in Mists doth lie,
Not to be clearly seen before we die;

The Resolution asserts her intention to retire to a loved retreat and give herself up to the delights and the improving influence of reading. *The Resolve* is another Retirement poem. *Solitude* begins:

Happy are they who when alone
Can with themselves converse,
Who to their Thoughts are so familiar grown,
They cou'd with silent Joy think all their Hours away,
And still think on, till the confining Clay,
Fall off, and nothing's left behind
Of drossy Earth, nothing to clog the Mind.

But very few persons (as Cowley, following Cicero, remarked) are fit for solitude.

"Taken as a whole," says Dr. Reynolds,[8] "the poems bitterly inveigh against life with its blighting sorrows, its fleeting, unreal joys, its injustice, its black despairs. The only break in the gloom comes in short periods of absorption in books, or in occasional religious ecstasies."

On Matthew Prior, Lady Winchilsea's more famous contemporary, personal misfortune had the effect of driving him into melancholy. He was naturally of a buoyant temperament, and in the greater part of his work,[9] consisting of love poems, official "odes," compliments to friends, and satiric tales or fables, his acknowledged master is Horace. Yet as early as 1702, he had translated the Emperor Hadrian's *Animula blandula vagula,* calling his version *The Dying Christian to his Soul;*[10] he admired Dr. Sherlock's *Practical Discourse Concerning Death,* and, in the 1718 edition of his *Poems,* published for the first time two long poems on serious subjects, the composition of which had occupied him a number of years.

In *Alma,* a poem in three cantos, the Hudibrastic manner prevents real consideration of the theme, the nature and origin of the soul, although one can feel that Prior is genuinely speculating on the subject. But *Solomon on the Vanity of the World,* a poem in three books, is serious reflection of a most melancholy kind. One of its "mottoes," from Bacon's *Advancement of Learning,* states that "The bewailing of Man's Miseries hath been elegantly and copiously set forth by Many, in the Writings as well of Philosophers, as Divines. And it is both a pleasant and a

[8] *The Learned Lady in England, 1650–1760,* p. 147. Dr. Reynolds emphasizes other aspects of Lady Chudleigh's life and work not pertinent here.

[9] Unauthorized edition 1707. Authorized edition 1709.

[10] In Dryden's *Miscellany Poems,* 1704, vol. V, p. 210.

profitable Contemplation." Prior's Preface echoes the utterances of Cowley, Dennis, and the other reformers of poetry in preferring scriptural to classic themes. His own effort has been to collect out of the great treasure-house of the books commonly attributed to Solomon "such Observations, and Apothegms, as most particularly tend to the proof of that great Assertion, laid down in the beginning of the *Ecclesiastes, All Is Vanity*." Thus the general tenor of his poem is that "The Pleasures of Life do not compensate the Miseries: Age steals upon us unawares; and Death, as the only Cure of our Ills, ought to be expected but not feared." This is, of course, simply a restating of Lucretius's Complaint of Life, and lines 110 and following in Book III of *Solomon* are actually a direct paraphrase of Lucretius. The only really beautiful lines are certain lyric passages in the third book which recall Fletcher and the late Elizabethans rather than his scriptural models (lines 575 ff.).

This change of tone in Prior may be attributed partly to the change of taste in the society around him, which demanded of its poets first of all orthodox piety, and partly to his own personal misfortunes, his downfall, imprisonment, and enforced withdrawal from public life, which increased the seriousness latent beneath his gaiety.[11] His earlier poetry had been lightly lyrical but the Preface to *Solomon*, with its references to Homer, Virgil, Tasso, Ronsard, and Spenser, indicates that, like other men of his time, he yearned to make an impression as an epic writer. He seems uncertain whether his work, which is cast in three soliloquies with narrative introductions, is actually "didascalic, or heroic." We of today are in no doubt that it is an extremely dull, didactic poem, in pseudo-epic style.

[11] L. G. Wickham Legg emphasizes his repeated illnesses and recurrent fits of melancholy. *Matthew Prior*, pp. 67, 119, 128, 169, 190, 230, 273.

Prior's reverse of fortune has apparently thrown him back into the religious vein of the seventeenth century, and into the epic form of expression.

Meantime, John Philips, one of Pope's circle, had done something both to stimulate admiration for Milton's versification, and to excite ridicule for pensive poetry by his clever parody, *The Splendid Shilling.* This piece,[12] in fluent blank verse, with Miltonic phrases and imagery, is in its plan a burlesque of *Il Penseroso,* describing one long, unhappy day in the life of a poet in hourly expectation of being arrested for debt. Its imitation of Milton was, however, so skilful as to call attention to the excellence of blank verse as a medium for reflective poetry.

> But when Nocturnal Shades
> This World invelop, and th' inclement Air
> Persuades Men to repel benumming Frosts
> With pleasant Wines, and crackling blaze of Wood;
> Me Lonely sitting, nor the glimm'ring Light
> Of Make-weight Candle, nor the joyous Talk
> Of lovely Friend delights; distress'd, forlorn,
> Amid the horrors of the tedious Night,
> Darkling I sigh, and feed with dismal Thoughts
> My anxious Mind; or sometimes mournful Verse
> Indite, and sing of Groves, and Myrtle Shades.

By such pleasing irreverence Philips sounded the first note of the anti-melancholy movement in poetry, but for the time being there were no new themes to take the place of those old and tried subjects of poetical meditation, the evils of life, the terrors (or perhaps the charms) of death, the happiness and profit of retirement.[13] Moreover, the old

[12] In its pirated form, this appeared in *A Collection of Poems* issued by Browne and Tooke in 1701. The author printed a correct folio edition in 1705. (*Dict. Nat. Biog.*)

[13] The Miscellanies of the period, besides those already mentioned, contain a good deal of melancholy material but no single piece of importance. We have, for instance:

themes were given a fresh impulse by a new poet of genuine, if limited talent, in the person of Isaac Watts, whose *Horae Lyricae* appeared in 1706.

In his Preface, Watts makes deliberate pretensions to be a serious poet filling a long-felt want for noble lyric.[14] He approves Dennis's *Proposal of Criticism* for the reform of poetry. He considers that Cowley and Blackmore by their sacred epics have proved " that the obstacles of attempting Christian Poesy are broken down, and the vain pretence of its being impracticable is experimentally confuted." He believes that lyrics on sacred subjects would be equally possible, and would be effective aids to the preacher in diffusing virtue and alluring souls to God. The shorter odes of Cowley and Blackmore, and a few of Norris's

---

1712. *Miscellaneous Poems and Translations, by Several Hands.* (Lintot's Miscellany.) Containing *An Epistle,* by Mr. Bate; Broome's paraphrase of *Habbakuk* III and parts of *Job* XXXVIII, XXXIX; Southcott's *Jeremiah's Prayer.*

1713. *Sacred Miscellanies: Or, Divine Poems Upon Several Subjects.* Viz: I *An Ode on Divine Vengeance, inscribed to Mr. Steele.* II *On the Last Judgment, and Happiness of the Saints in Heaven,* by N. Rowe, Esq. etc. (Curll's Miscellany).

1716. The edition in six volumes of Dryden's *Miscellany Poems.* Containing an anonymous *On Solitude; Against The Fear of Death* by Sir Robert Howard; *A Hymn to Darkness, Humane Life,* and *The Curse of Babylon,* by Yalden; *Considerations on the Eighty-eighth Psalm,* by Prior; a tranlation of Tibullus I, 1, by Charles Hopkins; *The Passing Bell* (anonymous); *The Plague of Athens,* by Sprat.

1717. *A Collection of the Best English Poetry, by Several Hands,* 3 vols. Containing Rochester's *A Satyr against Mankind; An Ode upon Solitude,* by Roscommon (separately paged and dated 1710, indicating that the volumes were made up by binding together numerous piratical issues of some years before).

[14] My quotations are from the 3d ed., 1715. Beneath Watts's portrait which forms the frontispiece to this edition is the motto, *Musas colimus severiores.*

"essays in verse" are cited as successful efforts in this direction.[15] He asserts that poets are in duty bound to furnish pleasure of a safe kind for young ladies and gentlemen who like poetry, and who may for lack of legitimate amusement be driven to the "dangerous diversions of the stage and impure sonnets." His own *Poems Sacred to Virtue* are so intended, for he says, "I thought it lawful to take hold of any Handle of the Soul to lead it away betimes from vicious Pleasures."

The Pindaric odes and other lyrics that follow are quite in the seventeenth century religious vein. The influence of the *Georgics* is traceable in the descriptive parts of the poem, *Divine Judgments,* the theme of which is that all good or ill comes to man by order of God. God sends the intense cold winter, when

The grazing Ox lows to the Gelid Skies,
Walks o'er the Marble Meads with withering Eyes,
Walks o'er the solid Lakes, snuffs up the wind, and dies.

The poem then makes a flight to the polar world, and there mourns the death by cold of prisoners in chain-gangs.[16] Even the atheist must tremble at the thought of God's omnipotence. Drought, disease, and dearth are also God's weapons. The poet exults in the thought of the terrible exhibitions of divine power against guilt.

Hail, Whirlwinds, Hurricanes and Floods,
    That all the leafy Standards strip,
    And bear down with a mighty sweep,

[15] Watts admires Milton, but with some reservations.

[16] Cf. Virgil's description of the miseries of the Scythians, *Georgics* III, 349–383, Ovid's account of his sufferings in his northern exile at Tomi (near the mouth of the Danube), in *Tristia,* especially III, 10, and Shaftesbury, *The Moralists,* in *Characteristics,* ed. Robertson, vol. II, p. 119.

The Riches of the Fields, and Honours of the Woods.
Storms that ravage o'er the Deep,
And bury Millions in the Waves;[17]
Earthquakes, that in Midnight-Sleep
Turn Cities into Heaps, and make our Beds our Graves.

The poem ends with the aspiration that God will reassure him as to his own fate. In *Death and Eternity* we have the usual seventeenth century emphasis on the sovereignty of Death.

The Tyrant, how he triumphs here,
His Trophies spread around!
And Heaps of Dust and Bones appear
Thro' all the hollow ground.
These Skulls what ghastly Figures now!
How loathsome to the Eyes!
These are the Heads we lately knew
So beauteous and so wise.

But what of the fate of the soul, embarked upon "that Sea without a Shore?" There it must sink or swim. Some friend, mourning our loss, shall remember that he too must die, and thus our very bones shall teach,

For Dust and Ashes loudest preach
The infinite Concern.

Watts's *The Day of Judgment* is too well known to need quotation. Its rhythmic sweep makes it an impressive poem, in spite of its grotesque images. After the manner of the milder religionists, Watts pauses at the brink of Hell and, without dwelling upon the torments of the damned, ends his poem peacefully and joyously with the song of the redeemed.

His poems on the vanity of life are numerous, but not especially noteworthy. *Seeking A Divine Calm in a Rest-*

[17] This is doubtless again the great storm of 1703, *ante* p. 82 and note 4.

less World, imitated from Casimir Sobieski[18] (IV, 28), ends with the thought,

> Earth's but an Atom: Greedy Swords
> Carve it amongst a thousand Lords. . . .

He also versifies "Remember thy Creator" from *Ecclesiastes* XII. *The Hero's School of Morality* recommends "A Turn among the Tombs" as a cure for ambition and an incitement to virtue, for tombs and monuments

> Tell me a thousand mournful things
> In melancholy Silence.

The Mourning Piece begins with a ghastly presentation of the old idea that all the world is a stage:

> Life's a long Tragedy: This Globe the Stage,
> Well fix'd, and well adorn'd with strong Machines,
> Gay Fields, and Skies, and Seas: The Actors many;
> The Plot immense: A Flight of Daemons sit
> On every sailing Cloud with fatal Purpose;

[18] Matthew Casimir Sarbiewski, 1595–1640, usually known as Casimir, and called "the Christian Horace," was a Polish Jesuit who wrote exclusively in Latin. He became famous outside of his own country more rapidly than at home. Dr. Watts translated many of his lyrics. For other English translations see Bowring, Sir John, *Specimens of the Polish Poets,* London, printed for the author, 1827. The (Cambridge) *Classical Journal,* vol. XXV, pp. 103–110 (1822) has an article *On the Life and Writings of Casimir,* signed Caecilius Metellus, who is, Bowring says, "Mr. Walker of Cambridge." This writer admires Casimir's skill in Latin verse, but finds the poetry uninteresting except in "the enunciation of moral truth." He notes parallels to Casimir's thoughts in Sir Thomas Browne and Bishop Jeremy Taylor. Mrs. Elizabeth Carter also translated portions of Casimir. I note that he loved solitude and sometimes described the natural scenery of his native Lithuania. See Brückner, A., *Geschichte der polnischen Literatur,* Leipzig, 1901, pp. 176–177.

And shoot across the Scene ten thousand Arrows,
Perpetual and unseen, headed with Pain,
With Sorrow, Infamy, Disease and Death.
The pointed Plagues fly silent through the Air,
Nor twangs the Bow, yet sure and deep the Wound.[19]

The idea of the poem as a whole is that the single man and woman run less risk of sorrow than those who are married. The latter suffer through each other and through their children. The second part of this poem is entitled *The Bright Vision* and presents the reverse argument, picturing the bliss of marriage, like that in Eden before the Fall.[20] The poet confesses that when he wrote the gloomy first part,

Melancholy's hateful Form
Stood by in sable Robe.

When he surveyed the bright scene of life, she made him look through a dark, long tube with a deceitfully colored glass. Now Urania breaks the glass, and he sees marriage as it is, a happy state. In the third part, the accounts are balanced. The married lover must enjoy wedlock in moderation, not forgetting that ill may come.

[19] This seems like a combination of the familiar "All the world's a stage" and Drummond's "This World a hunting is." Only, instead of Death as the Nimrod, Watts conceives a "flight of demons," who shoot from the clouds. The next important variation in the metaphor is made by Edgar Allan Poe in *The Conqueror Worm,* where angel spectators are added, who, at the end of the piece,

"Uprising, unveiling, affirm
That the play is the tragedy Man,
And the hero, the Conqueror Worm."

I have often wondered whether some of Poe's melancholy effects could not be accounted for by supposing him to have read at an impressionable age, Dr. Watts, Johnson's *Rasselas,* and the Bible.

[20] Here the influence of *Paradise Lost,* IV, 411ff. is obvious for several lines.

Watts gives his own peculiar pietistic turn to the themes of contemplation and retirement. *Meditation in a Grove* is a sort of religious pastoral. In this grove, there is no Phyllis. Instead, the poet's passion for Jesus is carved on the bark of every tree for swains to admire. *True Riches* shows the influence of Milton's *Il Penseroso* both in meter and in idea. The poet cares not what to-morrow may bring. He longs not for riches, for he has treasures that cannot be taken away.

I'm a Kingdom of my own.

Then follows a description of the garden of his soul, where all delights are.

Yet the silly wand'ring Mind,
Loath to be too much confin'd,
Roves and takes her dayly Tours,
Coasting round the narrow Shores,
Narrow Shores of Flesh and Sense,
Picking Shells and Pebbles thence:
Or she sits at Fancy's Door,
Calling Shapes and Shadows t' her,
Foreign Visits still receiving,
And t' herself a Stranger living.
Never, never would she buy
Indian Dust or *Tyrian* Dye,
Never trade abroad for more
If she saw her native Store,
If her inward worth were known
She might ever live alone.

The Adventurous Muse is inspired by Milton's epic though in form it is a Pindaric ode.

Urania takes her morning Flight
. . . .
Nor Rapin gives her Rules to fly,
Nor Purcell Notes to sing.

She flies straight to the Celestial Land, without even angelic guidance. While little skiffs humbly coast along mortal shores, afraid to lose sight of it, or of one another, Urania's poet cries:

> Give me the Chariot whose divine Wheels
> Mark their own Rout, and unconfin'd
> Bound o'er the everlasting Hills,
> And lose the Clouds below, and leave the Stars behind. . . .

His Muse

> Pursues an unattempted Course,
> Breaks all the Criticks' Iron Chains,
> And bears to Paradise the raptur'd Mind.

There Milton dwells:

> The Mortal sung
> Themes not presum'd by Mortal Tongue.

The poem ends with praise of Milton.

The enormous popularity of Watts,[21] especially of *The Judgment Day,* is sufficient evidence of the continuance into the eighteenth century of the seventeenth century emphasis on the vanity of life and the horrors of death and judgment. While Watts consistently offset these ideas by the thought of the saving power of Jesus and the bliss of the good in heaven, popular imagination seized most readily upon the gruesome parts of his poetry, and fed therewith that religious melancholy which Burton had described in the *Anatomy.* We may suppose that the new edition of *The Day of Doom*[22] by Michael Wigglesworth in 1711 was for the benefit of English readers, since there were by this time plenty of facilities for publishing in his New England home. This poem, in swinging ballad metre, describes with crude power the terrors of the great day. It takes the extreme Calvinist position in the determination of the elect, picturing with gusto the separation of friends and

[21] The *British Museum Catalogue* gives up the attempt to distinguish editions numerically after 12th ed. corr. of *Horae Lyricae,* London, 1770, and 28th ed. of *Hymns and Spiritual Songs,* London, 1767.

[22] First edition, 1662.

relatives, and the removal of unbaptized infants to "the easiest room in hell."

It is evident that Edward Young's first poem, *The Last Day,* 1713,[23] merely continues the seventeenth century tradition, though the usual themes are expanded at much greater length than by Flatman, Roscommon, Pomfret, Wigglesworth, or Watts. Nor is it necessary to look farther for his inspiration than to these poets, to Milton, and to the usual funeral and judgment day sermons.[24]

The poem, in three books, has a very rambling plan. In the opening lines of the first book, the poet prays for divine help to equal his theme.[25] He calls upon man to view the wonder and the beauty of the universe, but reminds him that, at the terrible sound of the last trump, all this beauty will be destroyed. And if the earth, once so beautifully rolling in state through space, shall in an instant become "one universal ruin," what of man himself? He must bow his proud head, acknowledge that he is made of clay,

and curse his form
That speaks distinction from his sister-worm.[26]

He must beg God, who once sweat blood to save him, to defend him at this supreme moment.[27] The wicked will beg the universe to hide them from the divine wrath,[28] but the universe will cast them forth to meet their doom,

[23] Quotations from Chalmers, *English Poets,* vol. XIII.

[24] W. Thomas, in his *Le poète Edward Young,* p. 310, is at great pains to suppose that the subject may have been proposed to him by John Philips or John Hughes. Whether or not this is true, the subject was simply "in the air."

[25] This idea derives from Milton and aligns Young with Dennis, Blackmore, Watts, and other reformers who believed that the most sublime religious ideas were the best subjects for poetry.

[26] *Job,* XVII, 14.

[27] *Dies Irae.*

[28] Cf. Flatman, *A Doomsday Thought, ante,* p. 62.

as the ports hurl back a fleeing traitor to execution. But the good man will be cared for, as the leviathan cared for Jonah, when he was cast into the sea. Here follows an elaborate retelling, with long descriptions, of the whole story of Jonah, the excuse for which is the analogy with God's redemption of man.[29]

The greater part of the second book is taken up by the description of the way in which the graves give up their dead, the scattered bones rejoin each other, and the souls find their proper bodies. The poet here seems unnecessarily literal!

Now charnels rattle; scatter'd limbs and all
The various bones, obsequious to the call,
Self-mov'd, advance; the neck perhaps to meet
The distant head; the distant legs, the feet.
Dreadful to view, see thro' the dusky sky
Fragments of bodies in confusion fly.[30]

[29] I suspect Young of trying here to repeat the success of Samuel Wesley, the elder, whose epic version of the Bible story had now reached gigantic proportions in *The History of the Old and New Testament in Verse,* London, 1703, 3 vols.

[30] Even this gruesome conception is capable of really poetical treatment. Cf. Dryden, *Ode to the Pious Memory of . . . Mrs. Anne Killigrew.*

"When in mid-air the golden trump shall sound,
  To raise the nations under ground;
When, in the Valley of Jehoshaphat,
The judging God shall close the book of Fate;
  And there the last assizes keep
  For those who wake and those who sleep;
  When rattling bones together fly
  From the four corners of the sky;
When sinews o'er the skeletons are spread,
Those clothed with flesh, and life inspires the dead;
The sacred poets first shall hear the sound,
  And foremost from the tomb shall bound,
For they are cover'd with the lightest ground;
And straight, with in-born vigour, on the wing,
Like mounting larks, to the new morning sing."

Westminster Abbey gives up its royal dead, and bodies arise from beneath other great buildings, for

> The most magnificent and costly dome
> Is but an upper chamber to a tomb.
> No spot on earth but has supply'd a grave,
> And human skulls the spacious ocean pave.[31]

Young describes the miscellaneous throng of Christians, Jews, Turks, and pagans before the judgment seat. None approach with more confidence than the philanthropists. Here Young inserts compliments to sundry benefactors mentioned by name, together with the pious hope that he, too, may be found among the saved.

The Judge now comes to judgment. The rest of the book consists of descriptions of the Son enthroned and contrasting descriptions of his lowly birth and humble life. The poet ranges from general pious aspirations and exclamations to detailed pictures like that of the unfurling of a great flag on which is a red cross which flushes the hills and dyes the ocean with red. At the end, he represents himself as kneeling in prayer for guidance in the right way through life.

The third book resumes the description of the judgment. The seal is broken, the book opened, the throngs divided into two parts; the seats of bliss above are described, and the boiling sulphurous furnace below. The condemned soul utters a cry of agony.

> Who burst the barriers of my peaceful grave?
> . . . .
> And cast me out into the wrath of God;
> Where shrieks, the roaring flame, the rattling chain,
> And all the dreadful eloquence of pain,
> Our only song?

This resemblance is noted by Dr. Johnson and by W. Thomas, *op. cit.*, p. 315.

[31] This idea is like Flatman's in *A Doomsday Thought*, *ante*, p. 62, and also like a passage in *Donne's Sermons*, p. 239.

The guilty soul acknowledges his sin, but prays that the punishment may not be forever. If he had never been born, he could not have sinned.

Father of mercies! why from silent earth
Didst thou awake and curse me into birth?
Tear me from quiet, ravish me from night,
And make a thankless present of thy light!
Push into being a reverse of thee,
And animate a clod with misery? [32]
　The beasts are happy! they come forth, and keep
Short watch on earth, and then lie down to sleep:
Pain is for man . . .[33]

He asks whether God can bear to

see me plunging in the dark abyss?
Calling thee Father in a sea of fire?
Or pouring blasphemies at thy desire?

He begs that God will not exalt himself by the misery of so insignificant a creature, and makes one last, small request:

[32] Cf. *Job* III, 20. "Wherefore is light given to him that is in misery, and life unto the bitter in soul?" Also the plea of the "reprobate infants" in Wigglesworth's *Day of Doom.*

"O great Creator, why was our Nature
　depraved and forlorn?
Why so defil'd, and made so vil'd
　whilst we were yet unborn?"

[33] Cf. Dryden's *Palamon and Arcite,* I, 484–491.

"Nay, worse than other beasts is our estate;
Them to pursue their pleasures you create;
We, bound by harder laws must curb our will,
And your commands, not our desires, fulfill:
Then, when the creature is unjustly slain,
Yet, after death at least, he feels no pain;
But man in life surcharged with woe before,
Not freed when dead, is doomed to suffer more."

Poetical Works of John Dryden, ed. Christie, p. 522.

> When I have wept a thousand lives away;
> When torment is grown weary of its prey;
> When I have rav'd ten thousand years in fire,
> Ten thousand thousand, let me then expire.

But his plea is in vain, for it comes too late.[34] The blessed move to heaven to fill the places left vacant by the fall of Satan and his angels. Here the poet's strength fails him. He descends from the regions of bliss to paint

> Dissolving elements and worlds in flame.

The world perishes like bubbles on a stream, or sparks scattered from a fire.[35]

In conclusion, the poet admonishes his readers that all this prospective dissolution is for man's sake, to put him in his proper place in a newly created and greater universe. Man, therefore, must begin now to look on himself with new respect, and live in a manner worthy of his great destiny. For his sake God hung the sun in the sky. When that service is done, "its beams shall fade away, And God shine forth in one eternal day."[36]

[34] Cf. Flatman, *A Doomsday Thought, ante,* p. 62.

[35] Cf. *ante,* ch. II, note 37.

[36] Young's *Ocean: an Ode,* 1725, should be mentioned as contributing to the melancholy tradition because of the slightly morbid tone of the concluding *Wish* for a humble and retired life, a tone for which we are unprepared by the raptures of the preceding descriptions of ocean. So placed, *The Wish* has almost the effect of an epitaph.

> "*The Wish*
> O may I steal along the vale
> Of humble life, secure from foes!
> My friend sincere, My judgment clear,
> And gentle business my repose!"

We must remember also that Young's plays, *Busiris* (1719) and *The Revenge* (1721), contained complaints of life and other melancholy passages, which are quoted by W. Thomas in his *Le Poète, Edward Young,* pp. 308–309.

The path marked out in the seventeenth century and pursued in the eighteenth by the dissenter, Watts, and the Anglican clergyman, Young, was followed presently by Aaron Hill, a man most influential in the world of letters at the moment, as friend of Pope and Swift, and much concerned with publishing enterprises.[37] Hill was kind-hearted, serious-minded, and devoid of literary taste, just the man to foster, in secular and middle-class circles, the tendency to the free, the diffuse expression of the melancholy mood. Perhaps directly inspired by Young, whom he knew personally, and whose poem, *The Last Day,* was then in its second edition, Hill in 1721 wrote *The Judgment Day.*

The course of thought in the first four sections of this poem is precisely like Young's. Common to both are (1) the poet's claim that he is treating a subject far greater than those usually found in poetry, his sense of insufficiency for his task, and his calling upon the Lord for aid; (2) admiration of the beauty of the universe and pathos at the thought that it must all perish in the last day; (3) the description of the sound of the first trump and of the wandering of the disembodied spirits through space in answer to its call. At this point the resemblance ceases, and even up to this point, it is plain that Hill, although his poem is more logically constructed than Young's, has none of the emotional power of the latter.

The greater part of Hill's poem is taken up with a description, all too detailed and pseudo-scientific, of the destruction of the material universe. He has a very definite idea of the precise manner in which this is to happen. The sound of the first trump dissolves the world. The

[37] Hill's character is drawn in a life-like manner in Dorothy Brewster's *Aaron Hill: Poet, Dramatist, Projector.* He edited the *Plain Dealer* from March 23, 1724, to May 7, 1725. No. 42 is a *Reverie in Westminster Abbey.* No. 32 is a *Meditation on Death.*

valleys heave upward, the forests are torn from their roots, the hills leap into the air, the rivers spout up, hissing as they meet the descending lightnings. Cities tumble in ruins, the mountains crumble, and the ocean swallows everything. This ocean then falls into the earth's center, which is so hot that the flood boils and recoils as steam. The steam rising towards the stars is followed by gigantic waves of liquid flame, which meet the sun, stars, and planets, throwing them into confusion. At the sound of the second and last trump, all these bodies clash and burn together in one great conflagration. The dark, cold planets, "hills of ice," dance about in the fire like huge hail-stones, until they too are melted. At last the whole subsides into the burning lake of damnation and there is a horrible silence. Now, above all, arches the region of heaven, a great dome shining in gorgeous colors, silver, azure, black, red, and gold.

The voice of the Eternal is heard, bringing about the resurrection. Scattered atoms come together, forming new and everlasting bodies, and the souls, which, since the

> Far, above all, thro' the dome's op'ning crown,
> Broad, as a world, the almighty's *Eye* looks down.

death of the earthly body, have been wanderers through space, descend to enter these. Adam now beholds his whole race; Caesar and Cato meet, as do the martyred Charles and his murderers.[38] Here the poet's "fancy" evidently fails him, and he hurries his conclusion. The Saviour calls the righteous to bliss; they obey and pass beyond the poet's sight. The close is didactic. Virtuous action is better than poetical composition; let action then be henceforth the author's sphere.

> All has been said, that's worth a wise man's ear,
> But much may be performed that's greatly new.

[38] A similar thought is in Young's *The Last Day*, II, 113–116.

The grotesqueness of all this to modern readers is apparent. The poem is verbally lurid without being really terrible. Especially absurd are the lions riding about the hot ocean on floating oaks, the elephants swimming desperately, and the indignation of the whales when they find out that the water they have sucked in is "no cooling flood" and angrily spout the boiling liquid to heaven. On the other hand there are a few — a very few — bits that are effective in almost a Dantesque manner.

> Thin troops of naked ghosts, long stript of clay,
> That, wand'ring 'twixt the spheres . . .
> Start, in loose shoals, and glide, like mists, away. . . .

The birds, skimming in frightened clouds over a darkening earth, are

> Wind-shaken, scorch'd, and wash'd by driving rains. . . .

There is an absence of allegorical personages, and no dominant influence of any previous poet, not even Milton, is seen throughout most of the poem. Hill's imagination, such as it is, is his own. It is noticeable that he omits the torments of the damned, in contrast to Watts and Young, and that he does not much emphasize the fears of the human race. In fact, he seems in the midst of his terrific relation to take a certain pleasure in contemplating destruction on so grand a scale.

The rest of Hill's poetry shows, amidst the usual epistolary compliment, occasional verse, satire, and mildly gallant love verses, the usual variations. That is, he makes the orthodox *Apology for Death,* in which death is declared to be really a blessing, and writes one poem on *Solitude,* and one on *The Happy Man.* He has a number of scriptural paraphrases, and sends his imagination roaming in *The Excursion of Fancy: A Pindaric Ode.* None of these has any distinction. They are mentioned merely as indications of the kinds of reflective poems which were sure to be tried by any poet of the day. One bit of Hill's verse which has found its way into a modern anthology is entitled *A Retrospect* and represents his highest level. It is a Complaint of Life.

Oh life! deceitful lure of lost desires,
How short thy period, yet how fierce thy fires!
Scarce can a passion start, we change so fast
Ere new lights strike us, and the old are past.

Schemes following schemes, so long life's taste explore,
That ere we learn to live, we live no more.
Who then can think, yet sigh to part with breath,
Or shun the healing hand of friendly death? [39]

The plague at Marseilles in 1720 frightened England thoroughly and may have united with the ever prevalent smallpox to bring the subjects of disease, death, and the uncertainty of the life of man prominently into mind. Defoe's *Journal of the Plague Year* (1722) recalls in some of its details the descriptions of the plague at Athens in Lucretius. The new edition of Creech's Lucretius in 1722 has notes which call attention to Sprat's poem, *The Plague at Athens*.[40]

If we may accept the date assigned to William Broome's *Melancholy: An Ode*,[41] it was written in 1723 though not published till 1729.[42] The occasion was the death of

[39] Quotations from *Works of the Late Aaron Hill*, 2nd ed. London, 1754.

[40] First published 1659, and frequently reprinted thereafter. Included in Dryden, *Miscellany Poems*, 1716. Dr. Watson Nicholson's *Historical Sources of Defoe's Journal of the Plague Year* includes the passage from Thucydides on which both Lucretius and Sprat are founded.

[41] Broome, a clergyman who held small livings, is known today only as having assisted Pope in his translation of the *Odyssey*. His poems are in Chalmers, *English Poets*, vol. XII.

[42] In Ralph's *Miscellaneous Poems by Several Hands*.

a beloved daughter. Its opening and closing lines and its meter are evidently influenced by Milton's *Il Penseroso*. It has one line taken pretty directly from *Hamlet*, while stanzas five and six recall *Job*.

Open thy marble jaws, O tomb,
Thou earth, conceal me in thy womb!
And you, ye worms, this frame confound;
Ye brother reptiles of the ground!

O life, frail offspring of a day!
'T is puff'd with one short gasp away!
Swift as the short-lived flower it flies,
It springs, it blooms, it fades, it dies.

The remainder of the poem is a moralization on the certainty of unhappiness, and the natural depravity of man. "All is show," says the poet,

All, to the coffin from our birth,
In this vast toy-shop of the earth.

At the end the poet renews his invocation to melancholy and bids adieu to the vain world.

In Broome's *Poem on Death*, Virgil and Milton furnish some of the descriptive detail. The opening lines are a description of Death enthroned.

High on a trophy, raised of human bones,
Swords, spears, and arrows, and sepulchral stones,
In horrid state she reigns! attendant ills
Besiege her throne, and when she frowns she kills;
Through the thick gloom the torch red-gleaming burns,
O'er shrouds, and sable palls, and mouldering urns;
While flowing stoles, black plumes, and scutcheons spread
An idle pomp around the silent dead:
Unawed by power, in common heap she flings
The scrips of beggars, and the crowns of kings:
Here gales of sighs, instead of breezes, blow,
And streams of tears for ever murmuring flow:

The mournful yew with solemn horror waves
His baleful branches, saddening even the graves:
Around, all birds obscene loud screaming fly,
Clang their black wings, and shriek along the sky.

The poet shudders with horror. An angel appears, and rebukes him for wishing to avoid the common fate when his "Saviour deigned to die." The poet, abashed, reflects that life is

A breath, one single gasp must puff away
A short-lived flower. . . .

that existence is really not worth while, and that "the poor reptile, man," is more blessed to die than to live, since by death

He mounts triumphant to eternal day.

In spite of the fact that histories of literature seldom mention Mrs. Elizabeth Rowe (Philomela — a pen name intended to remind readers of her patronym, Singer), both her prose and her poetry undoubtedly gratified popular taste throughout the eighteenth century and well into the nineteenth.[43]

Her first book appeared in 1696; while most of her verse was not published until after her death in 1737, it was evidently passed about in manuscript among a considerable circle much earlier. Her friend, Dr. Watts, paid her a poetical tribute in 1706 *On her Divine Poems,* and, in editing her *Devout Exercises of the Heart,* wrote a laudatory preface defending the "soft and passionate turn"

[43] *The Miscellaneous Works in Prose and Verse,* edited by her brother-in-law, Theophilus Rowe, in 1739, had a 5th ed. in 1772. *Devout Exercises of the Heart* had at least twelve editions before 1789, and *Friendship in Death,* twelve by 1786. She was popular in France and in America, and influenced the German romantic movement. See Wolf, *Elisabeth Rowe in Deutschland.*

of her religious meditations,[44] and condoning the occasional confusion of her style. Her somewhat sensational prose work, *Friendship in Death: in Twenty Letters from the Dead to the Living,* was published in 1728 with a dedication to Young, whose *Last Day* and *Paraphrase* on part of the book of *Job* she admired, and whose tone in the *Night Thoughts* she curiously anticipates at times in her prose.

She was the daughter of a nonconformist and herself a Calvinist in belief; nevertheless she declined to be classed intellectually and socially with dissenters,[45] and she had warm friends among Anglicans. Although herself a very quiet person, she knew some people of fashion. The Countess of Hertford[46] was her chief correspondent, but her circle included also Lady Winchilsea, the Earl of Orrery, the poet Prior (who, tradition says, wished to marry her), Mrs. Elizabeth Carter, and Bishop Thomas Ken of Bath and Wells, besides Watts and Young already mentioned. The variety of these intimacies is one of the indications that the love of melancholy literature was a tie that bound together persons of very different birth, breeding, beliefs, and tastes.

Her temperament in youth was serious and pious, and became positively morbid after the death of her husband, Thomas Rowe, who was thirteen years younger than she,

[44] There is little difference between Philomela's expressions of love for her husband and devotion to her God. Yet she suited the taste of her time. Pope admired her elegy on the death of her husband sufficiently to include it in the same volume with his *Eloisa to Abelard,* 2d ed. London, 1720, containing also his *Verses to the Memory of an Unfortunate Lady* and some other elegiac verse by Gay, Allan Ramsay, and Burchet. (*British Museum Catalogue.*)

[45] *Miscellaneous Works,* vol. II, pp. 68, 100.

[46] Who was also a friend of that quite different melancholy poet, Shenstone.

and to whose memory she was romantically devoted. She was fond of the retired life, of reading, drawing, music, and of writing, especially poems and letters. As a reader she showed a capacity equal to that of Jaques for sucking melancholy out of a song as a weasel sucks eggs. In fact from her wide reading, she selects for quotation in letters to friends solely the melancholy element, which she finds everywhere. She writes a letter explaining that Shakespeare's *Henry the Fifth* "gives the most solemn image in the world of the end of human greatness." She recommends Cowley's *Essays* (*Misc. Works*, vol. II, p. 67) and copies out the soliloquy from Dryden's *Aurengzebe* (*ibid.* p. 240; *ante* p. 46). She finds nourishment for melancholy in Pascal and is much interested in Milton (pp. 58, 62).

Among her contemporaries she quotes the soliloquy in Addison's *Cato,* which in her *Friendship in Death* (p. 13) she says she is sure the author repents having written, since it influences people to commit suicide. She quotes also " Mr. Pope's poem on death," i.e., *The Dying Christain to his Soul* (*Misc. Works,* vol. II, p. 178), admires William Law (p. 67), Watts's sermons and poems (pp. 68, 98, 113, 116) and Blackmore's lines,

> What are distinction, honor, wealth and state,
> The pomp of courts and triumphs of the great;
> . . . .
> If dread of death still unsubdu'd remains,
> And secret o'er the vanquish'd victor reigns,
> Th' illustrious slave in endless thraldom bears,
> A heavier chain than his led captive wears. (P. 57)

Nicholas Rowe's tragedy of *Jane Grey* comes in for praise and quotation.

> My soul grows out of tune, it loathes the world,
> Sickens at all the noise and folly of it;
> And I could sit me down in some dull shade,

Where lonely contemplation keeps her cave,
And dwells with hoary hermite; there forget myself,
There fix my stupid eyes upon the earth,
And muse away an age in deepest melancholy.
(Pp. 36, 38)

She copies out a long poem by her friend Mr. Birch, *On the Death of a Beloved Wife; written by her husband on her coffin* (pp. 126–30), and another by Mr. Grove, *On the Author's Recovery out of Sickness,* containing descriptions of his state of mind on the approach of death, and such reflections as

Sure life is but a huddled dream,
And time a swift, deceitful stream,
This vain world a shining bubble
Only full of wind and trouble.

She is in raptures over Thomson's *Seasons* and *Solitude* (pp. 55, 79, 102, 178) and even over *Sophonisba,* "a noble tragedy; I can't help preferring it to Mr. Addison's *Cato*" (p. 111). Most of all perhaps, she took delight in Young's poetry (pp. 61, 106, 107), although she died before the publication of the *Night Thoughts.* She is enchanted by Shaftesbury's *Moralists* (p. 44), and versifies a part of it (vol. I, p. 143, *On Love*), although she confesses to not quite understanding it.[47] These are only a few illustrations out of very many melancholy passages. Over and over again, she protests with Sophonisba,

I want to be alone, to find some shade,
Some solitary gloom; there to shake off
This weight of life, this tumult of mankind. . . .

[47] Mrs. Rowe's letters were printed almost without dates by Theophilus Rowe, but seem to be in approximately chronological order so far as dates are given or can be inferred. The letter mentioning the *Moralists* precedes one dated 1719.

Her own poetry, entirely negligible today except as it indicates tendency, includes *Despair* (*Misc. Works*, vol. I, p. 71), which is characteristic:

> Oh! lead me to some solitary gloom,
> Where no enliv'ning beams, nor chearful echoes come;
> . . . .
> There, in a melting, solemn, dying strain,
> Let me, all day, upon my lyre complain,
> And wind up all its soft, harmonious strings,
> To noble, serious, melancholy things.
> . . . .
> Here to my fatal sorrows let me give
> The short remaining hours I have to live,
> Then, with a sullen, deep-fetch'd groan expire,
> And to the grave's dark solitude retire.

Two other Retirement poems are in lighter vein, *To Chloe*, and *To Mrs. Arabella Fermor in the Country* (*ibid.*, pp. 84, 106). Two express her grief for her husband (pp. 115, 118–120). In these and in other elegies she calls upon the world of nature to mourn with her (pp. 75, 115, 116). In some translations from Tasso, there are " horror " passages. She turns *Revelations*, ch. XVI into verse (p. 78), and also writes *The Conflagration* (p. 86), another judgment day ode full of grotesque effects imitated from Young, but unlike Young, Watts, and Hill, ending with the descent of the wicked into hell

> Where, without intermission, without end,
> Howling and lamentations loud ascend;
> With flames and hellish smother, which appear
> To form about the globe a dreadful atmosphere.

Her personal letters more often than not take the form of smoothly flowing little essays on the vanity of life, on retirement, on the necessity of preparation for death (vol. II, pp. 44, 69–70, 77, 80). In fact, she warns her correspondents that if they forget their latter end it will not be her fault. When she herself is ill, or hears that there is an epidemic in the neighborhood, she takes pleasure in writing letters of solemn farewell to her friends. Many such letters were found in her cabinet when she died. She was well aware that her manner of life might be criticised as "the effects of melancholy," ill-nature, or selfishness, but she often insisted that she chose retirement not because she was "in the spleen," but for the sake of improving her reason and her morals.

It was natural enough to a woman of this temperament to project her imagination beyond the life of this world, and to conceive a series of letters supposed to be addressed to the living from the dead. Some of these are intended to be of a consolatory nature, but most of them are awful warnings, and they usually follow some sort of startling or romantic situation in a story cut short by death. Fifty years later, Mrs. Rowe would probably have written novels in letter form; as it is, her little book seems to be inspired by Drelincourt and Young in combination with her own ardent but rather commonplace imagination.

In Letter II, Leonora, who has seen her ghostly correspondent, is assured by her brother that the apparition is "the effect of spleen." In Letter I, a ghost appears in correct ghostly surroundings, which would have suited Young.

> The hour was come; the clock from a neighboring steeple struck *one;* no human voice was heard to break the awful silence; the moon and stars shone clear in their midnight splendor, and glimmered through the trees, which in lofty rows led to the centre of a grove, where I was engaged to meet you.

Letter XII is given up to describing the terror with which a libertine meets his end and suggests, though feebly, some of Dr. Young's warnings to Lorenzo in *Night*

Thoughts. In Letter XVI a dead brother warns a living, "you have but a few weeks more to live. . . . It is a serious thing, My Lord, to die." The series ends with a translation of *Thoughts on Death* from the *Moral Essays of Messieurs de Port-Royal,* containing an effective paragraph on what a man loses in death:

> When a man dies, he loses not only what is called his wealth, but the firmament, the sun, the stars, the air, the earth, and all the rest of nature: he loses his body, and all those sensations that gave him pleasure; he loses his relations, his friends, and all mankind; he loses all relief, all support, and in short, all the objects of his senses and passions.

Mrs. Rowe's *Letters Moral and Entertaining,* usually included with *Friendship in Death,* repeat many of the same effects. The most definitely "melancholy" are a meditation among the tombs in Westminster Abbey (Part III, Letter IX) and a poetical letter from "the abandoned Amoret," in hell, who writes thence to assure a friend that it is a very real place (Part III).[48]

Not only was the melancholy mood of the seventeenth century perpetuated by poets of religious training, such as Watts, Young, and Mrs. Rowe, but the secular group of Queen Anne writers, who were just beginning to depend on editors and the general public rather than on patrons and the court, showed themselves sensitive to the prevailing taste for melancholy themes. We find, in fact, that for a period of about ten years, between 1709 and 1719, each of the writers whose best work may be described as neoclassic and optimistic, paid his court in one fashion or

[48] For Mrs. Rowe's standing as a woman of learning, see Reynolds, *The Learned Lady.*

another to Melancholy. To modern readers, it is evident that, for these writers, the melancholy mood lacked reality and intensity enough to find for itself original expression or true form. Hence they contented themselves largely with repetitions and imitations, variations upon a very few themes. We are conscious of a narrow range of subjects and a want of sincerity, of emotional depth, and of philosophic insight. Nevertheless it is interesting to observe that they did, for a time, play or experiment with the old melancholy themes.

Steele and Addison, both of whom were sincere Christians and orthodox Anglicans, seem to have been in sympathy with Burton's views on religious melancholy. To them, the fanaticism of religious enthusiasts and the indifference of atheism or materialism were equally an evidence of an unsound state of mind. With the weapons both of ridicule and of persuasion, they set themselves to defining the limits and illustrating the uses of the melancholy mood in human life and in literature.

Steele, a man who flung himself heartily into the business of living, appears to have thought that a little melancholy musing was good for the system, like a dose of spring medicine. In *The Tatler* no. 181 (1710) he has a meditation on death, to which is prefixed a quotation from *Aeneid* V, 49.

> Dies ni fallor, adest, quem semper acerbum
> Semper honoratum (sic di voluistis), habebo.

He begins:

> When we are advanced in years, there is not a more pleasing entertainment, than to recollect in a gloomy moment the many we have parted with that have been dear and agreeable to us, and to cast a melancholy thought or two after those with whom, perhaps, we have indulged ourselves in whole nights of mirth and jollity. With such inclinations in my heart I went to my

closet yesterday in the evening, and resolved to be sorrowful. . . . With tempers too much given to pleasure, it is almost necessary to revive the old places of grief in our memory, and ponder step by step on past life, to lead the mind into that sobriety of thought which poises the heart, and makes it beat with due time, without being quickened with desire, or retarded with despair, from its proper and equal motion.

He then, in a famous passage, describes his feeling at the death of his father, at the death of friends in the army, at the death of his first love. But far from calming himself, he simply works himself into a perfect passion of tender feeling, when he is interrupted by the arrival of a present of a hamper of wine. He calls in some friends, and the evening ends in a drinking bout, "rather cheerful than frolicsome."

Spectator no. 133 (1711), by Steele, plays again upon the idea of mingled terror, delight, and sorrow to be found in such contemplations.

Addison's position is really the same though more thoughtfully taken. He believed that religion ought to be cheerful, and made fun of fanatics who were so exclusively concerned with the preparation for death that they ignored fitness for life and daily business (*Spectator* no. 494, 1712). Religious meditation in the solitude of the country, far from producing in his mind sad thoughts, led him to "actual sensations" of God, as his own phrase is (*Spectator* no. 465, 1712). The poetry that resulted was the hymn,

> The spacious firmament on high,
> With all the blue ethereal sky,
> And spangled heav'ns, a shining frame,
> Their great Original proclaim.[49]

[49] While this poem is quite orthodox, founded on the first three verses of the nineteenth Psalm, it was likely to please the deists and free-thinkers also, who reasoned in similar fashion from Nature to God. For instance:

Although his prose *Meditations in Westminster Abbey* (*Spectator* no. 26, 1711) has prefixed the familiar " motto " from Horace's *Odes,*

> Pallida mors aequo pulsat pede pauperum tabernas
> Regumque turris. . . .

Addison's thought does not take either of the characteristic Horatian turns. Horace's train of thought in connection with death would have been either, " Spring is here, let us enjoy it, for death is coming soon," [50] or, " Strive not for wealth or high place, for death will presently bestow upon another the fruit of your efforts." [51] Addison's mind is as well balanced in the presence of tombs as is Horace's. " I know," he says, " that entertainments of this nature are apt to raise dark and dismal thoughts in timorous minds and gloomy imaginations; but for my own part, though I am always serious, I do not know what it is to be melancholy; and can therefore take a view of nature in her deep and solemn scenes, with the same pleasure as in her most gay and delightful ones." In fact the " kind of melancholy, or rather thoughtfulness " produced by such a place is " not unpleasing." He reflects on the worthlessness of some lives, the promiscuity in burial, the special appropriateness of some epitaphs, but his leading idea is that a visit to such a place is a sort of moral tonic. It kills envy and inordinate desire, at the same time softening the heart and bringing about a more just conception of the relative values of human actions and desires. Thus

---

" All Nature's wonders serve to excite and perfect this idea of their author. 'Tis here he suffers us to see, and even converse with him in a manner suitable to our frailty. How glorious is it to contemplate him in this noblest of his works apparent to us, the system of the bigger World." Shaftesbury, *The Moralists,* in *Characteristics,* 5th ed. vol. II, p. 112.

[50] As in *Odes* IV, 7 and 12.

[51] As in *Odes* II, 14 and 18; III, 24.

Addison makes a distinction between unwholesome melancholy, which is mere self-indulgence in emotion, and wholesome melancholy, in which the mind is active for self-improvement.[52] In *Spectator* no. 289 (1712) he again expresses the idea of the moral usefulness of meditations upon death.

The famous soliloquy in Addison's *Cato* (1713), though it advocates suicide in a special case, does so not in the "melancholy" manner of a desperate man drawn on to self-murder, but on grounds of pure reason.

The case of Pope is different from that of Addison and Steele. In his earliest work, he seems to have had an inclination towards the melancholy *genre* of the seventeenth century. The first poem of his which can be certainly dated is the *Ode on Solitude*, 1709,[53] which sets forth after the manner of Martial the pleasures of a country life, but ends with a plaintive wish for obscurity:

> Thus let me live, unseen, unknown,
> Thus unlamented let me die,
> Steal from the world and not a stone
> Tell where I lie.

In 1712 he made a prose translation bringing out the full pathos of the death-bed utterance of the Emperor Hadrian, *Animula blandula vagula.*

> Alas, my soul! thou pleasing companion of this body, thou fleeting thing that art now deserting it! Whither art thou flying? to what unknown region? Thou art all trembling, fearful, and

[52] Cf. *Epictetus,* bk. II, ch. I, and Samuel Johnson, *Rambler* 2, March 24, 1749–50:

"It is the sage advice of Epictetus, that a man should accustom himself often to think of what is most shocking and terrible, that by such reflections he may be preserved from too ardent wishes for seeming good, and from too much dejection in real evil."

[53] Alluded to in a letter to Cromwell, July 17, 1709.

pensive. Now what is become of thy former wit and humour? thou shalt jest and be gay no more! [54]

He later made a poetical version in three stanzas, expanding the theme as it might shape itself in the mind, not of a pagan emperor, but of a dying Christian. This was published in Lewis's *Miscellany,* 1730, and in a revised form in the authorized edition of Pope's *Works* in 1737. By this time, the poem has become entirely non-melancholy through its orthodox Christian conclusion, expressed with an emotional fervor not found in Pope's more characteristic work. The dying man calls to the angels,

> Lend, lend your wings! I mount! I fly!
> O Grave! Where is thy Victory?
> O Death! Where is thy Sting? [55]

The fervor, however, is caught from the models Pope had been reading, Flatman,[56] Prior, and the Scriptures.

Pope's early translation of *The First Book of Statius: his Thebias* (published 1712 in Lintot's *Miscellaneous Poems*) shows that he was for the moment pleased with the sensationalism of "horror" passages. Typical lines are the description of the Fury, Tisiphone :

> Swift as she passed, the flitting ghosts withdrew,
> And the pale spectres trembled at her view:
> . . . .
> Blood stain'd her cheeks, and from her mouth there came
> Blue steaming poisons, and a length of flame.

Or these:

> The birds obscene, that nightly flock to taste,
> With hollow screeches fled the dire repast;

[54] Quoted by Steele in *Spectator* no. 532 (1712).

[55] For an account of the relations between Pope's version and Prior's earlier one, see Pope's *Works,* ed. Elwin and Courthope, vol. IV, pp. 408–410.

[56] One line is borrowed whole from Flatman.

And rav'nous dogs, allur'd by scent of blood,
And starving wolves, ran howling to the wood.[57]

Windsor Forest, 1713, also has a conventionally melancholy description of the ruined countryside about New Forest.

The levelled towns with weeds lie covered o'er;
The hollow winds through naked temples roar;
Round broken columns clapping ivy twined;
O'er heaps of ruin stalked the stately hind;
The fox obscene to gaping tombs retires,
And savage howlings fill the sacred choirs.

There is, also, in the same poem a passage on the happiness of retired country life, which vaguely recalls, as Pope's various commentators remark, Virgil's second *Georgic,* Horace, Lucan, or John Philips's *Cider.*

In 1717 Pope published two poems, each of which turns upon the fate of a woman unfortunate in love. The *Elegy to the Memory of an Unfortunate Lady* is a lament over the death by suicide of a young lady whose ghost haunts the moonlit glade. She is represented as dying in a foreign land, alone,[58] and as refused Christian burial

[57] All this is in Latin epic style, though not of the best period. Pope's maturer taste rejected this sort of thing, and he never again tried the "dreadful" manner. Warton classes Statius with Lucan, Claudian, and Seneca as likely to mislead young authors, because "his images are gigantic and outrageous, and his sentiments, tortured and hyperbolical." Quoted in Pope's *Works,* ed. Elwin and Courthope, vol. I, p. 43.

[58] The lines so much admired by Warton have a cadence similar to that of some lines in Collins's *How Sleep the Brave* (1746).

By foreign hands thy dying eyes were closed,
By foreign hands thy decent limbs composed,
By foreign hands thy humble grave adorned,
By strangers honoured, and by strangers mourned.

rites.[59] At the end, after the manner of an epitaph, a pathetic picture is drawn of the unmarked grave.

> So peaceful rests, without a stone, a name,
> What once had beauty, titles, wealth, and fame.
> How loved, how honoured once, avails thee not,
> To whom related, or by whom begot;
> A heap of dust alone remains of thee;
> 'Tis all thou art, and all the proud shall be.

The closing lines anticipate the death of the poet himself, when the muse shall be forgotten "and thou beloved no more."

The famous *Eloisa to Abelard* has many a melancholy touch in the description of Eloisa's surroundings.

> In these deep solitudes and awful cells,
> Where heav'nly-pensive contemplation dwells,
> And ever-musing melancholy reigns. . . .
> . . . .
> Ye grots and caverns, shagged with horrid thorn,
> Shrines! where their vigils pale-eyed virgins keep,
> . . . .
> In these lone walls (their day's eternal bound),
> These moss-grown domes with spiry turrets crowned,
> Where awful arches make a noon-day night,
> And the dim windows shed a solemn light. . . .
> But o'er the twilight groves and dusky caves,
> Long-sounding aisles and intermingled graves,
> Black Melancholy sits, and round her throws
> A death-like silence, and a dread repose.
> . . . .
> . . . . methinks we wand'ring go
> Through dreary wastes, and weep each other's woe,
> Where round some mould'ring tow'r pale ivy creeps,
> And low-browed rocks hang nodding o'er the deeps.[60]

[59] Young in his *Night Thoughts* III, later uses this same situation as a source of pathetic effect.

[60] Joseph Warton observed that Pope had been reading Milton. *Essay on . . . Pope,* 5th ed. corr. 1806, vol. I, p. 304, note.

All this is quite in the seventeenth century manner. But it is the end of pensiveness, pathos, and of any hint of love-melancholy in Pope. The *Works* collected and published by Lintot in 1717 contained poems of a very different kind which had been even more admired than these, namely *An Essay on Criticism* and *The Rape of the Lock* (first published 1712). Moreover Pope was at the moment immensely occupied with the translation of Homer. His later references to death occur chiefly in his imitations of Horace, and quite in the Horatian vein. Philosophically his attitude towards life and death is the deistic optimism of Shaftesbury and Bolingbroke, later the orthodox position of Warburton. But from 1709 to 1717 there is an evident inclination towards melancholy of the pensive kind, and towards pathetic description, owing to influences transmitted from the seventeenth century.

Swift's poems belong in the anti-melancholy group to be discussed later (ch. V).

In order to understand the work of Thomas Parnell, the poet of the *Night Piece on Death,* we must constantly bear in mind that he was a man of little originality, dependent in his literary work as in the conduct of his life on the advice of his friends, especially Swift and Pope. In religion, he was quite orthodox, and he suffered from a sense of personal unworthiness which he liked to pour out in the long, pious poems which were perhaps the literary form he would have found most natural if left to himself. These, however, were successfully suppressed by his friends,[61] and, with two exceptions, Parnell's poems, as published in Steele's *Poetical Miscellanies* (April, 1713) and in the collection made by Pope in 1721 after Parnell's death in 1718, are

[61] They were so bad that, when published in 1758, Gray spoke of them as "the dung-hill of Grub Street" (*Letters of Thomas Gray,* ed. D. C. Tovey, vol. II, p. 37) and Johnson took them for possible forgeries (*Lives of the English Poets,* ed. Hill, vol. II, p. 54).

"occasional," or didactic, or are directly imitative of well-known classic models of the non-melancholy sort.

The two exceptions are in the manner called melancholy by the seventeenth and eighteenth centuries, but which we should term simply reflective, or perhaps pensive. One of them is the *Hymn to Contentment*, or *Hymn on Contemplation*, by which and by the didactic poem, *The Hermit*, Parnell was best known to his own century up to the appearance of Goldsmith's *Life of Parnell* in 1776.[62] The *Hymn*[63] is evidently, in phrasing and metre, inspired by Parnell's reading of *Il Penseroso*, but in idea it is opposed to Milton's thought, for it condemns solitude as leading to restlessness and skepticism, unless solitary meditation is deliberately turned into religious channels.

> The silent heart which Grief assails,
> Treads soft and lonesome o'er the Vales,
> Sees Daisies open, Rivers run,
> And seeks (as I have vainly done)
> Amusing Thought; but learns to know
> That Solitude's the Nurse of Woe.
> No real Happiness is found
> In trailing Purple O'er the Ground:
> Or in a Soul exalted high,
> To range the Circuit of the Sky,
> Converse with Stars above, and know
> All Nature in its Forms below;
> The Rest it seeks, in seeking dies,
> And Doubts at last for knowledge rise.

Presently Contentment speaks:

> "Know God—and bring thy Heart to know.
> The Joys which from Religion flow."

[62] By that time, the immense vogue of Young's *Night Thoughts* and Gray's *Elegy* would naturally cause a biographer or critic to single out for mention any earlier production of like character.

[63] In Steele's *Poetical Miscellanies*, April, 1713. Quotations from Chalmers' *English Poets*, vol. IX.

The poet accepts her admonition:

Oh! by yonder Mossy Seat
In my Hours of sweet Retreat;
Might I thus my Soul employ,
With sense of gratitude and Joy.

Presently his thought takes a turn like that of Addison's *Hymn,* published a few months before Parnell's.

I'll lift my Voice and tune my String,
And thee, great Source of Nature, sing.

He then enumerates a long list of "natural objects," and concludes:

All of these, and all I see
Shou'd be sung and sung by me:
They speak their Maker as they can,
But want and ask the Tongue of Man.[64]

The other exception, *A Night-Piece on Death,* which it became the habit of the later eighteenth century to compare favorably with Gray's *Elegy*[65] was not published until 1721, when Pope, some three years after Parnell's death, made a selection of his friend's poetry.[66] I think it highly probable, however, that it was written about 1712 or early in 1713, that is to say about the same time as the *Hymn to Contentment,* which it resembles in metre. In thought it is loosely related to Addison's prose *Westminster Abbey,*

[64] Parnell is evidently thinking of *Psalms* XIX, 3, 4, and of Addison's line,

"What though no real voice is heard?"

[65] Cf. Johnson, *Lives of the Poets,* ed. Hill, vol. II, p. 55 and note 5.

[66] It attracted no special attention at the time. In Jacob's *Poetical Register,* London, 1723, Parnell is included merely as "an acquaintance of Mr. Pope's," and only three of his poems, not including the *Night Piece,* are mentioned.

for the poet visits "a place of graves" in order to learn wisdom, and makes somewhat the same general reflections when confronted by

> The marble tombs that rise on high,
> Whose dead in vaulted arches lie,
> Whose pillars swell with sculptur'd stones,
> Arms, angels, epitaphs and bones.

In mood and in vocabulary it recalls Parnell's own prose *Vision,* in the *Spectator* no. 501 (1712), sometimes called *A Vision of Grief.*

In this *Vision,* the author embarks on the River of Tears in a boat steered by Misfortune.

> When we landed, we perceived the Island to be strangely overcast with Fogs, which no Brightness could pierce, so that a kind of gloomy Horror sat always brooding over it. . . . We marched solemnly as at a Funeral, thro' bordering Hedges of Rose-Mary, and thro' a grove of Yew-Trees, which love to over-shadow Tombs and flourish in Church-Yards. [We approached] the most dusky silent Part of the Island . . . the grotto of Grief. It was a wide, hollow, and melancholy Cave, sunk deep in a Dale, and watered by Rivulets that had a Colour between Red and Black. These crept slow, and half congealed amongst its windings, and mixed their heavy Murmur with the Echo of Groans that rolled thro' all the Passages. In the most retired part sat [Grief] . . . in eternal Pensiveness, and the profoundest Silence. On one side of her stood Dejection just dropping into a Swoon, and Paleness wasting to a Skeleton. . . . The whole Vault had a genuine Dismalness in it, which a few scattered Lamps, whose blueish Flames arose and sunk in their Urns, discovered to our Eyes with Encrease. . . .
>
> [We emerged and began to compare experiences with others, which gave us some comfort. The darkness lessened.] We could now and then discern Tracts in it of a lighter Greyness, like the Breakings of Day, short in Duration, much enlivening, and called in that Country Gleams of Amusement. . . . Here the waters, that rolled on the other side so deep and silent, were much dried up. . . . [Patience handed me over to Comfort] and double Day at once broke in upon me.

The experience under the allegorical language we know[67] to have been this. Parnell's wife died in 1711, and for a year he suffered from melancholia so intense that his friends were alarmed for his sanity. By their efforts he was restored to a normal frame of mind, and began to take renewed interest in life. After 1712 he was writing steadily, submitting what he wrote to Steele, Addison, or Pope, while for his professional advancement he was depending on Swift.

The Night Piece on Death is free from any reference to personal grief, which would have offended the taste of Swift or Pope, and its orthodox Christian ending is such as would have been approved by Addison. It survives for us today by a certain actuality conveyed with very few touches. Parnell had to spend much of his time in retirement at Clogher in Ireland, where he was archdeacon. There, as the *Hymn to Contentment* hints, he took solitary walks, and such a walk, whether in England, or in Ireland, is sure to lead sometimes to a churchyard. Once, walking at night, Parnell was struck by the beauty of the dark sky with its stars reflected in the silent water below the churchyard hill, and by the pathos of the human effort to perpetuate distinctions of person or of fortune through differences in the manner of marking graves. This impression he successfully transferred to paper. Once having embarked on meditations concerning death, he continues in quite the seventeenth century manner. Ghosts rise "wrapp'd in shrouds" and urge him to

> Think, mortal, what it is to die.

The voice of King Death is heard in a "peal of hollow groans," but begins to speak against the fear of death, and against the external "forms of woe" in which grief expresses itself. The true view is

[67] Chiefly from references to Parnell in Swift's *Letters*.

Death's but a path that must be trod,
If man would ever pass to God.

If my dating of this poem is right, there is no further pensive strain in Parnell after 1712 or 1713. His didactic tale, *The Hermit,* reflects the doctrine, "Whatever is, is right." The rest of the volume of 1721 is non-melancholy.

John Gay, another member of the same circle, had more originality in expression than Parnell, but was equally dependent for his themes on suggestions from the stronger members of the group.

In the same collection with Parnell's *Hymn to Contentment* are two poems written by Gay, although printed anonymously. *A Contemplation on Night* [68] takes the same vaguely deistic or vaguely Christian position as Parnell's *Hymn* and Addison's "The spacious firmament on high."

Whether amid the gloom of night I stray,
Or my glad eyes enjoy revolving day,
Still Nature's various face informs my sense,
Of an all-wise, all-powerful Providence.

There is some description of night in a passage which Young may have had in mind in the *Night Thoughts.*

A *Thought on Eternity* draws from Horatian premises orthodox Christian conclusions.

Ah! what is life? with ills encompassed round,
Amidst our hopes, Fate strikes the sudden wound . . .
Who then would wish to stretch this narrow span,
To suffer life beyond the date of man?
The virtuous soul pursues a nobler aim,
And life regards but as a fleeting dream:
She longs to wake and wishes to get free;
To launch from earth into eternity.
For while to Thee she lifts her soaring thought,
Ten thousand thousand rolling years are naught.

[68] Quotations from Chalmers, *English Poets,* vol. X.

In this same year, 1713, Gay, then secretary to the Duchess of Monmouth, published *Rural Sports: a Georgic, inscribed to Mr. Pope.* His first lines are a sort of Retirement poem contrasting his own situation, confined to the city, with Pope's country retreat at Twickenham. He describes what would be his own chosen occupation on a pleasant summer day — watching the happy peasants rake hay. When the sun was hot, he would retire to the shade and read the *Georgics,* which are then very skilfully summarized. He describes the coming of evening and of night. Lines 91–94 have a reality which causes them to foreshadow the beginning of Gray's *Elegy* where the scene is similar.

> Or when the ploughman leaves the task of day,
> And trudging homeward whistles on the way;
> When the big-udder'd cows with patience stand,
> Waiting the stroakings of the damsel's hand. . . .

Lines 95–106 are unfortunately so generalized as to make no distinct picture. Lines 107–120 repeat in different language the idea of his *Contemplation on Night.*

But after 1713, Gay's contemplative mood is over. He is absorbed in burlesquing pastorals, in occasional verse, in plays, operas, and mock heroics, sometimes collaborating with others, sometimes merely under orders from Swift and Pope. His vein of pathos found expression in ballads of love — the dramatic monologues of the day — and was much appreciated. But there is no more pensiveness in the first person.

We find, then, that in the Age of Anne and throughout the first quarter of the century, the melancholy of the preceding age persists and the old subjects are treated with even more diffuseness. There is the same fascination with the thought of death, suicide, physical decay, and the Great Assize, the same complaint of the vanity of life, the same professed admiration for solitary retirement. Point of view and phrasing are still largely subject to the same literary influences, Lucretius, Virgil, Horace, Seneca, Martial, *Ecclesiastes, Job,* the *Psalms,* reinforced by the influence of Milton.

In the poems on Retirement, or Contemplation, there is an increasing tendency to expand into descriptions copied from Virgil's *Georgics* or from Milton, but up to 1725 almost no English poet had followed Lady Winchilsea's lead and sought inspiration from the direct and loving observation of nature at first hand. All the nature descriptions are bookish, and they therefore fail either to evoke a picture, or to give pleasure by sharpness or freshness of detail, except where they successfully imitate a fine original. Both Philips and Gay occasionally caught the true Miltonic or classic effect, but for the most part the descriptions are mere maps or lists.

There are, however, some differences in manner between this poetry and that of the last century, differences slight but important as hints of coming change.

First, in the Judgment Day poems particularly, and also in the poems on Contemplation, there is a tendency to dwell on the beauty of the universe as a whole. Poets frequently mount in imagination to some point in stellar space, and there hymn the wonders of planetary motion, passing, by a natural transition, from description to lyric praise of the Creator of such a world. These passages doubtless reflect the growing popularity of Milton's epic and the recognition of the analogy between "the sublime" in certain of his descriptions and in the poetry of the nature *Psalms.* But they are also symptomatic of the spread of the understanding of the Copernican system and the popular enthusiasm over Newton's discoveries.[69] We

[69] The use of these descriptions was probably a conscious effort after the sublime on the part of poets. John Dennis in *The*

find, in fact, that while an ardently religious mind like Watts accepts without question the necessity of the final cataclysm, secular poets tend to mourn the destruction of so beautiful a world, and to hint at the unreasonableness of condemning to eternal torment beings who are not responsible for their own existence in this world. In Hill's *Judgment Day* we notice, even, that a sort of scientific pleasure in the exact delineation of the final fate of the cosmos has almost superseded fear of the divine retribution for sin.

Secondly, we observe that the prevailing mood of the poems of Retirement is the Miltonic one. Melancholy is no longer an unmixed evil, but has both its uses and its mild joys, if indulged in moderation and properly dissociated from religious depression. The pleasures of melancholy are described with no feeling that they are abnormal, or dangerous, or that they will inevitably be followed by pain.

In the third place, while all the principal Queen Anne writers, except Swift, recognized possibilities in the old melancholy themes, and tried their hands at either the prose or the poetic expression of them, it is evident that for the most vigorous minds in the group, these subjects did not furnish real inspiration. Swift suppressed his melancholy, or hid it under satiric form. Steele and Addison

---

Grounds of Criticism in Poetry (1704) says, "The next Ideas that are most proper to produce Enthusiasm of Admiration, are the great Phaenomena of the Material World; because they too lead the Soul to its Maker, and shew, as the Apostle says, his eternal Power and Godhead." He quotes in illustration several descriptions of the sun and moon from *Paradise Lost,* his own paraphrase (1701) of the *Te Deum,* an apostrophe to the sun in *Aeneid* IV, 607, Godfrey's vision of the earth seen from heaven in *Hierusalemme* XIV, st. 9–11, and Milton's Paraphrase of *Psalm CXLVIII* in *Paradise Lost* V, 153 ff. *Critical Essays of the Eighteenth Century, 1700–1725,* ed. Durham, pp. 167–175.

advised it in small doses only, as moral antidote or tonic. Pope tried the existing fashion, achieving a certain distinction in parts of the *Elegy* and of *Eloisa,* but dropped it completely at the age of twenty-nine (1717) having found other moods vastly more fruitful. Gay and Parnell, under the influence of the stronger men, also abandoned contemplation, pensiveness, or gloom. Poets were plainly in need of new and larger experience, if poetry was ever again to rise to lyric heights and resume its place as a formative influence in the spiritual life of Englishmen.[70]

It remains to explain the loss of interest by Pope and his group in melancholy themes when these had been tried with some success and had proved congenial for a time at least. While the influence of Swift was, as we have said, anti-melancholy, and a good deal of poetic energy was absorbed in the writing of political satire, it is evident that these two facts do not, of themselves, sufficiently account for the abandonment of a vein of poetry which was to prove a veritable gold-mine to other poets some thirty years later. A more fundamental explanation is furnished by recognizing the changed and still rapidly changing world of readers for whom the Queen Anne poets wrote.

The twelve years of Anne's reign had seen a revolution in popular literary taste. Greater political stability in church and state following the Act of Settlement (1701), the Union with Scotland (1707), and the Peace of Utrecht (1713), relieved the tension under which Englishmen had

[70] Courthope says of the end of the seventeenth century, "It is indeed evident that unless poetry were recruited by new and abundant waters, it was in danger of perishing in a marsh. The eighteenth century brought the much needed supply. . . . The ancient spring of inspiration derived from national life and manners was renewed, and a long succession of poets . . . carried on the ethical impulse communicated to poetry by Pope." *The Liberal Movement in English Literature,* pp. 59–61.

been living for a century. Rapid commercial expansion and prosperity, an abundance of material things, was adding to the leisured, reading class more and more of the comfortable, city-bred, middle-class element. For these, the spread of journalism and the free use of the cheap pamphlet form of publication were providing a new literature, chiefly in prose, written by paid writers under orders from politicians, editors, and booksellers, and deliberately aimed to please the general reader, please him easily and at once. The *Daily Courant*, founded 1702, and Defoe's *Review*, 1704–13, accustomed readers to demand novelty. The *Tatler*, 1709–11, and the *Spectator*, 1711–12, did much to open their minds and awaken their taste for belles-lettres, music, and drama, and to popularize a knowledge of the classics, at least in translation, but the average reader was probably far less intellectually keen than in the days of Charles I, for this new public, though it had real common sense, was somewhat heavy-witted, fond of the clear and the obvious, the sensational, and the sentimental.[71]

In religion, the popular attitude was changing from intolerance to indifferentism, skepticism, or cynicism. The re-examination of theology by the light of reason in the early work of Toland, Tindal, and Collins, the anti-sectarianism of such books as Swift's *Tale of a Tub* (1704) and Hoadly's *Preservative against the Principles and Practices of the Non-jurors* (1717), the multiplication of dissenting sects, the fierceness of controversy within the church itself, had undermined the influence of religion, and made for worldliness and free-thinking.[72] The average

[71] For the increase in the number of readers and the improvement in their taste under Addison's influence, see Beljame, *op. cit.*, pp. 329–338.

[72] Lecky, *History of England in the Eighteenth Century* (N. Y., 1882–90), vol. I, pp. 269–341.

Toland's *Christianity not Mysterious* appeared in 1696; Tindal's *Rights of the Christian Church* in 1706, his more important work,

reader asked for secular reading matter, and his habitual frame of mind, in contrast with that of the late seventeenth century, was optimistic, objective, and not over-anxious about the state — or the fate — of his own soul.

These changes, already well under way by the end of Anne's reign, became more evident under the worldly-wise, prosperous administration of the Whigs, especially during the ministry of Walpole,[73] and were at their most influential moment about 1740. Optimism had many exponents, but one of the most important for literature, because of his eloquent and persuasive style, was Anthony Ashley Cooper, third Earl of Shaftesbury, who died in 1713.[74]

The nature of Shaftesbury's revolt against seventeenth century pessimism is very fully expressed in his *Letter to a Friend,* dated Dec. 2, 1704.[75] He first quotes the letter of his old master, John Locke (cited at the end of chapter II), ending " this life is a scene of vanity, that soon passes away, and affords no solid satisfaction but in the consciousness of doing well, and in hopes of another life. This is what I can say upon experience." From this breakdown of Locke's philosophical position, and from his apparent sanction of the conventional church doctrine which placed the reward of virtue in a future life, Shaftesbury strongly dissents. His own experience leads him to a different conclusion.

Christianity as Old as the Creation, in 1730. Collins's *Discourse of Free-thinking* was published in 1713.

[73] On the general prosperity during Walpole's administration, see Lecky, *op. cit.,* vol. I, pp. 355–404. Mr. Paul Elmer More, in his essays on Swift and Pope in *With the Wits,* regards the corresponding intellectual change as wholly disastrous for literature. According to him, " the high zeal of the imagination " was opposed and put to rout by the practical sense of England.

[74] On Shaftesbury's debt to Spinoza, and on his popularity and influence, see Robertson, *Pioneer Humanists,* pp. 181–229.

[75] In Shaftesbury's *Life,* ed. Rand, pp. 344–347.

[O]ur life, thank heaven, has been a scene of friendship of long duration, with much and solid satisfaction, founded on the consciousness of doing good for good's sake, without any farther regards, nothing being truly pleasing or satisfactory but what is thus acted disinterestedly, generously, and freely. This is what I can say upon experience, and this you will find sufficient at the last to make all reckonings clear, leaving no terrible account to be made up, nor terrible idea of those who are to account with.

The whole matter, he thinks, is a question of attitude, of will, of moral philosophy.

Life is vain ('t is true) to those that make it so. . . . For my own part . . . I have . . . no falling out with it . . . No harm in it at all that I know; *no vanity.* But (if one wills oneself) a fair, honest, sensible thing it is, and not so uncomfortable as it is made.

He then inveighs against the materialistic view that mere living on the animal plane is any satisfaction, and that human and rational pleasures, such as "friendship, justice, generosity, acts of love, and such like, the exposing of life, health, or fortune, spending it, throwing it away, laying it readily down for others — for friends, country, fellow-creatures, — are no happiness or satisfaction without a reward" in this life or another. He accuses the philosophers of his own day of being "hugely given to wealth and bugbears," i.e., to insisting on a system of visible or invisible rewards and punishments, and upbraids them with "making virtue burdensome and death uneasy." His own system is a better one.

For our part, let us, on the contrary, make the most of life and least of death . . . . Thank heaven, I can do good and find heaven in it. I know nothing else that is heavenly. And if this disposition fits me not for heaven, I desire never to be fitted for it, nor come into the place. I ask no reward from heaven for that which is reward itself. Let my being be continued or discontinued, as in the main is best. The author of it best knows, and I trust Him with it. To me it is indifferent, and always shall be so. I have never yet served God or man, but as I loved and liked.

Shaftesbury's *Inquiry Concerning Virtue or Merit* had already been published by Toland in 1699, though without the author's knowledge. The rest of his works came out in rapid succession between 1708 and 1710, and were collected in 1711 under the title of *Characteristics of Men, Manners, Opinions, Times,* of which a new edition, revised and enlarged, was published in 1713 immediately after his death. Other posthumous works continued to appear up to 1721. Signs of his influence are observable in Thomson's *Winter* (1726), and his ideas and emotions are continually repeated in the poetry of the second quarter of the century by Pope, Akenside, and a host of minor writers.[76] His books offered the public two novel attractions; the first, that his style was rapturous, the second that his system of ethics was based not on the revelations of religion or on the authority of the Church, but on a tolerant, hopeful view of ordinary human nature. As for the effect on poetry, it is obvious that Shaftesbury's confidence in the reliability of human, average reason, his conception of man as naturally virtuous, of the exercise of virtue as an end in itself and as constituting happiness, his identification of the good and the beautiful, and his indulgence of the " benevolent " sentiments which he found instinctive in all men, would all, if accepted, tend to diminish the attractiveness of the usual melancholy themes.

He held a brief for cheerfulness in religion:[77]

> The melancholy way in which we have been taught Religion, makes us unapt to think of it in good Humour. 'Tis in Adversity chiefly, or in ill Health, under Affliction, or Disturbance of Mind, or Discomposure of Temper, that we have recourse to it. Tho in reality we are never so unfit to think of it as at such a

[76] Moore, C. A., *Shaftesbury and the Ethical Poets in England, 1700-1760.* In Modern Language Association of America, *Publications,* vol. XXXI (1916), p. 277.

[77] *Characteristics,* 5th ed. vol. I, pp. 32–33.

heavy and dark Hour. . . . For then it is we see Wrath, and Fury, and Revenge, and Terrors *in the Deity;* when we are full of Disturbance and Fears *within.* . . .

If we would but contemplate the nature of the deity at a time when we ourselves were "in the best of Humours, and in the sweetest, kindest Disposition of our Lives," we should perceive that either there is no God, or else that "*he is truly and perfectly Good,*" and hence incapable of sending evil upon men, even by way of punishment.

In a passage in which he discriminates between the harmless and the harmful indulgence of fancy [78] he charges melancholy poetry (whether religious or Epicurean) with conducing to sensuality.

One of the latter [i.e., of the harmful fancies] is an Enchantress who appears in a sort of dismal Weed and with a most mournful Countenance, often casting up her Eyes, and wringing her Hands. . . . The Airs she borrows, are from the tragick Muse Melpomene . . . and if by her tragick Aspect, and melancholy Looks, she can persuade us that *Death* (whom she represents) is such a hideous Form; she conquers in behalf of the whole fantastick Tribe of wanton, gay, and fond Desires. Effeminacy and Cowardice instantly prevail. . . . The more eagerly we grasp at *Life,* the more impotent we are in the enjoyment of it. By this avidity its very Lees and Dregs are swallow'd. . . . Worth, Manhood, Generosity, and all the nobler Opinions and Sentiments of *honest Good,* and *virtuous Pleasure,* disappear, and fly before this *Queen of Terrors.* . . . The vicious Poets employ this *Specter* too on their side. . . . The gloomy Prospect of Death becomes the Incentive to Pleasure of the lowest Order. *Ashes* and *Shade,* the *Tomb* and *Cypress,* are made to serve as Foils to *Luxury.* The Abhorrence of an insensible State, makes mere Vitality and Animal-sensation highly Cherish'd.

Indulge Genio: carpamus dulcia, nostrum est
Quod vivis: Cinis, et Manes, et Fabula fies.

In characteristic accord with this point of view he elsewhere proves that Horace's final philosophy is Stoic, "or

[78] *Ibid.* p. 315.

Socratic, civil, or social,"[79] that Shakespeare's *Hamlet* is "one continue'd Moral,"[80] and that Milton's *Paradise Lost* has met with popular favor because of its "solid Thought, strong Reasoning, noble Passion, and a continu'd Thred of moral Doctrine, Pity, and Virtue."[80] From the public taste for such noble pieces, he concludes that it is not so much the public ear as the ill hand and vicious manner of our poets, which need reform.

In contrast to Swift, he approves the indulgence and the free expression of rapturous emotion, even of that fanatic passion called Enthusiasm, provided such enthusiasm is directed towards unselfish and exalted objects:

> The Transports of *Poets,* the Sublime of *Orators,* the Rapture of *Musicians,* the high Strains of the *Virtuosi;* all mere *Enthusiasm!* Even *Learning* it-self, the Love of *Arts* and *Curiositys,* the Spirit of *Travellers* and *Adventurers, Gallantry, War, Heroism;* All, all *Enthusiasm!*—'T is enough: I an content to be this *new Enthusiast,* in a way unknown to me before.[81]

And again:

> So far is he [i.e., the author, Shaftesbury himself] from degrading *Enthusiasm,* or disclaiming it in himself; that he looks on this Passion, simply consider'd, as the most *natural,* and its Object as the *justest* in the World. Even Virtue it-self he takes to be no other than a noble *Enthusiasm* justly directed, and regulated by that high Standard which he supposes in the Nature of Things.[82]

But he is careful to say that when the natural reaction from such states of exaltation comes in the shape of melancholy, reason must correct the distorted view of things thereby induced, and the best weapon to employ against it is ridicule.[83]

[79] Letter to Pierre Coste, 1706, in *Life,* ed. Rand, pp. 355–356.

[80] *Characteristics,* vol. I, p. 276.

[81] *Ibid.* vol. II, p. 400.

[82] *Ibid.* vol. III, p. 33.

[83] *Ibid.* vol. I, p. 13 and elsewhere.

Shaftesbury's philosophy, then, permitted enthusiastic outpouring so long as the emotion expressed was felt in connection with ideas of virtue or benevolence and was optimistic in character. In *The Moralists*, the first title of which was *The Sociable Enthusiast*,[84] he composed a sort of prose poem in praise of retirement, or the contemplative life, amid beautiful natural surroundings, as leading directly to ecstatic joy in nature, God, and man. These lyric outbursts, occurring chiefly in parts two and three, become the source, direct or indirect, of so many rhapsodic passages of natural description in the poetry of Thomson and his school that a summary of the contents of some of them may be useful here for future reference.

At the beginning of part two, Philocles recalls a long conversation which he has had with his friend, Theocles. He finds his friend roving in the field with a book, and rallies him on seeking retirement in order to read Virgil or Horace. But Theocles affirms that he is only putting himself in the mood in which these authors wrote, since "for the sake of such a life and habit, as you call contemplative, they were willing to sacrifice the highest advantages, pleasures and favours of a court," and launches into the praise of occasional solitude as a necessary relish to life. The two friends then discuss the nature of the highest good, which they conclude to be not a series of deeds, but a sentiment, benevolence, or love of mankind. Later they discuss the idea that virtue in itself is happiness, without any notion of rewards or punishments in the future state. Theocles, in a famous passage, asserts the order and harmony of the universe.

Later in the evening the two friends, accompanied by two guests, take a walk in the fields. "We fell naturally into the praise of a country life, and discoursed awhile of husbandry and the nature of the soil." Theocles argues

[84] *Life*, ed. Rand, p. 336.

from the order within a single plant to the necessity of believing in the order of the whole universe, though the finite mind cannot really grasp the idea of infinite harmony. Hence he proceeds to the notion of a Universal Mind, and thence to the idea of man's place in the universe, the union of all things, and the subordination of one order of beings to another. He concludes that the State of Nature is necessarily a social state.

At the beginning of part three, Theocles begins thus a prose poem in praise of country retirement:

> Ye fields and woods, my refuge from the toilsome world of business, receive me in your quiet sanctuaries, and favour my retreat and thoughtful solitude. Ye verdant plains, how gladly I salute ye. Hail, O, ye blissful mansions, known seats! delightful prospects! majestic beauties of this earth, and all ye rural powers and graces!

He passes to the adoration of nature-creatrix, as the source of beauty and perfection, and presently we find him speaking of nature and the Universal Mind, as though they were one and the same. This identity is presently explained by his exclamation, "Oh glorious nature! . . . Wise substitute of Providence! Empowered creatress." In a famous passage beginning, "Oh mighty genius! sole animating and inspiring Power!" he argues, but still rhapsodically, that the assurance of God's existence is wholly reasonable. All nature's wonders serve to excite and perfect this idea of their Author. Then follow paragraphs which are like little poems in themselves, expressing adoration for the stars, the sun, the planets, and for God, the Author and Controller of planetary motion. Theocles, in fact, speaks of his own rhapsody as "this vein of enthusiasm." Descending from heaven to earth, he praises the tilling of the soil in words recalling the *Georgics;* then the minerals in the mines, the movements of air and mists, the beauty of water and light, the awful sublimity of winter in the extreme Northern climes, the teeming fertility of the tropics. At this point we have apostrophes to the crocodile, the desert, Mount Atlas, the thick shade of the African jungle, and other "natural objects" and scenes not usually considered delightful by his contemporaries.

Here (section 2) Theocles interrupts himself with a sort of apology for having wandered so far from the present scene, but Philocles asserts that he likes the rhapsody and begs him to go on with a description of America. He claims that under his friend's influence he is beginning to have a growing passion for nature, even for "the rude rocks, the mossy caverns, the irregular unwrought grottos and broken falls of waters, with all the horrid graces of the wilderness itself." He reminds Theocles, however, that "all those who are deep in this romantic way, are looked upon, you know, as a people either plainly out of their wits, or over-run with melancholy and enthusiasm. We always endeavor to recall them from these solitary places. And I must own, that often when I have found my fancy run this way, I have checked myself, not knowing what it was possessed me, when I was passionately struck with objects of this kind." Theocles assures him that the passion for nature may be safely indulged, if he will always remember that the beauty of nature is a representative beauty only, designed to lead to the adoration of the Universal Mind. In fact, such rapturous admiration of beauty is conducive to philosophizing, which is the highest activity of the highest created beings in the universe — mankind.[85]

These are, in summary, the new ideas which Pope and his friends found more inspiring than the outworn melancholy of their predecessors, whether Epicurean, Stoic or

[85] *Characteristics,* 5th ed., vol. II, *The Moralists.*

Christian, and more suited to the tranquil prosperity of the reigns of the first and second Georges.[86] They are repeatedly recognizable in poetry up to 1750 or 1760. Often, however, we must suppose that the poet has been reading not Shaftesbury, but Thomson, who probably is echoing Pope, who, in his turn, is transmitting ideas received sometimes directly from Shaftesbury, sometimes at second hand through Bolingbroke.[87] Even more often we find it wholly impossible to trace the optimism of a particular poet with certainty to any of these sources.

For Shaftesbury's immediate appeal was not to the untrained mind, but to the aristocrat in literature. His philosophy did not become truly popular until it had been simplified and, as it were, translated into the language of the bourgeois reader.

I have been reading my Lord *Shaftesbury's Moralist* [writes Mrs. Rowe[88] to the Countess of Hertford] which has fill'd my head with

[86] Cf. Leonard Welsted, *Dissertation Concerning the State of Poetry* (1724). "May it not, my Lord, be reasonably hop'd, that the Peace, the Happiness, the universal Quiet and Tranquillity, which Great Britain and All Europe enjoys under the Influence of his Majesty's Councils, will have such happy Consequences for all the Studies of Humanity, as may, in Time, and under just Encouragements, bring them to that Standard or Perfection, which denominates a Classical Age?" *Critical Essays of the Eighteenth Century, 1700–1725,* ed. Durham, p. 358.

[87] Collins, J. C., *Bolingbroke,* pp. 137, 138. Bolingbroke's *Minutes of Letters to Mr. Pope,* which form the basis of the *Essay on Man,* were probably written between 1727 and 1733, but not published until 1754, after having been much revised. Sichel, W., *Bolingbroke and His Times,* vol. II, pp. 326–329, and Collins, *op. cit.,* p. 194. "[Bolingbroke's] deism . . . gave some form and impulse not only to Pope but also to Voltaire, and so to the whole century. . . . His thought, though not his own, was coined anew by Voltaire and Pope, and ran broadcast among the lands that read the *Dictionnaire* and the *Essay on Man.*" Elton, *The Augustan Ages,* p. 288. Cf. Moore, C. A., *op. cit.,* p. 324.

[88] *Miscellaneous Works in Prose and Verse,* vol. II, p. 44.

beauties, and love, and harmony, but all of a divine and mysterious nature. However superior his notions may be to my capacity, I have been agreeably led on thro' I know not what enchanting scenes of happiness. I wish you would read it, for it would make you the most charming and agreeable enthusiast in the world. Whether I am in my right senses at present I cannot tell. . . .

In the fields of philosophy and religion, his interpreter was Francis Hutcheson;[89] in poetry, his chief exponents were Thomson and Pope. His social ethics are to be found in popular form in Pope's *Essay on Man,* although Pope probably had received them already clarified by Bolingbroke. His personal ethics, based on the idea of self-development through submission to the influence of the world of physical nature, formed a large, though subsidiary, part of Thomson's *Seasons,* 1726–30. When thus separately developed, these two leading ideas were later perceived to be ethically opposed, for the eighteenth century continued to regard the contemplative attitude towards man and nature as "melancholy," and therefore anti-social. On the other hand, Pope's conception of man as a purely social being, without individual rights or importance, was regarded by the eighteenth century as a cure for melancholy.

The first effect on melancholy poetry of the acceptance of a more optimistic philosophy was, however, a new emphasis on the pleasures of melancholy, a new enthusiasm for the life of retirement, and a renewed assertion of its moral defensibility. These effects are most clearly seen in the descriptive poetry of James Thomson and his followers.

[89] Shaftesbury was probably more popular after Mandeville's attack on his ideas in the latter's *Fable of the Bees,* 1723, and Hutcheson's defense called *An Inquiry into the Original of Our Ideas of Beauty and Virtue,* 1725. Hutcheson occupied the chair of moral philosophy at Glasgow from 1729 until his death in 1746, and continued to spread Shaftesbury's ideas in his lectures.

CHAPTER IV

MELANCHOLY AND DESCRIPTION

1725–1750

In the poetry of the Romantic Movement, melancholy plays a large part, and this melancholy is often communicated through nature description, the poet's mood, whether merely pensive or sad, foreboding, gloomy, or desperate, seeming to arise naturally from the surroundings in which he finds himself.[1] The scene may be actually observed, as in Wordsworth's *Yew-Trees,* Coleridge's *Dejection,* Byron's *Elegy on Newstead Abbey,* Lamartine's *Isolement;* or it may be present to the mind's eye only, as in Shelley's *Alastor.* In either case, as Ruskin has made us forever sensible, the source of the effect is usually the pathetic fallacy, the representation of the outer world as feeling human emotions, or animated by human motives. Ruskin has further pointed out that the same fallacy exists when nature is reproached by the poet for remaining unmoved while he himself is suffering.

In order, therefore, to understand the melancholy of the eighteenth century, it seems necessary to inquire how early in that century descriptions of nature become the poet's vehicle for conveying the melancholy mood; and whether, in so using description, he makes his landscape suffer with

[1] "Sentiment de la nature, mélancolie, lyrisme: sur tous ces points, *qui au fond se réduisent à un,* Rousseau dépasse Richardson." Texte, Joseph, *Jean-Jacques Rousseau et les Origines du Cosmopolitisme littéraire,* p. 308. (The italics are mine.) Cf. Morel, *James Thomson,* pp. 352–3, and Babbitt, *Rousseau and Romanticism,* p. 305.

him, or, whatever his own mood, preserves his sense of objective reality. And first, let us go back for a moment to our starting point, the late seventeenth century.

In the seventeenth century, as literary histories recognize, there was almost nothing that we should now call "nature poetry." [2] It is true that the Elizabethan poets had had to a high degree the power of placing their men and women against a background clearly and beautifully indicated, just as Italian painters in Raphael's time, though not themselves landscape artists, were singularly competent to set in true Italian scenery their portraits and their madonnas. And in such men as William Browne of Tavistock and Robert Herrick, we even see an interest in landscape for its own sake. But these powers had gradually died of inanition, like the other impulses to poetic expression.[3] It is true also, that in Lucretius, Virgil, the *Psalms* and the other classical and biblical sources we have noted for the melancholy poetry of the seventeenth century, philosophic or religious reflection often grows out of the description of nature or is closely associated with it. But while seventeenth century poets admired and imitated these descriptive passages, they seem to have had either little impulse or little power to look about them and describe the English

[2] Reynolds, *Treatment of Nature in English Poetry between Pope and Wordsworth,* [2d ed.] Palgrave, *Landscape in Poetry from Homer to Tennyson,* p. 166. Neilson, *Essentials of Poetry,* p. 71.

"The poets [in the latter half of the seventeenth century] literally lose the best of their senses, and cease to perceive with joy, or interpret with insight, the colour and outline of things, the cadence of sound or motion, and the life of creatures. . . . The whole interest in the outwardly beautiful declines. . . . And this decline expresses the general invasion of poetry by ideas, arguments, and abstractions, which minister both to the rational spirit and to a false notion of literary dignity. The concrete interest confines itself chiefly to society and persons." Elton, *The Augustan Ages,* p. 211.

[3] *Ante,* ch. II.

landscape at first hand, independently of classical or biblical inspiration. Such lyric descriptions as do occur fall into three classes.

First, descriptions at the beginnings and endings of the many pastorals and elegies on the death of friends or public characters. These are always direct reflections of similar passages in classical originals, and, like the originals, are intended to induce in the reader the appropriate mood of gloom. *The Temple of Death,* by Sheffield, begins with such a description (already quoted *ante* p. 80), and we readily perceive that the scene has no relation either to real landscape or real feeling. Truth to outward fact and sincerity are both lacking.

Descriptions of another sort are found in the lyric passages of the tragedies of the day, and are also evidently intended to bring the spectator to a particular mood, in this case a mood consonant with the approaching portion of the action. This is a device common to playwrights of all ages, and was probably inherited by the late seventeenth century directly from Shakespeare and his contemporaries, whose descriptions had skilfully eked out meagre scenery. Such a passage occurs for instance at the beginning of Dryden's *All for Love,* act I, sc. 1, 17.[4]

Serapion (Priest of Isis):
Last night, between the hours of twelve and one,
In a lone aisle o' the temple while I walked,
A whirlwind rose, that, with a violent blast,
Shook all the dome: the doors around me clapp'd;
The iron wicket, that defends the vault
Where the long race of Ptolemies is laid,
Burst open, and disclos'd the mighty dead.
From out each monument, in order plac'd,
An armèd ghost starts up. . . .

[4] Quotations from Dryden, *Dramatic Works,* ed. Scott and Saintsbury.

Another very famous instance is in Congreve's *The Mourning Bride,* act II, sc. 1. In a different vein, but still lyrically descriptive, are these two soliloquies from plays by Dryden.[4]

Cortez (in *The Indian Emperor*):

All things are hush'd, as Nature's self lay dead;
The mountains seem to nod their drowsy head;
The little birds in dreams their songs repeat,
And sleeping flowers beneath the night dew sweat.
Even Lust and Envy sleep; yet Love denies
Rest to my soul and slumber to my eyes.

Antony (in *All for Love*):

Stay, I fancy
I'm now turn'd wild, a commoner of nature;
Of all forsaken, and forsaking all,
Live in a shady forest's sylvan scene;
Stretch'd at my length beneath some blasted oak,
I lean my head upon the mossy bank,
And look just of a piece as I grew from it;
My uncomb'd locks, matted like mistletoe,
Hang o'er my hoary face; a murm'ring brook
Runs at my foot . . .
. . . The herd come jumping by me,
And fearless, quench their thirst while I look on,
And take me for their fellow citizen.[5]

But the tragedies of the seventeenth century were so unnatural that it was quite unnecessary for such descriptions to reproduce a landscape actually observed by the poet. They were stage devices, accepted because they were in the theatrical tradition.

The third kind of description, however, foreshadows perhaps the eighteenth century descriptions of actual natural scenes. They occur in what Samuel Johnson later denominated " local poetry, of which the fundamental sub-

[5] In this passage the imitation of *As You Like It,* act II, sc. 1, is unmistakable.

ject is some particular landscape to be poetically described, with the addition of such embellishments as may be supplied by historical retrospection or incidental meditation."[6] Johnson's definition puts the emphasis where it belonged in his own time, on the element of description, but in the seventeenth century examples, Denham's *Cooper's Hill,* 1643, and Otway's *Windsor Castle,* 1685, the descriptions are merely introductory and the main purpose — the glorification of a place — is reached chiefly through historical allusion and pensive reflection.

Windsor Castle, the only very well known poem of the kind in the second half of the century, is dedicated to James II, and celebrates the virtues of Charles II. It opens with a description of St. George's Chapel with its banners of the Knights of the Garter, then passes to an old aisle of the church, whither the banner of one dead knight is carried when another succeeds him.

> I turn'd around my eyes, and, lo, a cell,
> Where Melancholy Ruin seem'd to dwell,
> The door unhing'd without a bolt or ward,
> Seemed as what lodg'd within found small regard.
> Like some old den, scarce visited by day,
> Where dark Oblivion lurk'd and watch'd for prey.[7]

The castle and the house are then described, though slightly, merely by the enumeration of some details, and the greater part of the poem is simply panegyric. While, therefore, these two poems, the first of their kind in England, describe actual places, the descriptions are so generalized that they do not make clear, individual pictures. But it is to be noted, as bearing on our subject, that the tone, since it is reminiscent of past glories, easily passes into a mournful, or even elegiac, strain.

[6] *Lives of the English Poets,* ed. Hill, vol. I, p. 78.
[7] Quoted from Chalmers, *English Poets,* vol. VIII.

Lady Winchilsea admired Denham and would have liked to celebrate, as he had done, the beauties of the country estate to which she had retired.[8] However, she despaired of success in so ambitious an effort, and therefore, as we have seen, set herself the much simpler task of describing carefully what she saw and how she felt, to the great advantage of her literary reputation to-day. But Pope's *Windsor Forest,* 1713, is mechanically composed on the models furnished by Denham and Otway, and achieves neither improvement nor novelty, except that the amount of description is much greater than that of reflection, so that it is the latter that furnishes the variety from what Pope considered the monotony of description.

Away from the London influence, however, poets living in the country followed their natural impulses and made verses on the scenes before their eyes. In Scotland, especially, there are signs just about this time (1725) of a reviving interest in the poetry of nature written on the principles of first-hand observation and sincere record of feeling.

In Edinburgh in 1724, Allan Ramsay published *The Ever Green,* a miscellany of Scotch poems written before 1600, and called attention in his preface to the excellence of the Scotch tradition on this point. The poetry of these good old bards, said he,

> is the Product of their own Country, . . . Their *Images* are native, and their *Landskips* domestick; copied from those Fields and Meadows we every Day behold.
>
> The *Morning* rises (in the Poets Description) as she does in the *Scottish* Horizon. We are not carried to *Greece* or *Italy* for a Shade, a Stream or a Breeze. The *Groves* rise in our own Valleys; the *Rivers* flow from our own Fountains, and the *Winds*

[8] See her Preface to the volume of 1713 in *Poems of Anne, Countess of Winchilsea,* ed. Reynolds, p. 9.

> blow upon our own Hills. I find not Fault with those Things, as they are in *Greece* or *Italy:* But with a *Northern Poet* for fetching his Materials from these Places, in a Poem, of which his own Country is the Scene; as our *Hymners* to the *Spring* and *Makers* of *Pastorals* frequently do.[9]

The poems of this collection are more often jocund than pensive, but a number of young Scotch poets of Ramsay's own time adopted the melancholy manner, and in such cases, the influence of Shakespeare or Milton is usually traceable.

John Armstrong of Roxburghshire, for instance, at the age of sixteen (1726) beguiled the tedium of a winter "passed in a wild, romantic country" by writing "an imitation of Shakespeare," describing the scenes that met his eye outdoors and in. The "imitation" is felt in the rhythm only, which is blank verse of no mean quality, sometimes too grandiose for the homely scene depicted. Armstrong's *Winter* differs from "local poetry" in that it is purely descriptive without trite generalizations or didactic reflections. It is spirited, not too long, a successful nature poem because it makes a single clear and truthful impression.[10] It seems strange that Dr. Armstrong never again even attempted its like, for his temperament, as described by Thomson in *The Castle of Indolence* I, st. 60, was noticeably melancholy.

[9] *Critical Essays of the Eighteenth Century, 1700–1725,* ed. Durham, p. 399.

[10] According to the publisher's advertisement in the 1770 edition of Armstrong's *Poems,* Thomson, just as he was finishing his own *Winter,* heard of Armstrong's treatment of a similar theme and sent for a copy, which he showed to Hill, Young, and Mallet. Mallet asked leave to print it, but later lost interest and neglected to do so. The piece thus remained unpublished until 1770, when the immense vogue of *The Seasons* made it worth while to resurrect any poetry of like nature. Chalmers, *English Poets,* vol. XVI, p. 540.

With him was sometimes join'd, in silent walk,
(Profoundly silent, for they never spoke)
One shyer still, who quite detested talk;
Oft, stung by spleen, at once away he broke,
To Groves of pine, and broad o'er-shadowing oak;
There, inly thrill'd he wander'd all alone,
And on himself his pensive fury wroke,
Ne ever utter'd word, save when first shone
The glittering star of eve — "Thank heaven! the day is done."

Nevertheless, in his *Art of Preserving Health,* 1744,[11] we find that he has gone over to the anti-melancholy party. Though his third book has a conventionally "horrid" description of a fifteenth century plague, "the sweating sickness," the fourth book, on *The Passions,* analyzes melancholy as arising from "pride in solitary scenes, or fear, or delicate self-love," and condemns enthusiasm on ethical grounds. And the inclemencies of British weather, described in the first book, have become to him simply "monstrous," not delightful as Burton says they are to the melancholy temper.

In 1726 also, and also in Scotland, the Rev. Robert Riccaltoun wrote a rather dull and conventional poem, later known as *A Winter's Day,* the relation of which to Thomson's *Seasons* will presently be pointed out.[12] Allan Ramsay's *Tea Table Miscellany,* 1724, is evidence enough that at the time when those two young Scotchmen, James Thomson and David Malloch, better known as Mallet, went up to London to seek their fortunes, Scotch lyric poetry had not suffered the exhaustion of the English, and that native poets were continuing to express quite simply and genuinely though in very general terms and still in the vernacular, their love of their own scenery with its wild hills, heaths, and cliffs, its mists and storms.

[11] *Ibid.* pp. 521–537.
[12] *Post.* p. 152 ff.

They had discovered also the interest and pathos that lie in a plain tale of unhappy love, even when the lovers are not of high degree. Mallet decided to see whether such a story would "go" in London poetical circles, and re-writing in the taste of the day an old ballad which he rightly guessed would have remained unknown in sophisticated society, he published anonymously his *William and Margaret.*[13] It is a melancholy tale, wherein Margaret's "grimly ghost" appears to William most appropriately at the midnight hour, in a sable shroud, which she clasps with her clay-cold hand. The poem, as a whole, faintly suggests Ophelia's song in the mad scene of *Hamlet,* and the phraseology here and there is otherwise reminiscent of Shakespeare. This maiden, like Cesario's sister in *Twelfth Night,* had let concealment prey upon her damask cheek and had died for love. She describes midnight somewhat as Hamlet does:

> This is the dim and dreary hour,
> When injured ghosts complain;
> When yawning graves give up their dead. . . .

and the ghosts disappear, as all ghosts should, at cock crow. The ghost also moralizes in seventeenth century fashion on the levelling effect of death.

> So doth the fairest face appear
> When youth and years are flown:
> Such is the robe that kings must wear
> When death has reft their crown.

And she also claims, as Job did, a humiliating relationship:

> The hungry worm my sister is.

[13] Quotations from Chalmers, *English Poets,* vol. XIV. Child, in his *English and Scottish Popular Ballads,* vol. II, p. 200, notes that Mallet used almost unchanged the 1711 version of *Sweet William and Fair Margaret.*

Under Hill's fostering care, the poem became a great success. Mallet presently claimed it, and it passed as his original poem throughout the eighteenth century, and even later.

In Wales, too, John Dyer, a young landscape painter, on a walking tour through his native country with Milton in his mind, borrowed the metre of *L'Allegro* and *Il Penseroso* to describe *The Country Walk,* which first appeared in Richard Savage's *Miscellaneous Poems and Translations,* London, 1726. Much of the description in this delightful little piece is the result of first hand observation, and many lines have a genuine reality, like that of Lady Winchilsea in her *Nocturnal Reverie.*

> I am resolved this charming day,
> In the open field to stray;
> I have no roof above my head,
> But that whereon the gods do tread!
> Before the yellow barn I see
> A beautiful variety
> Of strutting cocks, advancing stout,
> And flirting empty chaff about,
> Hens, ducks, and geese, and all their brood,
> And turkeys gobbling for their food,
> While rustics thrash the wealthy floor,
> And tempt them all to crowd the door.
> . . . .
> An old man's smoky nest I see,
> Leaning on an aged tree;
> Whose willow wall and furzy brow,
> A little garden sway below.
> Through spreading beds of blooming green
> Matted with herbage sweet and clean,
> A vein of water limps along,
> And makes them evergreen and young.
> Here he puffs upon his spade,
> And digs up cabbage in the shade.[14]

[14] Quotations from Chalmers, *English Poets,* vol. XIII.

During the course of his walk, the poet, as might have been expected, retires into the shade of the trees and lays him down on some green moss at the foot of an oak, where all is silent save for the sweet murmurs of a brook and the warbling of birds.

In the same Miscellany appears also the first version of *Grongar Hill*[14] by Dyer, a "local poem" celebrating the beauty of the view from a hill in South Wales near the poet's home. Dr. Greever, who has reprinted this first version,[15] notes that it is distinguished by the description of scenery "which Dyer has looked upon for himself, and liked for its own sake." But like Armstrong, Dyer, as he became more sophisticated, fell under the influence of London literary circles and lost the wish, or perhaps the power, to repeat such an effect.

Grongar Hill, is a Retirement poem, and in spite of its observation of nature at first hand, shows many of the conventional features left over from the seventeenth century. We have the usual ruin frequented by the usual appropriate animals, as in this passage descriptive of an old tower,

[14] Quotations from Chalmers, *English Poets,* vol. XIII.

[15] Dr. Greever points out that John Scott of Amwell knew of its existence. See Scott's *Critical Essays on Some of the Poems of Several English Poets,* London, 1785, p. 99.

Dr. Greever considers that the versification, while showing traces of Dryden and Pope, is something of a cross between the introductory lines of *L'Allegro* and *Il Penseroso* on the one hand, and the more lilting measures of these two poems on the other. The metre is chiefly iambic tetrameter, rhymed variously, with a tendency towards the couplet. In the same year Dyer made the poem over, using a rhythm more nearly like that of the greater part of Milton's companion poems, with an occasional hint of lyric rhythms caught from Shakespeare. This second version, the one now generally known, came out in Lewis's *Miscellaneous Poems by Several Hands,* London, 1726. See Greever, Garland, *The Two Versions of "Grongar Hill"* in *Journal of Eng. and Ger. Phil.,* vol. XVI, pp. 274–281.

Whose rugged walls the ivy creeps,
And with her arms from falling keeps,

. . . .

'T is now the raven's bleak abode;
'T is now th' apartment of the toad;
And there the fox securely feeds;
And there the poisonous adder breeds,
Concealed in ruins, moss and weeds,
While, ever and anon there falls
Huge heaps of hoary moulder'd walls.

Passing into a more cheerful, but still pensive strain, Dyer ends his poem with the pleasures of retirement:

Now, ev'n now, my Joy runs high,
As on the mountain-turf I lie;
While the wanton *Zephir* sings,
And in the Vale perfumes his wings;
While the Waters murmur deep;
While the Shepherd charms his sheep;
While the Birds unbounded fly,
And with musick fill the sky,
Now, ev'n now, my Joy runs high.
Be full, ye Courts, be great who will;
Search for Peace with all your skill;
Open wide the lofty Door,
Seek her on the marble Floor.
In vain ye search, she is not there;
In vain ye search the Domes of Care!
Grass and Flowers Quiet treads,
On the Meads, and Mountain-heads,
Along with Pleasure, close ally'd,
Ever by each other's Side:
And often, by the murm'ring Rill,
Hears the Thrush, while all is still,
Within the Groves of *Grongar Hill.*

But though some nature poetry occurs in the eighteenth century before Thomson, it was he who made that *genre* popular through publication in 1726 of his *Winter,* followed rapidly by poems on the other seasons. In the latest edition of *The Seasons* made in Thomson's lifetime, the influence of Shaftesbury is plainly visible, first in the rhapsodical descriptions of the larger aspects of nature, secondly, in the amount of space given to the ethical justification of enthusiasm. From a modern point of view, the effect of the fascination exercised by these modes of thought upon the young nature poets of the time was disastrous, for it seems to have delayed by fifty years or more the development of the true English nature lyric, by which I mean the "simple, sensuous, passionate" expression of the poet's personal response to the outdoor world.

It is comparatively easy to trace the process and the influences by which Thomson's *Winter*, first appearing as a poem of four hundred and six lines, almost lyrical in the unity of its theme and the sincerity of its feeling, was transformed in later editions into a long, discursive piece more like an essay in verse. The first version, 1726,[16] may properly be regarded as an expression of melancholy, the poet conveying his mood to the reader by the description of natural scenes in harmony with his own feelings. According to Thomson's own account, the idea of expressing a sort of melancholy pleasure in the gloom and discomforts of winter occurred to him as the result of reading Riccaltoun's unpublished poem on *Winter*, which, he says, "I still have." [17] Riccaltoun's poem,[18] fifty-seven lines long, is an expression of pleasure in the darkness, the storms, the general dreariness, gloom, and "horror" of winter, as suiting the black melancholy

[16] Reproduced in the edition of *The Seasons* by J. Logie Robertson, Oxford, 1891; of Thomson's *Winter* by William Willis, London, 1900; and in Zippel's critical edition of *The Seasons*, Berlin, 1908.

[17] Letter to Dr. Cranston, Sept. 1725. In *Memoir of Thomson* by Sir Harris Nicolas, first published in 1831.

[18] Given entire in the *Gentleman's Magazine* for May, 1740, vol. X, p. 256, as *A Winter's Day, written by a Scotch Clergyman: Corrected by an eminent Hand.*

in the poet's own soul, a melancholy for which no cause is assigned. This begins:

> Now, gloomy soul! look out — now comes thy turn;
> With thee, behold all ravag'd nature mourn.

It ends with an exhortation to time, not to bring back the spring,

> Fix'd my ill *fate,* so fix'd let winter be,
> Let never wanton season laugh at me!

In the course of the poem, there is suggested, though vaguely, the analogy between winter and death. Such a mood seems very far from the tone of the first part of *The Seasons,* as those poems exist today, but an analysis of this first version will show us where lies the sympathy between Riccaltoun [19] and Thomson.

The first sixteen lines announce the theme, Winter, sullen and sad, the season of gloom kindred to the soul of man. Lines 17–103 form a kind of prologue to the real subject by describing an autumn day, which induces in the soul a sort of philosophic melancholy. A few lines of transition bring us to the real subject. In lines 112–194 Winter himself approaches, "striding the gloomy blast." The poet describes the powers of rain and of wind, and expresses his own "pleasing dread" at the thought of the majesty of nature. He describes a great storm, which at midnight ends in "a noiseless calm." Seven lines make a transition to the first reflective passage, lines 202–215, in which the poet feels the littleness and vanity of human life by contrast with the might of nature, and prays the Almighty for goodness, knowledge, and real happiness.

[19] Peter Cunningham in an article entitled *James Thomson and "The Winter's Day"* in *Gent. Mag.,* April, 1853, pp. 368–9, discusses the evidence, collected by himself, that the poem, though printed in Savage's *Miscellany,* 1726, and in Chalmers, *English Poets,* 1810, as the work of Mallet, is really by Riccaltoun.

Resuming his description of winter in lines 216–252, he describes a heavy fall of snow. Then by a natural turn of thought, though evidently in imitation of Milton, he gives us, in lines 253–300, an indoor scene in which the poet retreats to a comfortable fireside, where by means of books he "holds high converse with the mighty dead," or talks with his friend Lycidas (David Mallet). Lines 301–324 describe a hard frost, lines 325–358 a sudden thaw, so destructive both on land and sea that men would succumb completely, did not Providence

> [light] them safe,
> Thro' all this dreary Labyrinth of Fate.

Lines 359–405, the second reflective passage, form a general conclusion. Winter is symbolic of death, of the perishing of all the restless hopes and ambitions that make up life. But as Winter is followed by Spring, death is to be followed by a new and better life in eternity, where virtue will receive its reward in

> Life undecaying, love without Allay,
> Pure flowing Joy, and Happiness sincere.

In all the models and sources cited by Thomson's most thorough commentator, Zippel,[20] only two, *Il Penseroso* and *L'Allegro*, affect the poem structurally, in the passage just

[20] Zippel, Otto, *Entstehungs- und Entwicklungsgeschichte von Thomson's "Winter,"* Berlin, 1908. *Nebst historisch-kritischer Ausgabe der "Seasons,"* Diss., Berlin, 1907. This critical edition supersedes by its thoroughness all former editions. Zippel's accompanying dissertation takes account of the work of Borchard, Mitford, Morel, Robertson, Tovey, and Willis. See Bibliography.

Zippel's list of models and sources seems to me reliable, except that it cites as sources passages in Browne's *Britannia's Pastorals* which I believe to be accidental parallels only, and that it practically ignores possible prose sources, such as Shaftesbury's *The Moralists.* Zippel adds a useful tabular view of the enlargements of *Winter* made by Thomson in editions after the first.

referred to, lines 253–300. All other parallels indicate merely what Thomson has been reading: they account for his phrasing and diction, but the imitation is not so close as to diminish Thomson's claim to originality. Every feature of his descriptions is such as he himself must have seen again and again in his Scotch home. The autumn landscape, the rains, the silent streams, the effects of snow and frost, the thaw, the appearance of clouds and sky, the behavior of animals and men under such conditions, have evidently all been matters of direct observation; the truth of his word-painting and the spontaneity of his feeling are easily recognizable.

Structurally also, the poem in its first form is satisfactory. The description of autumn passes naturally into that of winter, feeling arises naturally from the scenes described, and leads naturally into reflection. By following closely the progress of winter as it actually occurs, the organic unity of the poem is secured; a single tone is maintained, since the poet's mood remains in harmony with the conditions in the external world, shading from pensiveness to a deeper melancholy, as autumn shades into the winter. The analogy of winter with death, though a commonplace of man's thinking, is a real analogy. While there are two separate reflective passages, the first occurs very properly at the end of the autumnal prologue, and the two are directly related, since both contrast the

The important texts are:

A	(March, 1726)	405 lines
B	(June, 1726)	463 "
C	(1730, in the first collected ed. of *The Seasons*)	781 "
E	(1744) when *The Seasons* appears in vol. I of *Works. . . . with additions and corrections.*	1069 "

My quotations are from *The Complete Poetical Works of James Thomson*, ed. J. L. Robertson.

greatness of nature with the littleness of man, and contrast the transitory world with the eternal life of the soul. The proportion of lines of reflection to description is fifty-four to three hundred and fifty, or about one seventh, and the emotion, though mild, is just about strong enough to fuse the whole. Modern criticism might feel that the prologue descriptive of autumn, almost one hundred lines, is too long in proportion to the rest, and that there is, therefore, a tendency to split into two shorter descriptive units.

At any rate, analysis has shown that what Thomson has in common with Riccaltoun is the feeling of pleasure in the gloom of winter, the feeling which is most strongly expressed towards the beginning of the poem, but which is succeeded in the reflective passages by vaguely deistic aspiration towards virtue and by faith in a benevolent providence and the happiness of the future life. That Thomson naturally took delight in philosophical and pensive wanderings in the autumn and loved to disport himself in the beloved gloom of Scotch scenery, is affirmed in his letter to Dr. Cranston, already mentioned.[21] But apparently he owes to Riccaltoun the idea that the subjective expression of such pleasure might furnish the design for a descriptive poem.

Let us now examine the changes in the succeeding editions of *Winter* as they are tabulated by Zippel.

The B text (June, 1726) is longer than A by fifty-eight lines. The increase is due to three insertions in the passage descriptive of the snowfall. Eleven lines (B 233–247), as charming as anything Thomson ever wrote, tell how the robin redbreast, driven from the fields by hunger, visits a cottage where he alights

> On the warm hearth; then, hopping o'er the floor,
> Eyes all the smiling family askance,

[21] "Nature delights me in every form; I am just now painting her in her most lugubrious dress for my own amusement, describing Winter as it presents itself."

> And pecks, and starts, and wonders where he is—
> Till, more familiar grown, the table crumbs
> Attract his slender feet.

After line 252 (in the A text) are inserted in B twelve lines picturing the bear as he is seen in a Russian winter by a traveler who has lost his way. This is immediately followed by twenty-seven lines in a more lurid vein than anything else in the poem, describing an onslaught of hungry wolves which descend from the Appenines,

> Cruel as death, and hungry as the grave!
> Burning for blood, bony, and gaunt, and grim!

They tear and kill horses, bulls, human beings, and finally,

> lur'd by the scent,
> On churchyards drear (inhuman to relate!)
> The disappointed prowlers fall, and dig
> The shrowded body from the tomb, o'er which,
> Mixed with foul shades and frighted ghosts, they howl.

Here Thomson has left the Scotland he knows, and is letting his imagination work on suggestions caught from other people's poetry. The bear passage and the suggestion for the redbreast passage are from Armstrong's *Winter*. The detail of wolves which exhume bodies from graves is a literary convention borrowed by the English poets from classic times.[22] These additions do not change the general character of the poem; in fact, they are evidently intended to enhance the gloom of winter. But in going beyond the limits of the poet's own observation, these new passages mark a significant change in Thomson's method of compo-

[22] Cf. the *Glosse* to Spenser's *Shepheard's Calendar: September*. "'Saxon King.' King Edgare that reigned here in Britanye in the yeare of our Lord [957–975] which king caused all the Wolves, whereof there was store in this countrye, by a proper policie to be destroyed. So as never since that time there have ben Wolvs here founde, unlesse they were brought from other countryes. And there-

sition, and begin the process by which his little nature poem was finally transformed into a rambling, loosely connected piece, made up of moral reflections, nature descriptions, and personal compliment, a mixture of which Dr. Johnson very justly remarked, " The great defect of *The Seasons* is want of method. . . . The memory wants the help of order, and the curiosity is not excited by suspense or expectation."[23] For the resulting mélange no better name has yet been found than " a descriptive poem."

Great changes were made in the C text (1730) and almost as many in the E text (1744). For convenience, I shall describe the two processes together. The ninety-five lines describing the autumn day were removed to *Autumn,* a change which, considered by itself, was an improvement. But this shortening is overbalanced by the addition of new subject matter. Immediately after the sixteen opening lines come twenty-six lines of dedication to Lord Wilmington. Then follow thirty lines describing the malign influence of winter on men and beasts. After the snow storm, a peasant losing his way is frozen to death in the snow. Thirty-eight lines are given to reflection on the miseries of human life, ending with praise of the Jail Committee of 1729. After the onslaught of the wolves, there is a description

---

fore Hobbinoll rebuketh him of untruth, for saying that there be Wolves in England."

English poets welcomed the chance offered by Italian scenery to make "horrid" use of the wolf. Cf. Webster's Dirge in *The White Devil,* act V, sc. 4.

> But keep the wolf far thence that's foe to men,
> For with his nails he'll dig them up again.

The original is probably the passage in Statius, *Thebaidos,* X, 42–48.

[23] *Lives of the English Poets,* ed. Hill, vol. III, p. 299. Johnson, however, thought the defect inherent in the descriptive *genre.* "Of many appearances subsisting all at once, no rule can be given why one should be mentioned before another."

of an avalanche. Added to the compliment to Mallet is one to Pope, followed by a eulogy of James Hammond.[24] Forty-seven lines give the subjects of the philosophical conversations between the poet and his friends. Then follow descriptions of the winter evening amusements of country folk and city folk. Thirty-five lines flatter Chesterfield. Beginning again with the description of a frost, Thomson passes to winter in Russia, in Siberia, in Lapland, and at the North Pole. He pictures Sir Hugh Willoughby sent by Queen Elizabeth to discover the Northeast Passage, describes a lethargic race of human beings, dwelling in the far North, whom he calls "the last of men," and praises the civilizing influence of Peter the Great. He ends, as in the first edition, with the thaw, and the same general reflections. Many passages of the first edition are immensely expanded in the edition of 1744, more particularly the signs of coming storm, the catalogue of "the mighty dead," and the description of the frost. Thus the 1744 version of *Winter* is more than two and a half times as long as the first edition. Nevertheless, the two bits of reflection, fifty-four lines in all, remain almost unchanged. If to them are added the thirty-eight lines on the miseries of life, the 1744 version has a proportion of reflection to other matter of about one to ten. The new passage on the miseries of life is not organically related to the other two meditative passages, nor does it arise very naturally even from the account of the death of the peasant in the snow. The original design of the poem, the expression of pleasure in winter, is quite lost. No such feeling can be expressed in connection with body-snatching wolves on the one hand, or with the compliment to Lord Chesterfield on the other.

Most of the new material (listed by Zippel) is derived from books, not from the enlarged experience of the poet

[24] For Hammond's connection with the poetry of melancholy, see *post*, ch. VI.

with men or nature. The sources of the first version are Virgil (especially *The Georgics*), Horace, Pliny; the Bible (*Job, Psalms, Gospels, Acts*); Spenser, Milton, Shakespeare; Philips's *Cider,* Pope, Riccaltoun. In later editions, he increases his indebtedness to his former models and adds passages suggested by Lucretius, by Armstrong's *Winter,* Mallet's *Excursion, The Tatler,* Savage's *The Wanderer,* and Aaron Hill's *The Northern Star.* In the other *Seasons* he does not greatly increase his range of allusion to the classics (adding only Plutarch and Ovid) or to the Elizabethans. But he at once includes, in whatever portion of *The Seasons* he happens to be writing, by allusion, paraphrase, or expansion, such bits as please him out of the work of his friends. Besides those contemporaries already mentioned, Zippel finds parallels with poems by Leonard Welsted, with Gay's *Rural Sports* and *Wine,* Philips's *The Splendid Shilling,* and Denham's *Cooper's Hill.* A rather curious situation develops in the case of Savage and Mallet. Both these, writing after the first edition of *Winter* had appeared, are evidently imitating Thomson; he in turn imitates them. These mutual borrowings were undoubtedly intended as compliment and advertisement, and were taken in good part.

External evidence exists that Thomson continually asked for criticism from his friends and conscientiously endeavored to mold himself and his work to please them. This proof is found in Thomson's letters and in the marginal corrections made on an interleaved copy of the first volume of the 1738 edition of Thomson's *Works* (British Museum), and the point remains the same whether we ascribe the corrections to Pope, with earlier critics, or to Lyttelton, as Professor Macaulay and Zippel apparently have good reason for doing.[25] Under the pressure of the

[25] Macaulay, G. C., *James Thomson,* p. 59. Zippel, Otto, *Thomson's Seasons,* critical ed. pp. VI–IX, XXII–XXXI.

ideas and example of his particular circle, he tried to moralize his song. But in his philosophy he was a satellite, not a leader. Since his religion and his philosophy remained always vague, confused, and even contradictory, his later attempt to write a purely philosophical poem was a lamentable failure; *Liberty* failed to sell, in spite of the admiration excited by *The Seasons*.[26] Dr. Johnson complained that he could not get through it.[27] The effect of London upon the young Scotchman was, within five years, to destroy entirely the impulse towards lyricism, and though he worked constantly on perfecting his *Seasons*, he wrote no new nature poetry.

Dr. Myra Reynolds in her book on *The Treatment of Nature in English Poetry*[28] points out a similar transformation in the work of other poets of the time.

> As a rule, such significant poetry of Nature as appeared during the transition period was the work of men who had spent much of their youth in the country or in country villages; it was practically their earliest poetic venture, and usually the work of their youth; and, in most cases where there was an extended literary career, the poetry of Nature speedily gave way to work of a didactic or dramatic sort, in which Nature played but a small part. [Exceptions to this statement are Collins, Cowper, Blake. Illustrations of it are Armstrong, Dyer, Thomson, Akenside, Allan Ramsay, William Pattison, Mickle, Bruce, Beattie.]
>
> The import of these facts in this period seems to be merely that there was a genuine and widespread love of Nature on the part of many isolated poets, who, by the circumstances of their lives knew Nature better than they did literature, but that this love was not sufficiently robust in individual cases to withstand the cramping influences of city life and literary coteries. The developing tradition was carried on not so much by the persistent influence of a few as by the constant springing up of the same spirit in many minds.

[26] Brewster, Dorothy, *Aaron Hill*, pp. 198–199. Johnson, *Lives of the English Poets*, ed. Hill, vol. III, p. 289.

[27] *Ibid.*, p. 301.

[28] 2d ed. pp. 329–332.

While Thomson's descriptions in the first *Winter* are in general accurate and have many truthful touches, there is a considerable tendency to transfer the poet's feeling to the outer world. Winter is sullen and sad (2), the breeze sobs amid the Boughs (49), the Fruits forsake the Parent Bough,

> That, in the first, grey, Glances of the Dawn
> Looks wild, and wonders at the wintry Waste (63).

There are "weeping Grottos" (76). Winter comes, striding the gloomy Blast (113). The Cock is pensive (128). The Clouds doubt which Master to obey (158). The Moon is sad (159). The Demon of the Night warns the devoted Wretch of Woe and Death (189). The Clouds are weary. The Sky saddens. The Labourer-Ox does a little philosophizing and "demands the Fruit of all his Toil" (230). The winter morn, late-rising o'er the drooping World, lifts her pale Eye, unjoyous (313). The Rivers, underneath the ice, swell impatient for the day (329). The northern Seas are sullen, the Pole is ungenial (331). There are almost no cheerful touches. But in the last edition the melancholy has been much obscured by the introduction of passages in a different mood, such as the description of winter sports, of winter-evening amusements in city and country, and of sledding in Russia.

Thomson's *Juvenile Poems* include *A Complaint on the Miseries of Life, A Pastoral between Thyrsis and Corydon upon the Death of Damon, A Pastoral Entertainment* (which I take to be a paraphrase of the Epicurean picnic in Lucretius), *An Elegy on Parting, On a Country Life,* and *Upon Happiness.* All these show some tendency to lament poetically amidst suitable surroundings, to luxuriate in solitude.[29] But after the composition of the

[29] M. Morel in his chapter on *La Philosophie du Poème* (*James Thomson,* II, ch. V.) points out that, on the whole, Thomson can

Winter of 1726, Thomson can scarcely be reckoned as a melancholy poet, in the modern sense.

He remains, however, melancholy in the eighteenth century, technical sense, for in the other *Seasons*, and especially in *Summer* and *Autumn*, he makes liberal use, in forms expanded and embellished to suit his personal taste, of the time-honored " melancholy " sources and devices. The poet advocates retirement not once, but five times in *Summer* 9–14, 458–468, 516–563, 1379–1397, and *Autumn* 1235–1373, paraphrasing carefully in the last passage the end of the second *Georgic* with its praises of simplicity, obscurity, and rural industry. There is a kind of " Night Piece " at the end of *Summer* (1664–1729) and another in *Autumn* (1138–1171). One of the effects of spring is love-melancholy, the symptoms of which are described quite according to Burton (*Spring* 1022–1110). The pathos of the nightingale's lament for her young (*Spring* 712–726) and of the failure of the father of the family to return to his wife and children (*Autumn* 1145–1159, *Winter* 310–317) are repeated from Lucretius. The life of man is compared to that of insects fluttering in the sun until

> Fierce Winter sweeps them from the face of day.
> (*Summer* 342–351.)

There is also a set Complaint of Life in the classical manner (*Spring* 272–308), in which the Golden Age is first lauded and then the present bemoaned as " these iron times, These dregs of life " when

---

be called neither pessimist nor optimist. He is satisfied merely to express the beauty of nature and his love for her various aspects. So far as Nature teaches anything, it is that disturbances are passing accidents — that there is no death, only a transformation of life. He always associates with nature the thought of human life and of nature's usefulness to man, but in his latest poetry he no longer views it suffused with his own melancholy feeling.

Even Love itself is bitterness of soul,
A pensive anguish pining at the heart. . . .

Storms destructive of life and property appear again and again. In an "excursion of fancy" to tropical climes, there is a long passage (*Summer* 629–1102) describing the horrors which there threaten the life of man. The crocodile, the hippopotamus, and the elephant seem to be regarded as not especially dangerous, but the serpent, the scorpion, the tiger, leopard, and hyena, sand storms in the desert, the typhoon at sea, with its terrors increased by prowling sharks, and tropical fever and plague, are all congregated in an attempt to be sensationally terrific, until the poet exclaims,

But 'tis enough; return, my vagrant Muse;
A nearer scene of horror calls thee home . . .

and lets us down with a mere thunderstorm in the Welsh mountains.

Throughout *The Seasons* we see the ideas of Shaftesbury constantly paraphrased in defense of this sort of melancholy enthusiasm. The passage just mentioned at the end of *Autumn* does no more than praise the simple retired life as harmless, inexpensive, and pleasurable. But elsewhere Thomson, like Shaftesbury, asserts that moral improvement is the unfailing effect of the solitary contemplation of nature. Thus:

I solitary court
The inspiring breeze, and meditate the book
Of Nature, ever open, aiming thence
Warm from the heart to learn the moral song.
(*Autumn* 669–672.)

Again, evening is the time

For those whom wisdom and whom nature charm,
To steal themselves from the degenerate crowd,
And soar above this little scene of things —

To tread low-thoughted vice beneath their feet,
To soothe the throbbing passions into peace,
And woo lone Quiet in her silent walks.
(*Autumn* 964–969.)

Walking thus on an autumn evening, when " the desolated prospect thrills the soul," the poet feels himself seized and wrought upon by this beneficent influence.

He comes! he comes! in every breeze the Power
Of Philosophic Melancholy comes!
His near approach the sudden-starting tear,
The glowing cheek, the mild dejected air,
The softened feature, and the beating heart,
Pierced deep with many a virtuous pang, declare.
O'er all the soul his sacred influence breathes;
Inflames imagination; through the breast
Infuses every tenderness; and far
Beyond dim earth exalts the swelling thought.
Ten thousand thousand fleet ideas, such
As never mingled with the vulgar dream,
Crowd fast into the mind's creative eye.
As fast the correspondent passions rise,
As varied, and as high — devotion raised
To rapture, and divine astonishment;
The love of nature unconfined, and, chief,
Of human race; the large ambitious wish
To make them blest; the sigh for suffering worth
Lost in obscurity; the noble scorn
Of tyrant pride; the fearless great resolve;
The wonder which the dying patriot draws,
Inspiring glory through remotest time;
The awakened throb for virtue and for fame;
The sympathies of love, and friendship dear,
With all the social offspring of the heart.
(*Autumn* 1004–1029.)

" Public Zeal " is elsewhere (*Summer* 1616) asserted to be the greatest of the virtues and parent of all the rest, and life as a whole is declared to be unsatisfactory only to the selfish.

But to the generous still-improving mind
That gives the hopeless heart to sing for joy,
Diffusing kind beneficence around,
. . . .
To him the long review of ordered life
Is inward rapture only to be felt.
(*Summer* 1641–1646.)

Equally in accord with Shaftesbury's position, Thomson represents the contemplation of nature as leading not only to love of Him,

The world-producing Essence, who alone
Possesses being . . .

but to a positive power of abstract reasoning upon His nature and relation to the created universe (*Summer* 1730–1805). Thomson also offsets the description of nature in aspects hostile to man by the thought characteristic of Shaftesbury, Bolingbroke, and Pope, that Creative Wisdom has undoubtedly ordered all things well, in a manner beyond the criticism of "little haughty Ignorance" (*Summer* 318–340). Rhapsodic outbursts very like those of Shaftesbury in *The Moralists* are the passage beginning "Hail, Source of Being! Universal Soul" (*Spring* 556–571), the adoration of God apparent in His works (*Spring* 849–866) and of the power of the sun (*Summer* 97–174), and the apostrophe to Nature (*Autumn* 1352–1373).

There is no external evidence to show just how conscious Thomson was of the sources of his ideas, but he pays a tribute to Shaftesbury, in *Summer* 1551–55, as the friend of man and lover of nature, who knew how

To touch the finer movements of the mind,
And with the moral beauty charm the heart.

In the preface which appears in the second and later editions of *Winter*, Thomson aligns himself with the reformers of poetry, and urges upon poets the choice of great and serious subjects, of which he cites Hill's *Judgment Day* as an admirable instance. He thinks no subject "more ready to awake the poetical enthusiasm, the philosophical reflection, and the moral sentiment than the works of Nature." For this reason "the best, both ancient and modern poets have been passionately fond of retirement and solitude." He mentions the *Book of Job* and *The Georgics* as sublime instances of the poetry of nature.

The great number of editions of *The Seasons* throughout the eighteenth century, the admiration and respect in which their author was held in spite of his failures in other kinds of composition, his strong influence upon contemporary poets, all these things indicate that his series of nature poems abundantly satisfied popular taste. Modern readers must remember that the very miscellaneousness of these poems — their frequent change of subject with only a mechanical transition, the continual infusion of moral reflections by the way, the frequent resemblance to descriptive passages in Lucretius, Virgil, or Ovid — was a source of delight to readers whose literary taste had been nourished on the classics, in the original or in translation, on satiric and didactic verse, and on the essays of the *Tatler* and the *Spectator*. Doubtless Thomson's contemporaries recognized what we also must recognize today, that whether he is borrowing, or mixing, or imaginatively rethinking the thoughts of others, Thomson is always in rhythm, diction, and general tone a genuine poet. Then, too, after the long attempt to equal the classics in epic kind, Englishmen must have taken great pride in the production of such a series as *The Seasons,* rivaling them in the descriptive *genre.*

But for descriptive poets of less genius than Thomson, the pursuit of his method was far from being so easy as it seemed. Freed by his example from the convention that repressed the public display of personal emotion, his imitators poured out floods of pathetic feeling in their descriptions of nature. Encouraged by his successful miscellaneousness, and unrestrained by his almost unfailing good taste, they tried to include in a single poem philosophical argument and moral exhortation, allusion to current events, compliments to friends and eulogy of patrons or of public men deceased, all of which was more properly the material of poets of the non-melancholy school, who for the most part eschewed description and devoted themselves to the study of society for material, and to argument for the method. Thomson's imitators also copied his idyllic episodes, which replaced in public favor the despised pastoral, and they pushed to farther extremes the device called the "excursion of fancy." Not confining themselves to any one scene, country, continent, or even to the earth, they ranged in fancy over land and sea, from the pole to the equator, and explored the stars. They thus spun out their reflections and observations to great lengths, which they divided into books or cantos, with invocations after the epic manner. In fact they wavered between lyric and epic design, endeavored to be subjective and objective at the same time, and while trying to be comprehensive succeeded only in being incoherent. This poetry was still, as we have seen, called melancholy, or enthusiastic, but instead of separate short lyrics on Retirement, or Life, or Death, we have all these subjects and many more, mechanically included in that poetic omnibus of the eighteenth century, the descriptive poem. Moreover, they too often attempted rhapsody, and since it was impossible to sustain intense emotion at such length, the results were for the most part either tumid or flat. Mallet's *Excursion*

(1728), Savage's *Wanderer* (1729), Ralph's *Night* (1729) and *The Tempest* (1727), Dyer's *Ruins of Rome* (1740), Young's *Night Thoughts* (1742–45), William Thompson's *Sickness* (1745), are all constructed on the omnibus model. In all these, the unfortunate consequences may be seen of free self-expression unformed by organic idea and unlimited by the external pressure of rhyme, stanza form, or classical model. But the popularity of *The Seasons* was so enormous, it was no wonder that the eager hordes of poets leaped to the conclusion that the road laid out by Thomson led directly to success.

Even before *The Seasons* appeared as a whole, Thomson's friend, Mallet, had published *The Excursion,* in 1728. As Dr. Johnson readily perceived, the diction is copied from Thomson.[30] The poem is in blank verse, in two cantos. How far afield it ranges may be shown by a synopsis.

It begins with an invocation to Imagination to bear the poet away from the haunts of vice and folly, vanity, and man, to the country, where blameless virtue walks. Here follows a description of spring, then of the dawn, presently of full morning, and of the view from a high hill. Following Shaftesbury and Thomson, the poet is led by the sight of such a view to thoughts of the Creator, and to the pious wish,

> Thus, ever fix'd
> In solitude, may I, obscurely safe,
> Deceive mankind, and steal through life along,
> As slides the foot of Time, unmark'd, unknown.[31]

Resuming description, he pictures for us the noon hour; then a storm, a flash of lightning, a cottage in flames, a traveler struck dead by a tree. Such exhibitions of the power of nature lead to thoughts of the divine power.

[30] *Lives of the English Poets,* ed. Hill, vol. III, p. 401.
[31] Quotations from Chalmers, *English Poets,* vol. XIV.

The storm clears and evening approaches.

> Onward she comes, with silent step and slow,
> In her brown mantle wrapp'd, and brings along
> The still, the mild, the melancholy hour,
> And Meditation, with his eye on Heaven!

The poet walks, musing in sober mood, and presently finds himself in a grove of cypresses. At the left is a high rock, the haunt of the raven, down which pours a foaming waterfall. Before him on the blasted heath rise the ruins of a church. Within is a place of tombs, which the poet describes with the usual details of skulls, bones, ivy, falling roof and arch, columns gray with moss, and so forth.

> All is dread silence here, and undisturb'd;
> Save what the wind sighs, and the wailing owl
> Screams solitary to the mournful moon,
> Glimmering her western ray through yonder aisle,
> Where the sad spirit walks with shadowy foot
> His wonted round, or lingers o'er his grave.

But after this rather ghastly description the poet somewhat sentimentally hails the venerable dome as a refuge where the weary are at rest, and where great and small mingle, with the distinctions of rank and wealth lost forever. He notices and describes one of the monuments commemorating the virtues of Thyrsis, wisest and best of men, to whom he pays tribute. While he is still occupied with his reflections, morning dawns.

Now he urges his fancy to a conscious flight, and she leaves the present scene, traveling with immense rapidity first to the North Pole; then to the eastern desert, where hags and sorcerers perform their wicked rites with appropriate "horror" machinery; then to the south (by which he means the Caucasus) where the poet describes the view from the top of the mountains. She then flies to Italy, and there is a description of a city ruined by an earthquake. Here, of course, the horrors are piled high, and the poet is led to reflections on the dark and inscrutable purposes of heaven. After a description of the complete ruin around about, he ends, rather as a seventeenth century writer might have done, with the thought that all God's ways are holy.

Next his fancy leaves the earth, for he reflects that the wonders of God are even more fully displayed in the heavens. The poet mounts by a path which the vulture's eye has not observed, nor the foot of eagle trod. From the heavens he looks back at the earth and around on the whole universe. Here he shows off his astronomy, uttering an apostrophe to light and describing Venus, Mars, and Saturn. He thinks again on the Creator of planetary motion and praises Newton, the discoverer of its laws. By contrast, he is led to think of the littleness of earth. He sees a sun and its attendant worlds expire, and another sun born. He thinks of the ministering spirits who attend these worlds, and ends with the thought of infinity, where

> no landmarks are,
> No path to guide imagination's flight.

It is, perhaps, needless to say that nothing in this so-called poem indicates that Mallet has ever seen any of the objects he describes, or independently thought any of the generalizations which he utters. The poem is a jumble of Milton, Shaftesbury, Thomson, and Hill, with considerable biblical suggestion and much display of astronomical reading. The plan of the poem, so far as it has any, is the order of the times of day. Within this general chronological plan, there is also a geographical plan, arising from the course of the walk, which the poet takes. Since a walk may begin and end anywhere, the poem also may begin where it likes, wander at will, and end at pleasure. Once the device is adopted of letting the fancy soar away from earth, there are no bounds to the scenes which may be described, and no limits to the length of the poem.[32]

Mallet has also left *A Fragment* in the manner of *L'Allegro,* describing the walks of health.

> There plunged amid the shadows brown,
> Imagination lays him down,
> Attentive, in his airy mood,
> To every murmur of the wood.

He wrote also a *Funeral Hymn,* which is in stanzas, but which distinctly recalls Milton's *Il Penseroso* in its subject matter.

Another rather curious case of the results of imitation is to be seen in the work of James Ralph, whose *Miscellaneous Poems* were published in London in 1729, with a dedication to the Earl of Chesterfield. Ralph, it will be recalled, was the ne'er-do-well companion of Benjamin Franklin on his first journey to England late in 1724. He was born and brought up in America, where the civilization and the scenes about him were totally different from those present to the English poet of the same time. Yet, within four years Ralph had apparently forgotten all about actual America, and was writing descriptive poems after the manner of Thomson, but with none of Thomson's inspiration.

The little volume contains *Night,* in four books, *Zeuma, or the Love of Liberty,* in three books, *Clarinda: or The Fair Libertine, The Muses' Addresses,* and *The Tempest.* The preface makes a great pretense of having chosen lofty and serious subjects in imitation of Milton, Watts, and

[32] That is to say, both poets and critics of the eighteenth century seem to have considered the order of details in a descriptive poem either arbitrary or accidental. Cf. Johnson, *Lives of the English Poets,* ed. Hill, vol. III, p. 225.

Thomson. Then begins a discourse on the relative merits of blank verse and rhyme. While Ralph admires both, his own choice for serious poetry is blank verse.

The poem *Night* again illustrates the dangers of the descriptive-reflective manner, when there is no plan except the presentation of pictures, from which any appropriate thoughts may arise. The opening lines may obviously lead anywhere:

> Lo! sable night ascends the dusky air,
> And spreads her deep'ning shadows all around;
> Her silent influence stills the noisy world,
> And wakes the studious soul to solemn thought.
> . . . .
> Wrapp'd in thy shades; What wonders will arise,
> And thro' the deepest gloom delight my soul!

In the briefest possible summary, the content of the poem is as follows:

Contemplation is invited to guide the poet's muse. He describes the coming of night. Revolving time brings on the various seasons, and first, naturally, spring. Very early in the year, there is an unseasonable hail storm and a frost. At last the spring comes fully, and there is a description of a spring evening. The seas are calm. The lovesick maiden meets her lover in the groves. There is a shower at night, which beats on the roof and lulls the sleepers within to deeper sleep. This peaceful scene is contrasted with the night as it is passed in time of war, when anxious parents are awake, and Desolation and Horror stalk over the scene while plunderers ravage the dead. (These are compared to wolves tearing the carcasses of bears which have been slain in the hunt by Russians.) Again by contrast, the poet imagines a scene in America where nature in her most peaceful aspect lulls the unthinking savage to repose. But any man who is truly miserable is denied the relief of sleep.

Black melancholy glooms his mournful thought,
And gives a dreadful horror to the night:
All sad she rises o'er the pensive fields,
And with her dusky wing embrowns the dark'ning green;
Where e'er she turns, contagion flies along,
And fades the honours of the blooming tree;
Infects the odours of the springing flow'rs,
And veils the beauty of their silken leaves:
Now plaintive down the headlong wave she glides,
And wakes lone echoe with the sadd'ning sound;
Now on the sighing breeze sublimely rides,
And murmurs solemn in the waving boughs:
Ascending thence, the *Stygian* vapour shades
The twinkling glories of the heav'nly vault;
And all the planets of malignant rule,
Gleam on the midnight earth their baleful rays.

In the second book, summer comes. The laborer in the fields longs for night in vain. There is a description of great heat followed by the refreshment of evening dews. There is a comparison with the sufferings of travelers in the deserts of Arabia, relieved by the finding of a spring. A moonlight night is described, and there is a fanciful passage in which the poet wonders who inhabits the moon. There are flashes of heat lightning. All nature sleeps, and weary laborers are at rest. Meantime, maidens are bathing in the moonlit stream, till, disturbed by a passing traveler, they run away and hide. The poet lies in the shadows made by the moon, and thinks on the shining path of virtue, which leads straight to the mansions of heaven. He calls on his friend, Nisus, to roam along the fields in conversation. He rejoices in the beauty of the shining vales, hills, and streams. The land of peace which he sees is contrasted first with Greece, depopulated by plagues:

the glutted grave
No longer opens her destructive jaws,
But, choak'd with heaps of dead, can hold no more.

So on the blasted heath whole tribes are hurl'd,
And rot, and moulder in the tainted wind.

Then it is contrasted with the Orient, where slavery and idolatry reign, where tornadoes and poisonous creatures and beasts of prey threaten death; with certain islands in the Atlantic, where at night malarial vapors kill; and with tropical seas where there are sudden storms, which wreck ships and drown the sailors. The morning comes, and Nisus is urged to retire far from man's deceitful race, since he can never stain his spotless life with fashionable dissipations.

The third book is devoted to autumn nights. There is an elaborate description of a ruined castle, once the home of Chaucer, now haunted by the ghost of the builder. The poet walks in the evening, and meditates on the beauty of the scene presented by the laborers going home from work, and on the pleasures of retirement with Nisus, his virtuous friend. Occupations of peasants at night are described — drinking, dancing, and sleeping. A contrast is made with the condition of peasants in Italy, whose harvests are destroyed by earthquakes, as Sodom was destroyed. It is now midnight. The poet describes the Aurora Borealis. In a passage imitative of Mercutio's Queen Mab speech in *Romeo and Juliet,* he describes the dreams sent to lovers, to friendless wanderers, to poor slaves. In some lines imitated from *Comus,* he suggests that angels are sometimes sent to drive away the horrors of night from virtuous souls. Again, recalling Shakespeare, he describes the antics of the will o' the wisp. Copying Thomson's *Winter,* he gives us a description of a tempest, with a shipwreck and the drowning of the mariners.

The fourth book is occupied with winter nights and imitates Thomson in its effects. After a few lines of general description, we have a fog in which a wanderer loses his way and is finally drowned, and an ice storm during which a man, clinging to a cliff, falls into the sea.

> And on his mangled limbs, the scaly monsters feed.

He next describes a flood, which is compared to the violence of Niagara; then a snow storm, followed by clearing. This, he thinks, is the time to "explore the twinkling glories of the sky." While gazing at the stars, the poet thinks now of man as he appears in the social life of cities, now of death and the melancholy sound of funeral bells. He reflects that "horrid night" covers all the northern skies and is spread for half a year over "sad Greenland's coast." He describes storms in the polar seas and the hardships suffered by fishermen, who are often crushed to death in the ice. Meantime, the rich sleep wrapped in down,

> Nor dream the sorrows which the luckless feel,
> Dark-roaming thro' the melancholy gloom,
> And beg a shelter from the blast in vain:
> With harden'd hearts the living bar their doors,
> And all relief deny: the silent dead
> Are only kind; so, in the dreary vault,
> On heaps of mould'ring bones, they seek repose
> And bless the friendly shade. . . .

In conclusion the poet prays that if, in the future, wealth is forced on him, and he shows any tendency to avarice, the heavenly powers will take away his fortune. There follow contrasting descriptions (anticipating Blair) of the death of the rich man and of the poor man.

I have described this poem at such length, partly in order to show the close imitation of Thomson, and partly to indicate the sometimes absurd wanderings of "the fancy" in the descriptive-reflective poem. It will also have become clear, I hope, that there is an association well established by 1730, between the description of nature and either pensive or gloomy reflection.

Certain details of the descriptions, too, had become so fixed by repetition as to be in themselves considered either pensive or horrible, so that the mere use of them in a poem was sufficient to stamp it as melancholy, regardless of whether or not the poet's feeling really penetrated his description. Thus, autumn and evening are pensive, winter and night, gloomy. The shade of the deep woods by a stream, or the top or bottom of a cliff by a waterfall, or any moonlit path, are appropriate places for solitary contemplation. The nightingale or the thrush assist meditation. The presence of the redbreast adds pathos to a lonely grave. A ruin covered by ivy and haunted by owls, bats, ravens (birds of ill omen), or adders, toads, foxes (emblematic of desolation) is almost an inevitable feature. A deeper shade of melancholy is attained through descriptions of a graveyard or charnel house, preferably in a state of ruin, thickly shaded by cypress and yew, haunted by ghosts, frequented by wolves, and offering unpleasant evidences of physical decay. The horrible or terrible is achieved by laying the scene in the frozen north or a tropical desert, and bringing on carnivorous animals, or by describing war, pestilence, famine, earthquakes, avalanches, storms, floods, and shipwrecks. In descriptions of planetary space, comets are used for terrible effects, because of the possibility of their destroying other heavenly bodies.

Probably these elements are often instinctively included, their use sanctioned by long tradition, but they are often somewhat mechanically and ineffectively brought in, in accordance with a critical theory such as that of John Dennis, who in *The Grounds of Criticism in Poetry*, 1704, lists

> the several Ideas which [next to religious thoughts] are capable of producing . . . enthusiastick Terror; viz., Gods, Daemons, Hell.

Spirits and Souls of Men, Miracles, Prodigies, Enchantments, Witchcrafts. Thunder, Tempests, raging Seas, Inundations, Torrents, Earthquakes, Volcanos, Monsters, Serpents, Lions, Tygers, Fire, War, Pestilence, Famine," etc.[33]

Supremely terrible is the wrath of infinite power, and Dennis quotes in evidence his own paraphrase of *Psalm* XVIII, which is a description of a destructive thunderstorm.

A description of this character is frequently inserted, just for the sake of sensation, in a poem which is otherwise non-melancholy. There is such an instance in Ralph's *Zeuma* in the same volume with his *Night.* This has a preface giving the early history of America, and is the story of the resistance of an Indian King of Peru to the Spaniards. It is in blank verse, and attempts to be an heroic poem. In Book II there is inserted a description of a ruined temple, once used by the Indians for human sacrifice. Here we have the regular details of ivy, darkness, feeble lamps, crimson stains on the pillars, with bones and the skulls of fierce enemies on the walls, and ghosts. Much is made of the impression of ghastly solitude. In Ralph's *Clarinda,* also, there are several pensive descriptions of the solitary places in which Clarinda meets her lover, but after the lady goes to London, she leaves

> The pleasing Horror of the gloomy Wood,
> The plaintive Murmurs of the falling Flood . . .

and mingles in scenes more like those of the *Rape of the Lock.*

The Tempest, by Ralph (first published in 1727), attempts to refute the Lucretian argument against the fear of death. Lycus, living in pensive retirement in a foreign land, reasons that life is miserable, because of the possibility of inherited disease, accidents involving the loss of fortune,

[33] *Critical Essays of the Eighteenth Century,* ed. Durham, p. 190.

disappointment in love, duels, loss of reputation, the downfall of the great, tyranny, the loss of strength in old age, uncertainty as to when death will come, and the pangs of conscience. Therefore, death is a kind conclusion to our ills. However, on his voyage home, there is a storm and his ship is wrecked.

> Then Lycus found the Fears of Death prevail,
> . . . .
> And, ere the Surges rav'd around his Head,
> All pale with Horror, shudder'd at his Fate.
> . . . .
> Till the sad Soul could fear grim *Death* no more,
> And thro' the *Storm* ascended from the *Waves*.

The later work of Dyer, too, shows the overwhelming influence of Thomson in its mingling of melancholy reflection and excursions of fancy with the description of actual scenes. It will be recalled that two of Dyer's earlier poems, both of which were short, had an almost Miltonic charm in their pictures and in their rhythms, but the *Ruins of Rome*, 1740,[34] in spite of the lines admired by Dr. Johnson,[35] is merely a rather dull descriptive poem, following at long distance *The Seasons*, or sometimes Thomson's most unpoetic *Liberty*.

Now, Dyer had actually been to Italy and seen the scenes he describes, but the details which he recalls are of the most obvious kind, and are buried under a heap of allusions to Scipio, Marius, Caesar, Cicero, the Horatii, and the Curii. He is inspired with a desire to serve his country, as these served Rome. The view from the top of the Palatine hill at once recalls the days when all the buildings and columns at his feet stood in their glory in the days of Imperial Rome. But now they are all reft of their graces.

[34] Chalmers, *English Poets*, vol. XIII.
[35] *Ibid.*, p. 222.

So Time ordains, who rolls the things of pride
From dust again to dust. Behold that heap
Of mouldering urns (their ashes blown away,
Dust of the mighty!) the same story tell;
And at its base, from whence the serpent glides
Down the green desert street, yon hoary monk
Laments the same, the vision as he views,
The solitary, silent, solemn scene,
Where Caesars, heroes, peasants, hermits, lie
Blended in dust together; where the slave
Rests from his labours; where th' insulting proud
Resigns his power; the miser drops his hoard;
Where human folly sleeps.—There is a mood
(I sing not to the vacant and the young),
There is a kindly mood of melancholy
That wings the soul, and points her to the skies. . . .
. . . .
'T is sweetly soothing sympathy to pain,
A gently wakening call to health and ease,
How musical! . . .
How sweet thy diapason, Melancholy!

Before the end of the poem, Dyer manages to insert reflections on the decay of poetry since the time of Virgil, and to cover most of the history of Rome, ending with a description of the horrors of the barbarian invasion. He closes with an apostrophe to luxury, which has ruined Assyria, Greece, and Imperial Rome.[36]

Young himself, whose *Night Thoughts* will be separately treated in the next chapter, is obviously partly inspired by Thomson. It was the adoption of Thomson's manner which gave him opportunity to spin out at such great length miscellaneous argument, reflection, and description, in a composition lasting over several years and conceived, not as a whole, but as a series of postscripts to his first thought.

[36] This description and the reflections at the end evidently owe something to the descriptions of Parthia, Rome, and Athens in *Paradise Regained*.

Blair's *Grave* has far more coherence, but it, too, shows the new freedom of manner, the liberty to range over vast subject matter, inaugurated by Thomson.

Savage's *The Wanderer*, 1729,[37] though intended in praise of "the still, compar'd with active life," does no more than follow the Thomson recipe without much reality or poetic power. Invoking Contemplation, the poet seeks solitude in the wilds of a "grey, leafless wood" on a mountain side. He finds the cave-like dwelling of a hermit, in discourse with whom he learns — in five cantos — that the object of life is to avoid deserving its ills, but at the same time to learn to bear them with fortitude. A sort of novelty is attained by working in the story of Christ's patience in suffering, a meditation on the sorrows of a bereaved husband tormented by superstition, spleen, and the impulse to suicide, from all of which he is rescued by religion. The third canto describes the vices of city life; the fourth, the joys of the reviving spring. In the fifth the hermit discourses on the apparent triumph of vice over virtue in this world, the usefulness of suffering, and the proper attitude towards death, ending with the astonishing statement that he himself is dead. The poet in a vision sees him vanish into heaven, with the parting admonition:

> Justly to know thyself, peruse mankind;
> To know thy God, paint nature on thy mind;
> Without such science of the worldly scene,
> What is retirement? — Empty pride or spleen;
> But with it wisdom.

The entire poem seems to a modern reader devoid of real idea or charm in rhythm or phrase, and overloaded with descriptive maps and lists which somehow fail to evoke a picture. One suspects that the attention it received in its own time was largely due to the general sympathy for its author's misfortunes.

[37] Chalmers, *English Poets*, vol. XI.

Between 1740 and 1750, we begin to perceive a distinct trend in melancholy poetry towards a more organic structure, greater simplicity and charm in language, and the more direct and personal expression of feeling, — in other words, towards real lyric. This movement appears in the work of seven young men, Akenside, Hammond, Shenstone, Gray, Collins, Joseph and Thomas Warton, who, all born after 1710, seem happily to have escaped the literary influences of the late seventeenth century. Leaving for a later chapter the first five named, with whom the striving for form seems to have been self-conscious, let us consider the work of the youngest two, the brothers Warton in whom the improvement seems chiefly due to the loving imitation of a great model, Milton's minor poems.

Joseph Warton's *The Enthusiast: or The Love of Nature* was written in 1740, and published in his *Odes on Various Subjects,* 1746. It is a Retirement poem in blank verse, asserting the poet's preference for natural scenes, sounds, and flowers over all the works of man. It draws a picture of society in its first state, but here he follows not the tradition of a Golden Age, but Lucretius, Book V, representing primitive life as rude and hard, yet free from the curse of war and commercialism. He asserts that the failure to prefer the primitive state to a high degree of civilization, is evidence of a corrupt nature. He rhapsodizes upon the nature theme after the manner of Thomson, probably following Shaftesbury. Presently he swings into a passage like some famous lines in *Il Penseroso:*

> . . . near some crowded city would I walk,
> . . . .
> Or wandering near the sea, attend the sounds
> Of hollow wind and ever beating waves.

Here follows a conventional "horror" passage, but presently, resuming the Miltonic imitation, the poet is found walking in the moonlight and invoking Contemplation to lift his soul above this little earth. In this mood there appear to him Philosophy, Solitude, Wisdom, Virtue, and Innocence. Virtue tells him that she and all her train are about to forsake England, which is given over to vice. The poem ends prettily with the poet's longing to be borne to the western hemisphere, to fields yet unpolluted with the sword of war; there he would hunt with the simple Indian, feeding on dates and herbs, despising luxury and avarice, and heeding not " the distant din of the tumultuous world."

> So when rude whirlwinds rouse the roaring main,
> Beneath fair Thetis sits, in coral caves,
> Serenely gay; nor sinking sailors' cries
> Disturb her sportive nymphs, who round her form
> The light fantastic dance, or for her hair
> Weave rosy crowns, or with according lutes
> Grace the soft warbles of her honeyed voice.

In the other " odes " the imitation of Milton is even more marked, as is obvious in such a passage as the following, from the *Ode To Fancy:*

> To meet the matron Melancholy,
> Goddess of the tearful eye,
> That loves to fold her arms and sigh;
> Let us with silent footsteps go
> To charnels and the house of woe;
> To gothic churches, vaults, and tombs,
> Where each sad night some virgin comes,
> With throbbing breast and faded cheek,
> Her promised bridegroom's urn to seek.
> Or to some abbey's mouldering towers,
> Where, to avoid cold wintry showers,
> The naked beggar shivering lies,
> While whistling tempests round her rise,
> And trembles lest the tottering wall
> Should on her sleeping infants fall.[38]

[38] Quotations from Chalmers, *English Poets,* vol. XVIII.

The range of Joseph Warton's subjects is shown by the titles, *To Health, To Superstition, Against Despair, To the Nightingale, To Solitude.* In the last named poem, Solitude is represented as an allegorical figure, dressed in black, and crowned with cypress. She walks at midnight by the pale moon's light, listening to the crowing cock, or the owl, or the howling mastiff, or the distant-sounding clock. The poet longs to leave the city and dwell calmly with her. These poems are all short, logically constructed, and in a pensive tone, recalling Milton in rhythm, and phrasing, though an occasional "horror" passage is inserted after the manner of Thomson. For instance, in the ode *To Superstition,* Superstition vanishes when Reason lifts her head and Ignorance and Fear disappear with her.

> So by the Magi hail'd from far,
> When Phoebus mounts his early car,
> The shrieking ghosts to their dark charnels flock;
> The full gorged wolves retreat; no more
> The growling lionesses roar,
> But hasten with their prey to some deep-cavern'd rock.

Among these *Odes* is one *To Evening,* which anticipates Gray's *Elegy* in the atmosphere of one of its stanzas.

> Hail, meek-eyed maiden, clad in sober gray,
> Whose soft approach the weary woodman loves;
> As homeward bent to kiss his prattling babes,
> Jocund he whistles through the twilight groves.

The last stanza, and in fact the poem as a whole, parallels Collins's ode *To Evening,* which appeared in the same volume.

> O modest Evening! oft let me appear
> A wandering votary in thy pensive train;
> Listening to every wildly warbling throat
> That fills with farewell sweet thy darkening plain.

Suggestions for such a poem are, of course, present in Milton's *Il Penseroso,* all the images have been used before in other pensive poetry, and the metre had been first used for elegy by Hammond. Nevertheless the combination is new and may have helped to determine Gray, who was even then working on his *Elegy,* in the choice of metre and tone.

Most of the poetry of Thomas Warton falls in the period after Gray's *Elegy,* and hence is not for discussion here, but *The Pleasures of Melancholy,*[39] written in 1745 when he was seventeen, and published anonymously in 1747, already shows the ideas and feelings common to Thomson and Shaftesbury, but modified by the chastening influence of Warton's marked admiration for Milton.

The poem is three hundred and fifteen lines long, written in blank verse, and has prefixed the motto

Praecipe lugubres Cantus, Melpomene!

Contemplation is invoked to lead the poet to the haunts of melancholy, and certain scenes appropriate to melancholy musings are called up. Such are: a ruined abbey at twilight under the early moon, silent save for the hooting of an owl upon an ivy-clad tower; a gloomy pine walk; a burial vault at midnight around which ghosts are hovering; a wakeful couch at dead of night, lying on which the poet meditates on passages of Spenser and Milton; or perhaps a fireside on a winter evening, which also induces meditation. After this description of suitable surroundings, the poet describes the pleasures of melancholy. He thinks of Pope's mournful Eloisa; he describes the night in terms reminiscent of Young, and then a wet morning in a manner that recalls Thomson. He waxes enthusiastic over the pleasure of books, for reading, it seems, is one of the melancholy occupations, and here he expresses his preference

[39] *Ibid.* The title was doubtless suggested by Akenside's *Pleasures of Imagination,* 1744. For Akenside, see *post,* ch. V, VI.

for Spenser rather than Pope. He loves the sound of an organ and choir in a Gothic church. He thinks there may even be pleasure in the pensive mood arising from unfortunate love, a sort of delight in tragedy, or even in the life of an exile in Siberia, and here we have descriptions of northern scenes, evidently influenced by Thomson. He describes the ruins of Persepolis in a way recalling Dyer's *Ruins of Rome*. The whole poem ends with a renewed invocation to Melancholy and to Contemplation, who is hailed as fairer than the muses.

There is here hardly an image or an idea not gained from books. Milton is the most evident source, but one hears also distinct echoes of Thomson, Pope, Young, and Dyer. However, the taste for pensive pleasures is evidently quite genuine, and perhaps nothing is to be expected of a young man of seventeen, with bookish tastes, beyond a restating of other people's ideas in his own language. The logic of the poem is comprehensible, for the poet does not pretend to be transported to the different scenes but calls them up in a natural fashion before the inward eye of solitude. Thus the poem is conceived as a single whole, held together by its unity of feeling. The descriptions therefore form a series of pictures expressing the poet's thought but not accidentally determining it, just as the case is with Milton's *Il Penseroso*. Thomas Warton's *Poems*, published in 1777, and his later work as editor of Milton and Spenser, show him working congenially with his brother to further the return to nature, the admiration and imitation of Milton's minor poems, and the appreciation of the charm of old buildings and historical places. That he was destined to add a new note to pensive poetry — the more genuine and sincere appreciation of the mystical beauty of Gothic art — does not appear in this earliest poem. What does appear is the marked admiration for Milton.[40]

[40] For a full statement of Warton's contribution to English poetry, see Rinaker, *Thomas Warton,* ch. II and IX.

In these twenty-five years, then, we find that a large amount of melancholy poetry has been written and eagerly read, which does not express either religious gloom or the pessimistic philosophy of Epicureanism, Stoicism, or scientific materialism. Melancholy has been secularized and associated with the enthusiastic description of nature. In this form, it is considered not as evidence of a morbid mental or physical state, but as a truly beneficial mood, associated with health, simple living, benevolence, and the love of God.

In form this poetry is for the most part diffuse, illogical, and too mildly phrased to be permanently interesting. In spite of the example of Thomson, whose descriptions are almost always true, beautiful, and permeated by sincere feeling, the "school" as a whole is characterized by affectation and sentimentalism.[41] Nevertheless poets and readers have really awakened, largely under the influence of Thomson, to the thrilling quality of life, and have realized afresh the inspiration that lies in the love of nature and of humanity. The increasing admiration for Milton's minor poetry has somewhat counteracted the tendency to diffuseness and taught a few poets the secret of making a poem out of a single mood. The almost unfailing use for descriptive poetry of either the *Il Penseroso* metre or blank verse, instead of the stanza and couplet forms transmitted by Dryden and Waller and preferred by Pope and other poets of the non-melancholy camp, bears witness to the growing love of both Milton and Shakespeare in the hearts of the poets of melancholy.

[41] On this point see the very suggestive pp. XXIII–XXVIII of Professor Bernbaum's Introduction to his volume of selections, *English Poets of the Eighteenth Century*.

CHAPTER V

THE PERSISTENCE OF MELANCHOLY AND ITS ETHICAL CONDEMNATION, 1725–1750

BUT religious melancholy was by no means extinct. We have seen it surviving through the first quarter of the century in the later work of Prior, the early work of Young, and in the poetry of Watts, Hill, Mrs. Rowe, Broome, and others. During the second quarter of the century it still continued in some circles, undiluted by either the "sociable enthusiasm" or deistic optimism of Shaftesbury, and it furnished the impulse for both poetry and prose which became very popular.

Robert Blair,[1] a Scotch divinity student living in Edinburgh, far from London influence, with his mind turned inward upon himself not outward toward the aspect of the Scotch landscape round about him, was working steadily on his poem, *The Grave,* almost every idea of which was suggested by seventeenth century authors. Blair's cast of mind may be inferred from his friendship with William Law, author of *A Serious Call,* whose daughter he married, and with Isaac Watts, with whose ideas of life and literature he thoroughly agreed. He was in sympathy also with the reforming purposes of Addison, whose character he greatly admired. Of authors contemporary with himself there are few traces in his poem, though he had apparently read Mallet's *Excursion* and Thomson's *Seasons.*

[1] My entire treatment of Blair is based on a dissertation by Carl Müller, *Robert Blair's "Grave" und die Grabes- und Nachtdichtung,* Weimar, 1909. For a list of resemblances to sources, see pp. 32–55.

The influence of Thomson is not visible in the subject matter of *The Grave,* but the structure of the poem — general meditations arising from scenes vividly present to the imagination — is doubtless largely due to the reading of Thomson. Blair, like Thomson, uses blank verse but he employs a large number (17½%) of feminine endings. His verse therefore differs from that of either Milton or Thomson, and approaches more nearly that of Shakespeare's latest plays. It resembles Shakespeare's also in its skilful use of alliteration and in a peculiar sonorousness.

The most marked influences on the subject matter are: the familiar passages of *Job;* certain passages from Shakespeare about death, sleep, the grave, ghosts, about midnight as the time for dreadful deeds, and about the decay of the body after death; the passages from Milton's epic which describe Sin and Death; certain meditative poems by John Norris; Addison's *Spectator* papers on *The Pleasures of the Imagination* and *Westminster Abbey;* Young's *The Last Day,* Parnell's *Night Piece on Death,* Tickell's *Elegy on the Death of Addison,* and Mallet's *Excursion.* Young's *Night Thoughts,* which appeared after the greater part of Blair's poem was written, apparently had no effect on his work in completing *The Grave.*[2] The poem was nearly finished by 1731, having been written apparently only for the author's own satisfaction, without any thought of immediate publication. Watts was eager to have it printed and offered it to two booksellers, but in vain, because it was by an unknown young man living three hundred miles from London. After the success of the first of Young's *Night Thoughts* in 1742, Blair's work was recognized as having similar elements of popularity

[2] But Young from the fifth *Night* on shows plainly the influence of Blair. Müller, *op. cit.,* p. 67. Thomas, W., *Le Poète Edward Young,* pp. 358–359, 410.

and was brought out in 1743. It is treated here before Young's work in order to show that many of the ideas which appear in Young were ready to his hand in the work of seventeenth and eighteenth century authors and were making their appeal to another serious poet at about the same time. The enumeration of the details of Blair's poem will make it obvious that there is practically nothing new therein, although the combination of ideas, the design, and the treatment of details are such as to constitute originality.

The first few lines announce the theme, the Grave. Then begins a description of a cathedral where the illustrious dead lie, surrounded by blasted elms and haunted by specters. With a ghastly vividness Blair brings before our eyes a school boy frightened as he passes the graves at night, and then a widow lying prostrate on her husband's tomb.[3] The author then falls into a series of meditations, arising from such scenes. The grave severs friendships, it stops the jester's jokes, it has put an end to the great civilizations of antiquity, whose kings now rot in state. He describes a pretentious funeral and reflects on the uselessness of all the pomps which indicate the noble birth of a dead man. No monument is lasting, tyrants and slaves moulder side by side. The grave reveals the truth underneath flattery, it degrades and destroys beauty, it lays low the strong man, the student, the orator, the physician, the miser. He meditates on the strange horror which men have of death, reasoning in truly seventeenth century fashion that, if there were no life after death, no one need hesitate to die. As it is, since life is eternal, to attempt to evade life by suicide is sinful as well as useless. He wonders

[3] Both of these descriptions are realistic, as though Blair had seen these scenes with his own eyes, but the suggestion of the first may be derived from Shakespeare's "schoolboy, with shining morning face," and of the second from the famous passage in Congreve's *Mourning Bride,* act II, sc. 1.

why the dead never return to tell us what death is. Death's arrows fly thick about us, but mortals seem as unconscious of this fact as is the sexton who so placidly digs graves day after day.[4] It is strange that all men are so unmindful of the universal fact. He then enumerates the various classes of people who must meet undistinguished in death. Since death came into the world through sin, he recalls the happiness of man in Eden and the misery of his fall, and describes the general ruin wrought by sin. He then apostrophizes Death as an insatiable, devouring monster. But the Son of God has foiled Death; henceforward Death shall be welcome as the path to life, for in the resurrection body and soul are reunited and the end of the good man is peace.

> Thus at the shut of even, the weary bird
> Leaves the wide air, and in some lonely brake
> Cow'rs down, and dozes till the dawn of day;
> Then claps his well-fledg'd wings, and bears away.[5]

It will be seen that in spite of the orthodox, pious close, like that of Parnell's *Night Piece*, the poem as a whole is chiefly about the mystery, the horror, and the inevitability of death. Anyone who has visited the graveyard opposite St. Giles church in Edinburgh, and looked at the seventeenth century gravestones and tombs, with their ghastly skulls, skeletons, and warning epitaphs, which must even then have been covered, as they are today, with the green slime due to the dampness of the Scotch mists, will recognize where Blair got many of his most effective realistic touches, especially towards the beginning of his poem.

The persistence in certain quarters of the melancholy mood of the late seventeenth century is further illustrated

[4] Observe the combination of an idea from Watts's *Mourning Piece*, *ante* p. 91 and the gravedigger scene in *Hamlet*.

[5] For the poem, see Chalmers, *English Poets*, vol. XV.

by the *Night Thoughts* of Edward Young. The elaborate study of Young by M. W. Thomas,[6] and the sympathetic interpretation of certain phases of his influence given by M. F. Baldensperger[7] and M. J. Texte,[8] make it unnecessary here to analyze his work as a whole. It remains simply to show his relation to the changing modes of melancholy poetry before 1750.

The Complaint; or, Night Thoughts[9] (1742–1745), consisting of nine *Nights* in all, is essentially a rejection of the optimistic philosophy of Shaftesbury and Pope, and a reaction against the doctrine of the unimportance of the individual.[10] In the rhapsodic tone of some of its descriptions, in the use of blank verse, and in its expansive manner, the work is doubtless nearly related to the descriptive-reflective method of Thomson. But whereas Thomson's meditations had been humane, benevolent, and for the most part objective, Young, a sick soul, a disappointed man, invariably proceeds from reflections on the misery of humanity to reflections upon his own wretchedness. He thus contributed to reflective poetry at this stage a strong infusion of self-pity, an elaborate self-analysis during a mood of grief.[11] We remember that Shaftesbury had sanctioned the free out-pouring of emotion, provided such enthusiasm expended itself on humanity in general, on the beauty of nature, or the power and goodness of God. Through the poetry of Thomson and his imitators such outpouring of feeling had become common, and was in popular writing and talking alluded to as an act of virtue.

[6] Thomas, W., *Le Poète Edward Young.*

[7] Baldensperger, F., *Young et ses "Nuits" en France.* In his *Études d'Histoire littéraire.*

[8] Texte, J., *Jean-Jacques Rousseau et les Origines du Cosmopolitisme littéraire,* pp. 370–382.

[9] Chalmers, *English Poets,* vol. XIII.

[10] Thomas, *op. cit.,* pp. 342–348.

[11] *Ibid.* pp. 458–459.

Young turned the current inward upon the self, outdoing Thomson in length and discursiveness.[12] It might almost be said that Young makes of himself an epic hero, such is the seriousness with which he takes the adventures of his soul. Thomson luxuriates to the point of sentimentality at times over the woes of others, both man and beast, but there is only one passage in the *Night Thoughts* (I, 238) where the author makes even a pretense that his sorrow is common and that he mourns for others.[13] M. Thomas points out that such moral egoism somewhat wearies us.

Yet this attitude is only a return to the attitude of the seventeenth century religious writers, for whom personal salvation, the fate of the individual soul, was a matter of first importance. This becomes particularly clear in *Nights V–IX*, which deal at length with

> Th' importance of contemplating the tomb;
> Why men decline it; suicide's foul birth;
> The various kinds of grief; the faults of age;
> And death's dread character. . . .

In *Night IX*, some four hundred lines towards the beginning of the book constitute a regular " Meditation on Death " and repeat some of Blair's ideas and some of Young's own best effects from his earlier composition, *The Last Day*. And we must always remember that Young, born in 1681, was educated under seventeenth century influences, that much of his earlier work (*A Poem on the Last Day*, 1713; *A Paraphrase on Part of the Book of Job*, 1719; *A Vindication of Providence: or, A True Estimate of Human Life*, 1728) was morbidly pessimistic,[14] and that his second tragedy, *The Revenge*, indicates an

[12] The *Night Thoughts* are more than twice as long as the *Seasons*.

[13] Thomas, *op. cit.*, pp. 458–459.

[14] For an analysis of these works, see Thomas, *op. cit.*, pp. 308–341.

admiration for Shakespeare, from whom melancholy suggestions are easily caught. Indeed, if Young's career is considered in its entirety, the *Night Thoughts* seem like a relapse into the mood which was the natural expression of his temperament, after a single, albeit successful, excursion (*The Universal Passion*, 1725–1728) into the more objective *genre* of satire in the French mode.[15]

In the work of Thomson, the personal impression of nature becomes lost eventually in the descriptive details, and the accompanying reflections often seem only mechanically related, but Young's subjectivity extends to his nature descriptions and amounts to pathetic fallacy. He understood perfectly, says M. Thomas, the influence of natural scenery upon the course of thought, and the use that he made of it in his poem proves how far he had separated himself from the English neo-classic poets. Henceforward, melancholy remains indissolubly united to the shadows of evening, the darkness of midnight, or to the moonlight falling from a clear heaven,[16] for Young's degree of melancholy is too deep for mere noonday retirement amid sylvan shadows. By his philosophy, then, Young recalls the religious melancholy of the seventeenth century; in his treatment of nature, he is influenced by the growing fondness of readers for description, but narrows his choice of scenes to such as may appropriately be viewed through a mist of tears.

15 This view differs from that of M. Thomas, who regards Young's melancholy as progressively diminishing. Young's final position in the *Night Thoughts*, however, is simply the orthodox consolation offered by seventeenth century Anglican divines. Professor Bernbaum, *op. cit.*, p. xxvi also considers Young reactionary in thought, though novel in form.

16 "Un homme s'abandonnant à sa douleur en face d'un paysage dont les ténèbres et l'aspect désolé semblent renforcer les plaintes de l'affligé, voilà ce qui constitue la nouveauté . . . des Nuits." Thomas, *op. cit.*, p. 577.

The principal influence on Young's poem discovered and enumerated[17] by M. Thomas are to be found in the work of Jeremy Taylor; in the essays in verse of Cowley and the prose essays of Addison and Steele; in certain passages of Thomson's *Seasons,* more particularly in *Winter;* in Parnell; in the two little poems of Gay; and occasionally in Pope's imitations of Horace. He does not borrow from Lucretius, but is generally influenced, as was the seventeenth century, by ancient philosophy as a whole, and especially by Seneca. The opening apostrophe to Night and many of his phrases recall Shakespeare. In the description of the starry heavens he is largely influenced by Milton (*Paradise Lost,* VIII, 66–168) and by Thomson (*Summer,* 32–42 and 94–111). He owes something also apparently to Pascal, and to Fontenelle's *Conversations on the Plurality of Worlds,* often issued in English in the late seventeenth and early eighteenth centuries. Like Thomson, he is enthusiastic over the wonder of Newton's discoveries.

The history of the popularity of the *Night Thoughts* at the end of the eighteenth century in France[18] and Germany,[19] makes it plain that there were two great elements of appeal in these poems. In France, Young was accepted as the artist of a new *genre, le sombre;* in Germany he was regarded as the apostle of the freedom of the individual, the apostle of the self. But in England neither of these elements was startlingly novel. The importance of the individual was, as I have said, the great seventeenth century religious doctrine in England. As for the melancholy *genre,* it had existed in English poetry from the beginning, though this melancholy had had different flavors in Old English and mediaeval poetry, in the

[17] *Ibid.* pp. 363–374.

[18] Baldensperger and Texte, *op. cit.*

[19] Kind, J. L., ***Edward Young in Germany.***

lyric of the Renaissance, in the contrasted religious and Epicurean lyrics of the seventeenth century, and in the meditative essays or the pensive verse of the early eighteenth century. Therefore, though Young was instantly accepted as interesting and became increasingly popular with the general reader of his own day, his popularity was not sensational; he was not the fashion or the rage, as he was a little later in Germany and France. In fact, English admiration was tempered with some sense that the *Night Thoughts* went to extremes. Shenstone wrote in 1743,[20]

> Dr. Young's *Complaint* is the best thing that has come out this season (these twenty years, Pope says) except mine.

Later in the same year, he is distinctly irreverent. Speaking of the complaints of an elderly aunt, he suggests that she

> shall fetch a long-winded sigh with Dr. Young for a wager; though I see *his* Suspiria are not yet finished. He has *relapsed* into "Night the Fifth." I take his case to be wind in a great measure, and would advise him to take rhubarb in powder, with a little nutmeg grated amongst it, as I do.[21]

Mrs. Elizabeth Carter thought his writings in general "original," having "some passages strikingly sublime, others deplorably creeping."[22] Gray criticised their "redundancy of thought," and Johnson spoke of his descriptions as only "bright stepping stones over a miry road," and of his manner in general as "the noise of a tea-kettle," not to be compared with "the roaring of the ocean" of Shakespeare's or Dryden's verse.[23] Akenside rebuked him

[20] *Works in Verse and Prose of William Shenstone,* London, 1769, vol. III, p. 81.

[21] *Ibid.* p. 107.

[22] Pennington, *Memoirs of the Life of Mrs. Elizabeth Carter,* 3rd ed., vol. II, p. 170.

[23] *Lives of the English Poets,* ed. Hill, vol. III, p. 399, n. 6.

by name in his *Hymn to Chearfulness,* though he later disguised the allusion. Mason is plainly making fun of German bad taste, when he writes to Gray [24] that he has met a Hanoverian lady who thinks the *Elegy* " pretty " but who bursts into sentimental *schwärmerei* over Dr. Young and the " dear Nitt-Toats! "

Like the imitators of Thomson, the followers of Young made sad havoc of poetry when they attempted to employ his methods. The poetry of William Thompson, Dean of Raphoe, is a particularly flagrant case in point. In the year 1745, he produced a long poem called *Sickness,* first published in three books, and later expanded into five.[25] It is perfectly evident, as Davenport, his biographer, says, that the author was " just warm from the perusal of the *Night Thoughts.*" This perfectly ordinary man had got from Young the notion that the perfectly ordinary experience of any individual might be the subject for *quasi* epic treatment. Accordingly, he begins his Book I, entitled *Sickness,* as Milton began *Paradise Lost.* He bewails the fact that the muse " has so long idly breathed soft elegies or pastoral strains." He begs Urania to inspire him, as she has the sacred writers, more particularly the author of the book of *Job,* who sang " themes correspondent to thy servant's theme." How nearly he imitates Young's manner, is evident in the opening passages.

> I sing to you, ye sons of men! of dust,
> Say rather: What is man, who proudly lifts
> His brow audacious, as confronting Heaven,
>
> . . . .
>
> But moulded clay? an animated heap
> Of dust, that shortly shall to dust return?
> We dream of shadows when we talk of life,

[24] *Letters of Thomas Gray,* ed. Tovey, vol. I, p. 264.

[25] Thompson was not included in Johnson's edition of the *English Poets,* but does appear in Chalmers, *English Poets,* vol. XV.

. . . .
Mere tales to cheat our children with to rest;
And, when the tale is told, they sink to sleep,
Death's image! so inane is mortal man!
Man's but a vapour, toss'd by every wind,
. . . .
Man's a brisk bubble, floating on the waves,
Of wide eternity: . . .
. . . .
Man is a flower [etc., etc.]

Now begins the real story. On Valentine's Day, two lovers, Ianthe (who, he says, is a real person) and Thomalin (evidently Thompson himself) are out for a walk. Ianthe sings a song to St. Valentine, reminiscent of Thomson's *Spring* and of the *Pervigilium Veneris*, and the lovers embrace. In the midst of this ecstasy, Thomalin realizes that he feels ill. The approach of fever (smallpox?) is described in a periphrastic manner and at great length, with metaphors in the epic style. The poet recognizes that disease is sent by heaven to purify men from sin, because in health we have no time to think of truth. But now what cares the sick man for Anacreon, Horace, Virgil, Homer, Tibullus, Ovid, Sappho, Cicero, or Seneca? Sickness whispers to the ear that life is vain, and man can depend on virtue alone. Though virtue cannot save from death, it takes away death's sting. A Christian looks beyond to Eternity, where he shall fill a place "next to God." At the end of the book are elaborate notes by the author, explaining the sources of his allusions.

Book II is entitled *The Palace of Disease*, and is an invocation to Spenser, who, he says, had visited similar scenes.[26] He also invokes the protection of Lady Hertford,

[26] "Every Book of the *Fairy Queen* is fruitful of these visionary Beings, which are invented and drawn with a surprising Strength of Imagination." John Hughes, *On Allegorical Poetry* (1715) in Durham, ed., *Critical Essays of the Eighteenth Century*, p. 97.

afterwards Duchess of Somerset. He then describes the palace of disease with many a line borrowed from Milton and Spenser. The personifications described at length or alluded to, are: Disease, Havoc, Famine, Gout, Dropsy, The Stone, Angina, Ephialtic, Catarrh, Pleuritis, Vertigo, together with the six Furies, War, Intemperance, Melancholy, Fever, Consumption, Variola. Then follows a list of persons who have died of smallpox, and a lament over their talents and virtues. The notes and allusions show that Thompson had in mind in writing this book passages from Virgil (*Aeneid, Georgics,* and *Eclogues*), Homer, the Bible, Lucretius, Spenser (whom he calls the beginner of English poetry), Ovid, Horace, Lucan, Pliny, Tasso, Addison, and Milton (whom he prefers to Virgil).

Book III describes his suffering during the smallpox, and argues in favor of the reasonableness of a Christian's hope. He praises the science of physic and the comforts of friendship. This book has few allusions, is in a less inflated style, and its blank verse is fairly skilful.

Book IV is entitled *The Recovery.* Again the poet asks, What is man? He feels the approach of death, and prays for mercy,

> While on this isthmus of my fate I lie,
> Jutting into Eternity's wide sea,
> And leaning on this habitable globe,
> The verge of either world!

Mercy sends Hygeia to the Well of Life. There follows a description of the Well, and of the descent of Hygeia (an imitation of Milton) to the poet's bedside, where she

---

Hughes quotes part of the description of the Cave of Mammon from *Fairy Queen,* bk. II, including the lines:

> And after him Owls and Night-Ravens flew,
> The hateful Messengers of heavy things,
> Of Death and Dolour telling sad Tidings.

touches his breast and head, and "infuses" three drops into his mouth. He begins to feel better, but still cannot sleep. Then follows an apostrophe to Sleep in imitation of Milton, Shakespeare, Sidney, and probably of classic and contemporary authors as well.

> . . . dewy feather'd Sleep!
> The shield his pillow, in the tented field,
> By thee, the soldier, bred in iron war,
> Forgets the mimic thunders of the day,
> Nor envies luxury her bed of down.
> . . . .
> At thy approach the wrinkled front of Care
> Subsides into the smooth expanse of smiles,
> And, stranger far! the monarch, crown'd by thee,
> Beneath his weight of glory gains repose.

At last he sleeps. He describes the progress of health and rejoices in his recovery. His imagination revives and, leaving the earth, soars "amid the pomp of planetary worlds." He celebrates the restoration of his capacity for emotion.

Book V, *The Thanksgiving,* is an intolerable medley. He argues for many lines that the restoration of health ought to have an improving effect upon a meditative mind in the spring season. He describes a rural scene, and then, for some unintelligible reason, makes an excursion to the battle ground at Tournay. He reflects on the abuses of modern poetry, and ends with a hymn to the ever blessed and glorious Trinity, which contains these lines:

> Come, Contemplation! therefore, from thy haunts,
> From Spenser's tomb (with reverent steps and slow
> Oft visited by me; certes by all,
> Touch'd by the Muse): from Richmond's green retreats,
> Where Nature's Bard the Seasons on his page
> Stole from the Year's rich hand: or Welwyn groves,
> Where Young, the friend of virtue and of man,

Sows with poetic stars the nightly song,
To Phoebus dear as his own day! and drowns,
The nightingale's complaint in sadder strains
And sweeter elegance of woe, O come!

There are many expressions from Milton's minor poems, some from the *Psalms, Revelations,* and *Zechariah.* He introduces into his notes a short hymn written "when very young" in the great epidemical cold of 1732. Apparently we have here another mind, pre-occupied like Blair and Young in the seventeenth century manner with the idea of death, and at about the same date.

But hark! the passing toll,
In a long, sadly solemn knell,
Alarms anew my soul.

No lovely prospect meets my eye,
  But melancholy fear,
Attended with the hollow pomp
  Of Sickness and Despair.

Thompson seems to be a clear case of the strong influence upon an average mind of reading Young. In a note at the end of Book V, he says:

A recovery from the smallpox a few years ago, gave occasion to the preceding Poem. I only at first (in gratitude to the Great Physician of Souls and Bodies) designed to have published this Hymn to the Trinity upon a Recovery from Sickness. But the subject being very extensive and capable of admitting serious reflections on the frail state of humanity, I expatiated further upon it. . . . I do not remember to have seen any other poem on the same subject to lead me on the way, and, therefore, it is to be hoped, the good-natured reader will more readily excuse its blemishes.

The hymn which he would naturally have written evidently begins with the line,

Father of Heaven and Earth! Coeval Son!

It is merely pious, reflecting hymnology and something of Milton. It was plainly Young who taught him to "expatiate," heaping up classical allusion, nature description, and Miltonic rhapsody. Though he mentions Spenser admiringly, the influence of that poet is scarcely recognizable. It is from Young that he has learned this elaborate treatment of the experiences of an individual. Unfortunately, however, in the case of Thompson the experience was not significant, or he is not able to handle it so as to make it seem so.

Some of Thompson's other poetry uses the Spenserian stanza. Like other poets of his day, he wrote *Garden Inscriptions* over various spots in his grounds where he had placed emblems, busts, and pictures of his favorite authors. One of these was to be placed "Over Young's *Night Thoughts*." Other objects of his admiration were Spenser, Shakespeare, Milton, Pope, Chaucer, Cowley, Addison, Virgil, Horace, Thomson, and "Mr. Philips's *Cider*."

Young's success apparently stimulated writers to try similar effects in prose, also. The Reverend James Hervey published very promptly (1746–47) two volumes of *Meditations and Contemplations*.[27] The contents of these volumes in later editions are *A Meditation Among the Tombs, Reflections on a Flower Garden, A Descant Upon Creation, Contemplation on the Night and Starry Heavens* and *A Winter Piece*. These became very well known and were greatly admired throughout the latter part of the century. The author's footnote to *Reflections on a Flower Garden* says that his work was formed on the plan sug-

[27] But we have, also, quoted in the *Gentleman's Magazine* for May 1738, from an Edinburgh weekly called *The Reveur, A Meditation on the Grandeur of Nature and her Works, in an Evening Walk,* which reads like Shaftesbury transmitted through Thomson and then rendered into prose.

gested by the *Spectator* no. 393, a portion of which he quotes:

> Many Authors have written on the *Vanity of the Creature,* and represented the Barrenness of every thing in this World, and its Incapacity of producing any solid or substantial Happiness. As discourses of this Nature are very useful to the Sensual and Voluptuous, those Speculations which shew the bright Side of Things, and lay forth those innocent Entertainments, which are to be met with among the several Objects that encompass us, are no less beneficial to Men of dark and melancholy Tempers.

While it may be true that Hervey was using the *Spectator* paper as a sort of text for his essays, it is plain from the whole course of his thought and from many of his phrases, that the chief influences on his work are Young's *Night Thoughts* and Thomson's *Seasons.*

Of course, the voice of common sense was from time to time raised in protest against the morbidness, the easy self-indulgence, the sentimentalism, the contented inaction of all this. England was, after all, a satisfactory place in which to live in the early eighteenth century, and the stimulus to her intellectual life was very naturally to be found not in the retirement of country estates but in the city of London, with its bustling crowds, its political activity, its assemblies and conversaziones, its theaters and concerts, its coffee-houses, book-shops, and printing offices. There were many poems, letters, and little essays depicting the attractions of this busy life, and many ridiculing the inconvenience, stupidity and grossness of the country. The influence of plays and of novels made for objectivity in literature. While by 1725, the tone of comedy had become sentimental,[28] it was a cheerful not a melancholy sentimentalism that there prevailed. The scandal novel of

[28] This fact is established by Professor Krutch's dissertation, *Comedy and Conscience.*

Mrs. Manley and the adventure novel of Defoe both tended to cultivate in readers a taste for objectivity. The self-analysis of *Pamela* (1740) was promptly ridiculed by *Joseph Andrews* (1742), and although *Clarissa Harlowe* (1748) was genuinely melancholy and had moments of almost lyrical reflection, we notice the nearly simultaneous appeal to the novel reading public made by *Tom Jones* (1749), healthy-minded, humorous, and full of animal spirits.

The ascendancy of Swift and Pope in literary circles during the first half of the century was a strong influence against the indulgence of melancholy moods. It is true that the Dean's melancholy was deep-rooted, really a disease and ending in madness. Nevertheless, throughout his work in prose and poetry, there is no expression of it, or indeed of any of his personal feelings, intended for public perusal. What he thought of human nature, in his blackest moods, we find in the dreary tale of the Struldbrugs, and the obscene account of the Yahoos in *Gulliver's Travels* (1727). His power of exact observation taught him that country simplicity was an illusion; its actual occupations and discomforts are depicted with rough humor by Swift in his poem, *The Country Life*, and by his friend, Dr. Thomas Sheridan, in *A Letter to the Dean when in England* and in the two fragments by Sheridan usually published along with Swift's poems:

The Blessings of a Country Life.

Far from our debtors; no Dublin letters;
Not seen by our betters.

The Plagues of a Country Life.

A companion with news; a great want of shoes;
Eat lean meat or choose; a church without pews;
Our horses away; no straw, oats, or hay;
December in May; our boys run away; all servants at play.

Swift satirizes the commonplaceness of the usual reflective essay upon the life of man in his *Tritical Essay upon the Faculties of the Mind* and in that amusing practical joke, *A Meditation upon a Broomstick.* The thought of his own death is made the occasion, in his poem, *On The Death of Dr. Swift,* of sardonic reflection upon the unimportance of the individual and the general heartlessness of society. Such a poem is really melancholy enough, but the expression of it is intellectual, objective, and satiric, not emotional, subjective, and direct. Melancholy, like true love, is in Swift's opinion not for public exhibition. Only occasionally in a letter to a friend do we find some pages that are a revelation of acute suffering and fundamental despair.

I have already said (*ante,* pp. 119, 128) that Pope turned from his early experiments in melancholy to the writing of witty moral essays and social satires. By the time of the publication of the *Essay on Man,* 1732–34, his ethical position was fixed. Adopting Shaftesbury's system of practical morals as interpreted by Bolingbroke, Pope regards man as actuated by a combination of selfishness and of love for other men, or by "self-love and social." However, he believes that an enlightened selfishness is in the long run as beneficial to society as a genuine love of others (*Essay on Man, Epistle III*). Unlike Thomson, Pope was very little interested in the idea of the expansion of the soul and the cultivation of benevolence through the contemplation of the natural world, although, like Thomson, he has much to say of the beautiful order of the universe, and of looking through nature up to nature's God, and like Thomson also, he believes that virtue constitutes happiness. Pope's emphasis is rather on the necessity of recognizing one's human limitations, on the impossibility of everyone's being happy at the same time, on the acceptance of life as it is, and on an active participation in the life of the social whole. Virtue and happiness are identical: therefore, for man, virtue is

> At once his own bright prospect to be blest,
> And strongest motive to assist the rest.
> *Epistle IV*, 351–2.

The method of the *Essay* is exposition and argumentation, almost unvaried by description. Pope's ease and plausibility in versified reasoning and the popularity of the practical optimism of the *Essay* gave a great impulse to the writing of didactic essays in verse, and, as I have indicated in Chapter IV, worked against the tendency to melancholy lyricism. Pope came to view with easy contempt his own early descriptive poetry, in which "pure description held the place of sense" (*Epistle to Dr. Arbuthnot*, 148). But of all who followed him in the argumentative method, perhaps only Thomson and Young in the first half of the century succeeded as well as he in keeping the train of thought clear. Akenside's *Pleasures of Imagination*, 1744, Brooke's *Universal Beauty*, 1735, also present aspects of Shaftesbury's philosophy, but in a confused fashion; nature descriptions of some beauty are suddenly invaded by argument, and the reasoning is simply interrupted, not illustrated, by the word painting.

I have spoken of Philips's *The Splendid Shilling*,[29] 1701, which seems to ridicule a causeless melancholy by depicting in the same language the real discomforts of the debtor pursued by duns. I have noted also the soliloquy in Addison's *Cato*, act V, 1713, where suicide is faced in Stoic mood without the morbid hesitation of a Hamlet, and Armstrong's condemnation of enthusiasm in *The Art of Preserving Health*, 1744.[30] (*Ante*, pp. 87, 115, 147.) Many other voices made up a chorus of disapproval which grew in volume in the second quarter of the century.

[29] Chalmers, *English Poets*, vol. VIII. [30] *Ibid.* vol. IX.

Parnell's *The Hermit,* published in 1718, is a moral tale in which a hermit, who, through too much solitude, has acquired views of life colored by religious melancholy, is instructed by an angel in disguise that he must trust God, who has ordered life wisely, however incapable finite man may be of understanding the divine plan.

William Somerville [31] in *The Hip,* supposedly written "the day after the great meteor, in March, 1715," laughs at the superstitious fear of death caused by the event. Somerville's *The Chase,* 1735, is a descriptive poem in pentameter couplets, containing a good deal of accurate, realistic detail, but in it the natural scenes are merely background, against which the separate pictures of the hunt stand out in relief. The incidents are related uncolored by the author's personal impression, and the difficulties of the hunted animals are recorded without sympathy, merely as incidents observed. The whole is clear, bright, rapid, non-melancholy and it "generally pleased the world," as Shenstone said.[32]

Matthew Green's *The Spleen,*[33] 1737, a poem which found readers in great number, reverts to Burton's view of melancholy as a disease. It first describes remedies against the spleen — temperance in food and drink; hunting, bowling, or any form of exercise; laughter (and among subjects for laughter are listed "experiment on felons' ears"!); attendance at plays, tragic, comic, or "moral"; music; books (in bad weather); coffee-houses, with their card games and talk; pleasant gossip with women. Causes of spleen, and therefore to be avoided are: dissenters' meetings; processes of law; gambling and extravagance; party politics; religious enthusiasm; schemes for reform;

[31] *Ibid.* vol. XI.

[32] *Works in Verse and Prose of William Shenstone,* London, 1769, vol. III, p. 55.

[33] Chalmers, *English Poets,* vol. XV.

money getting; dancing attendance on a patron; the free exercise of "the fancy" in romantic dreams; the composition of poetry (though he inserts a passage in praise of Glover's epic, *Leonidas*); ambition. Green then describes the happy life, much in Pomfret's style. Contentment requires only two hundred a year, a farm some twenty miles from town, two maids, a serving man, a boy, and a housekeeping "niece." This description sometimes recalls *L'Allegro* and sometimes Herrick's accounts of his establishment. It is altogether material and comfortable, yet withal charming.

At the close, and in a more serious mood, the poet examines by reason and "the light of day"

> Th' enthusiast's hope and raptures wild.
> . . . .
> The melancholy man such dreams
> As brightest evidence, esteems.

These men are, he thinks, too prone to dread the specters of the brain. For his part, he thinks a man's thoughts had best confine themselves to earth. For the future man must trust God. Green takes an agnostic position, but seems to believe in a sort of law of compensation. On the whole,

> [God] for his creatures must decree
> More happiness than misery,
> Or be supposèd to create,
> Curious to try, what 'tis to hate.

Under the guidance of such thoughts, the poet makes,

> Neither becalm'd nor over blown,
> Life's voyage to the world unknown.

In his poem *The Grotto*, Green has inserted a digression to warn "Delia" not to be pensive.

Samuel Johnson's *London*, 1738, and *The Vanity of*

Human Wishes, 1749, are both arraignments of contemporary society, but their method is not that of the complaint but of classical satire with a strong infusion of the moral essay, both being adaptations to contemporory taste of satires of Juvenal. The second of these has an orthodox Anglican conclusion. It urges man to pray, not for deliverance from the ills of life, but for

A healthful mind,
Obedient passions and a will resigned;
For love, which scarce collective man can fill;
For patience, sovereign, o'er transmuted ill;
For faith, that, panting for a happier seat,
Counts death kind nature's signal of retreat;
These goods for man the laws of Heaven ordain,
These goods he grants, who grants the power to gain;
With these celestial wisdom calms the mind,
And makes the happiness she does not find.

Though Johnson's view of life was really melancholy, he was consistently opposed to the expression of melancholy anywhere except in the privacy of a religious exercise, and as a critic, he was continually impatient of it in any but its classical forms. At this date, however, the Johnsonians were not yet a group in control of the literary situation. At the middle of the century, when this study ends, Johnson may be said to have just about reached the position he so proudly boasts in his letter to Chesterfield, five years later. He was, for his own merits, "known" and beyond needing patronage or caring for it.[34]

Dr. Mark Akenside's poetry reveals a temperament

[34] Dyer's *The Fleece* (1757) is excluded from this study by its date, but it has the same bright, hard tone as Somerville's *The Chase*. It fails to reproduce the melancholy atmosphere of its model, *The Georgics,* and its descriptions, made in a scientific spirit, were admired for the amount of useful information they afforded on Great Britain's wool-raising industry. Akenside's help in finishing the poem would have militated against melancholy.

naturally pensive. His *Hymn to Science*, printed in 1739 in the *Gentleman's Magazine* (vol. IX, p. 544) is a Retirement poem showing the influence of *L'Allegro* and *Il Penseroso*. *To the Evening Star*, which according to Bucke[35] was written in 1746, is an exquisite blending of many melancholy strains from Spenser, Shakespeare, Milton, Greek myth, and possibly also from Collins, the Wartons, and Gray. One of his acquaintances remembers that he admired Gothic architecture and was fond of gazing on Westminster Abbey by moonlight from a bench in St. James's Park.[36] Nevertheless, he must on the whole be counted in the opposition to melancholy. As a doctor, he thought it unhealthful; as a deist, he deemed it unreasonable; as a lover of the classics, he stood for the golden mean in conduct and expression. Accordingly, his most famous poem, *The Pleasures of Imagination*, despite its use of blank verse and the Hutcheson "jargon" of which Gray complained,[37] is, even in its first version (1744), nearer to Pope's moral essays than to *The Seasons*. His loveliest poem, the *Hymn to the Naiads* (written 1746)[38] is filled with Greek joy in nature rather than English melancholy. And his *Odes on Several Subjects*, which appeared anonymously in 1745 when Akenside was only twenty-four, assert the young man's definite intention to observe a classical moderation in the expression of the pensive mood.

The first of these ten odes, *Allusion to Horace* (*Odes IV, 2*) declares that his muse, abjuring pessimism and satire, will devote herself to the creation of beauty, which ministers both to pleasure and to health.

[35] *On the Life, Writings, and Genius of Akenside*, p. 52. It was first published in 1772.

[36] Dyce's *Life of Akenside* in *the Poetical Works of Mark Akenside*, Aldine ed., 1845, p. 60.

[37] *Letters of Thomas Gray*, ed. Tovey, vol. I, p. 119.

[38] Not published until 1758. Dyce, *op. cit.*, p. 39.

Nor where the raven, where the owl
By night their hateful orgies howl,
  Will she her cares imploy;
But flies from ruin and from graves,
From ghastly cells and monkish caves,
  To day-light and to joy.

On the Winter Solstice, 1740 describes the season much in the manner of Thomson, but in octosyllabic stanzas. When

Black storms involve the louring sky
And gloomy damps oppress the soul. . . .

townspeople gather about the fire to drink, sing, or dance,

While mute and shrinking with her fears,
Each blast the cottage matron hears,
  As o'er the hearth she sits alone:
At morn her bridegroom went abroad,
The night is dark and deep the road;
  She sighs and wishes him at home.

But Akenside gives his poem a cheerful turn by traveling forward in imagination to the spring, which will come in due time. He is

Secure that health and beauty springs
Thro' this majestic frame of things,
  Beyond what he can reach to know,
And that heav'n's all-subduing will,
With good, the progeny of ill,
  Attempers every state below.

How pleasing wears the wintry night,
Spent with the old illustrious dead!
While, by the taper's trembling light,
I seem those awful courts to tread
Where chiefs and legislators lie. . . .

Like Milton and Thomson, he loves to spend the evening reading classical poetry and philosophy. But unlike them, he would welcome an invitation to leave his fireside and join a genial party where the toasts are all of "love and May."

There is a similar swing of the pendulum from gravity to a determined gaiety in the *Hymn to Chearfulness, The Author Sick.* This begins with the customary description of the gloom of a wintry night,

While winter's voice, that storms around,
And yon deep death-bell's groaning sound,
Renew my mind's oppressive gloom,
Till starting horror shakes the room!

But he calls to his aid Cheerfulness, daughter of Love and Health. She can cure the sick, assist the despairing lover, and arouse the modern muse to eloquence, as she once inspired the singers of ancient Greece.

Hark, when thy breath her song impells,
How full the tuneful current swells!
Let melancholy's plaintive tongue
Instruct the nightly strains of Y——g;
But thine was Homer's ancient might,
And thine victorious Pindar's flight.

The glories of Alcaeus, Sappho, Theocritus, Anacreon, and Horace, too, were due to their power to express joy. Here he attacks Young's pessimistic view of the constitution of the universe.

See where the pale, the sick'ning sage
(A prey perhaps to fortune's rage,
Perhaps by tender griefs oppress'd,
Or glooms congenial to his breast)
Retires in desart-scenes to dwell,
And bids the joyless world farewell.
Alone he treads th' autumn shade,
Alone beneath the mountain laid,
He sees the nightly damps arise,
And gath'ring storms involve the skies;

He hears the neighb'ring surges roll,
And raging thunders shake the pole:
Then, struck by every object round,
And stunn'd by every horrid sound,
He pants to traverse nature's ways:
His evils haunt him thro' the maze:
He views ten thousand daemons rise
To wield the empire of the skies,
And chance and fate assume the rod,
And malice blot the throne of God.

Akenside invokes Cheerfulness — as Shaftesbury or Pope might have — to teach such a pessimist

To trace the world's benignant laws,
And judge of that presiding cause
Who founds in discord beauty's reign,
Converts to pleasure every pain;
Subdues the hostile forms to rest,
And bids the universe be blest.

For his own poetry, he would choose moods "indulgent and tender," of such a degree of sadness

As just the struggling breast may chear,
And just suspend the starting tear,
Yet leave that charming sense of woe,
Which none but friends and lovers know.

To Sleep begins very like Statius — and Young.

Lo, Midnight from her starry reign
Looks awful down on earth and main,
The tuneful birds lie hush'd in sleep,
With all that crop the verdant food,
With all that skim the crystal flood,
Or haunt the caverns of the rocky steep.
No rushing winds disturb the tufted bowers;
No wakeful sound the moonlight valley knows,
Save where the brook its liquid murmur pours,
And lulls the waving scene to more profound repose.

The poet begs sleep to bring him, not dreams of gratified ambition nor of great power, but only blameless visions of posterity benefited through his efforts to teach the love of virtue. A turn quite characteristic of Akenside's proud self-reliance is his assertion that he can deal with the lovesick dreams himself, without calling upon Morpheus to arrange such matters for him. In two odes, *To a Gentleman, whose Mistress had Married an Old Man,* and *To A Friend on the Hazard of Falling in Love,* we have common sense advice against love-melancholy. Akenside's poetry, in short, includes only a single example of melancholy lyricism, the ode *To the Evening Star,* on the part of a young scientist determined to be only reasonably pensive.[39]

William Whitehead,[40] who became poet laureate in 1757 after the office had been refused by Gray, continually expressed in poetry his disapproval of the enthusiast, to whom he invariably attributed selfish motives. *In a Hermitage* supports the view that the man who has led a natural life will at its close want no such monitors as are found in the hermit's cell.

> The gloomy grot, the cypress shade,
> The Zealot's list of rigid rules,
> To him are merely dull parade,
> The tragic pageantry of fools.

It is only fools who, having indulged every appetite, come finally to loathe all enjoyment and " act alive the farce of death."

[39] Quotations from the first edition of the *Odes.* For the relation of this version to that of later editions, see Dyce, *op. cit.,* pp. 34–37. The alterations made by Akenside do not indicate any change in his attitude towards melancholy.

[40] Chalmers, *English Poets,* vol. XVII. Whitehead's first publication of his *Poems,* 1754, lies a little beyond my terminating date, but his views may be presumed to have been known somewhat earlier, through conversation and manuscript circulation.

Then, fill'd with all which sour disdain
  To disappointed vice can add,
Tir'd of himself, man flies from man,
  And hates the world he made so bad.

Whitehead's *The Enthusiast: an Ode,* 1754, begins by describing what he conceives to be the typical attitude of the lover of retirement. The poet in the spring takes a country walk, and pauses to admire the scene.

I stop, I gaze; in accents rude
To thee, serenest Solitude,
  Bursts forth th' unbidden lay:
Begone, vile world; the learn'd, the wise,
The great, the busy, I despise,
  And pity e'en the gay.

These, these are joys alone, I cry,
'Tis here, divine Philosophy,
  Thou deign'st to fix thy throne!
Here, contemplation points the road
Thro' Nature's charms to Nature's God!
  These, these, are joys alone!

In this mood he bids farewell to human cares, hopes, fears, pleasures, and pains.

Yet still I felt, or seem'd to feel,
A kind of visionary Zeal
  Of universal love,
When lo! a voice! a voice I hear!
'Twas Reason whisper'd in my ear
  These monitory strains:
"What mean'st thou, man? would'st thou unbind
The ties which constitute thy kind,
  The pleasures and the pains?

"The same Almighty Power unseen,
Who spreads the gay or solemn scene
  To Contemplation's eye:
Fix'd every movement of the soul,
Taught every wish its destined goal,
  And quicken'd every joy.

"Art thou not man? and dar'st thou find
A bliss which leans not to mankind?
Presumptuous thought and vain!
Each bliss unshar'd is unenjoy'd,
Each power is weak, unless employ'd
Some social good to gain.

"Enthusiast, go, unstring the lyre;
In vain thou sing'st if none admire,
How sweet soe'er the strain;
And is not thy o'erflowing mind,
Unless thou mixest with thy kind,
Benevolent in vain?"

The concluding line of the poem reminds the enthusiast "That man was made for man."

And what, amidst all this welter of poems, melancholy, non-melancholy, and anti-melancholy, would be the effect upon the average reader? If we may judge by the number of editions and the sales of these various pieces and the comments, now pro, now con, now excited, now nonchalant, the general effect was a broadening of taste. Then, as now, the omnivorous reader liked novelty, and picked his way through the mass of new productions by the path of eclecticism. Perhaps it may not be unfair to select as illustrative the mental habits of Mrs. (really Miss) Elizabeth Carter, for though she was genuinely learned in the classics,[41] so were many readers of her day, and though her own time reckoned her as a remarkable woman, she can to-day claim no preëminence in literary history. She

[41] Able to read and write Greek and Latin. Her translation of Epictetus has stood the test of modern scholarship and has recently been republished in *Everyman's Library*. In the correspondence between Mrs. Carter and her friend Miss Talbot, the two ladies discuss the characters and motives of ancient heroes as eagerly as though they were contemporaries. See her *Letters*, ed. Pennington, 3rd ed. London, 1819, vol. I, p. 199, and Pennington, *Memoir*, 3rd ed. London, 1816, vol. I, pp. 380–381.

was, however, an actual force in the determination of popular taste, because she belonged to the influential group which recognized Johnson as their leader in literary matters. Not that Mrs. Carter always agreed with the great Doctor; she had too much real independence and too large an element of whim in her nature to agree absolutely with any of her friends. But the group formed itself naturally upon a community of likes and dislikes. From about 1750 to about 1780, or beyond, any book which came out had to meet at once the opinion of this circle, and if they damned it, it could make its way, if it succeeded at all, only with difficulty. We may, then, take Mrs. Carter's attitude towards melancholy before 1750 as indicative of what average taste would shortly be.

Elizabeth Carter, a maiden lady living with her father in the small town of Deal in Kent, within sound of the sea, took long walks in the early morning, and spent hours of her day and more hours of her night in reading books, serious or pleasant, in the study of the classics and of half a dozen modern languages, and in the contemplation of the view from her window. She read sermons, history, novels, plays, and poetry, and spent a part of every year with her literary friends in London, exchanging opinions on literature and life. She was not excessively religious, though a genuine common-sense piety is visible in all her writings and actions. She did not consider herself much of a poet, but she wrote poetry occasionally, and her father's friend, Edward Cave, who was running his new *Gentleman's Magazine* successfully on his perfect intuition of average taste, insisted on printing some of it in his pages, and introduced her to Johnson, then just making his mark. Most of her poetry remained unpublished until late in her life, but it was circulated among her friends, and therefore known. It was by no means good enough to influence other poetry, but may be quoted as evidence of a certain state of mind, a state ready to accept Thomson, Blair, and Young, Akenside, the Wartons, Collins, and Gray, as well as Swift, Addison, and Pope.

After the appearance of two or three small poems,[42] we find Mrs. Carter translating, in 1736, Horace's *Odes IV, 7.* This is one of the classical sources of melancholy poetry. It compares human life to the four seasons, and points out that the seasons return, but that when a man dies

> Nor Wit, Descent, nor Piety can aid,
> To rescue thee from Death's eternal shade.

She translates also Horace's *Odes I, 22, Integer Vitae,* but characteristically omits all reference to the laughing Lalage. Her only attempt at satire is a poem expanded from two lines of Juvenal. The idea is that it is vain to trust fortune, and the soul must find satisfaction in its own intrinsic worth. In 1738, she has a poem descriptive of the starry heavens and in the form of a contemplation at night. This poem was, doubtless, inspired by her knowledge of astronomy, a study of which she was very fond.[43] The sight of the stars leads her to thoughts of the Creator, but her muse descends to earth again in order to compliment Wright, the astronomer.

In 1739, she wrote her *Ode to Melancholy* which runs thus:

> Come Melancholy! silent Pow'r,
> Companion of my lonely hour,
> To sober thought confin'd:
> Thou sweetly-sad ideal guest,
> In all thy soothing charms confest,
> Indulge my pensive mind.
>
> . . . .

[42] Quotations from her *Poems on Several Occasions.* In vol. II of Pennington, *Memoir,* 3rd ed. London, 1816.

[43] *Ibid.* vol. I, pp. 24–26. She translated (1739) a work of Algarotti's, *Sir Isaac Newton's Philosophy Explained for the Use of Ladies.*

I from the busy crowd retire,
To court the objects that inspire,
Thy philosophic dream.

Thro' yon dark grove of mournful yews
With solitary steps I muse,
By thy direction led;
Here, cold to Pleasure's tempting forms,
Consociate with my sister-worms,
And mingle with the dead.

Ye midnight horrors! awful gloom!
Ye silent regions of the tomb,
My future peaceful bed:
Here shall my weary eyes be clos'd
And ev'ry sorrow lie repos'd
In Death's refreshing shade.

Ye pale inhabitants of night,
Before my intellectual sight
In solemn pomp ascend:
O tell how trifling now appears
The train of idle hopes and fears
That varying life attend.

The following eight stanzas develop the thought that only religion can make death a welcome visitor. The concluding thought is of the resurrection which leads to an eternity of active life and bliss. The resemblances to *Job,* to Young's *Last Day,* to Thomson, to Parnell are easily recognizable. In 1739 she wrote *An Ode,* which is in the form of a prayer, and begins in deep gloom, but ends in hope. In the same year, we have *Thoughts at Midnight.* She prays the Almighty for death, because at that moment her soul is ready for it. In 1741 there are some lines *Written Extempore on the Seashore — By Moonlight:*

Thou restless fluctuating deep,
Expressive of the human mind,
In thy forever varying form,
My own inconstant self I find.

The ocean's calm is broken and the peace of friendship gives way to "the gloom of spleen."

In an undated poem to the memory of a friend, whose name is not given, we have the metre of Gray's *Elegy.*[44] This is placed by her editor immediately after another poem to the same friend written in 1747. A poem *To Miss D'Aeth,* 1744, is in praise of the life of retirement, but the nature descriptions are in the cool manner of Pope, not of Thomson or Young, mosaics not rhapsodies. *Written at Midnight in a Thunder Storm,* 1743, draws an analogy between the storm and the Judgment Day. Reason teaches her to despise fear; just so

> Unmov'd mayst thou the final storm,
>   Of jarring worlds survey,
> That ushers in the glad serene
>   Of everlasting day.

It will be seen that Mrs. Carter's early poetry is continuously pensive and at the same time didactic. Horace, religion, and the love of the outdoor world, more particularly of storms and of night, are miscellaneously combined. There is a considerable tendency to mild melancholy, partly religious, partly bookish, quite genuine, but not very deep. Now, in her daily life Mrs. Carter was known as an active, cheerful, industrious, conversational, common sense body, whose regular occupations included the making of shirts and of puddings, yet her inner life was all of a pensive tone. A number of other poems before 1750, are in this melancholy mood.

Special mention is required of the *Ode to Wisdom,* written in 1746, and published anonymously in the *Gentleman's Magazine.* Richardson saw this poem in manuscript while he was writing *Clarissa Harlowe,* and made Clarissa

[44] Which she might have begun to use from reading Hammond or Shenstone.

sing a single stanza, describing the flight of an owl from an old tower in the late evening. Mrs. Carter's friends recognized the stanza as hers, and the great popularity of *Clarissa* was an immense advertisement for her poem, but the lady, who shrank from notoriety, was indignant at the use of the verses without permission. Richardson wrote her a note, in which he protested his ignorance of the authorship and his innocence of all piratical intention. The apology was accepted and a delightful friendship between the two began.[45]

An example of her way of taking extreme pleasure in the outdoor world is found in one of her letters written about the year 1746.[46] It is significant, as showing that there were other mortals, besides Thomson, who rejoiced in winter.

> I am now nearly as gay and wild as ever, and want to be flying all over the face of the earth, though this weather something cramps my genius, for I cannot meet with anybody here romantic enough to take moonlight walks in the snow, and travel as people do in Lapland. If I was happy enough to be at Canterbury, what excursions should you and I make through trackless paths, and enjoy a season that less whimsical folks shudder at. Certainly we odd mortals, that take delight in such things as make the rest of the world very sententiously pronounce us mad, enjoy infinitely more pleasure than the sober, prudent part of mankind, who sit close to a fire, because they are cold. To us every season has its charms; and even the gloomy prospects of winter have a kind of dark sullen beauty, that strikes the mind with no disagreeable sensation.

There is an instance in the same year, of her never-failing delight in the aspect of the sky at night.[47]

> I waked last night at some unseasonable hour, and seeing the stars glitter, I could not help getting up to take a view of the

[45] *Letters*, vol. I, pp. 203, 207. *Memoir*, vol. I, pp. 100–102.
[46] Quoted in *Memoir*, vol. I, p. 107.
[47] *Ibid*. vol. I, pp. 105.

sky, and I think I never saw a finer glow of constellations in my life. Orion and Sirius quite dazzled me. This sight did me a great deal of good, and after a little contemplation upon it, I returned very quietly to sleep. To be sure it is a great happiness to accustom one's self to take extreme pleasure in objects so easily acquired.

But her pleasure in twilight, moonlight, the stars at midnight, the sea, storms, and winter gloom was indulged without deluding herself into the belief that such enjoyment was a virtue. It was for her a harmless pleasure to be snatched at odd hours, which, in such a busy life as hers, were more or less stolen from household duties, serious literary work — the translation of Epictetus — or social intercourse. She visited the poor as a Christian obligation, as a matter of course, and without sentimentalizing over them. In later life, she applies to her love of ruins the term "romantic," but tries by reasoning to account for it and harmonize it with her religious beliefs. Her analysis takes the form of a little prose essay, which is inserted twice, in almost the same form, in letters to friends.

Reflections Suggested by the Sight of Ruins, August, 1767.

Did you ever try to account for that astonishing mixture of deep awe, soft melancholy, and exquisite delight, which the imagination experiences from such views of ruin and desolation? Is it that the soul, while it is subdued by a sad proof of the weakness of all that is strong, and of the littleness of all that is great below, while it feels a tender sympathy in the overthrow of human art and magnificence, at the same moment exults and triumphs in its own superiority to all mortal things, and looks through the devastations of time to its own eternal prospects? I think there is something in this beyond mere refinement; at least I feel with regard to myself, that if I had any doubts of immortality, the sight of a ruin would affect me only with unmixed and insupportable gloom and horror.

I wished for you the other morning to share with me in a situation of this kind. After a pretty long walk, I sat down on the roots of an elm, and listened to the music of a spring which bubbled at my feet, and formed a small lake, shaded by the hanging branches of some venerable trees which surround the ruins of an ancient seat. I just remember the death of the last possessor. The house survived him long enough for me to have a much more perfect idea of it, as I have often walked over it with great delight in its untenanted state. The apartments, unfurnished and solitary, had a striking air of sombre greatness, particularly a cedar gallery, which was a noble room, and had two very magnificent chimney-pieces. There was a little gloomy chapel, which I was once so lucky to see solemnly gilded by the rays of the setting sun; a picture which, young as I then was, and with a set of gay companions, made a very strong impression on my imagination. We drank tea in a kind of pavilion, fronted by a marble colonnade, which looked upon a garden, where one mount rising above another reminded me of the pensile groves of Babylon.

Such do I once remember the house of which I now sat and contemplated the melancholy ruins. The estate was divided, and the building was sold for the materials, and for the most part levelled with the ground. So little influence have the objects which form the pride and pleasure of one age upon the varying temper of the next.

In the midst of my reflections on the desolation within my view, I surveyed the scenes of nature around me, and derived great comfort from the observation of one who made wiser reflections than I, that the *"earth abideth forever."* . . . [T]he creations of Divine Wisdom charm equally and universally through every revolution of time, and amidst all the caprices of inconstant taste; and thus continue the only real standard and uncontested examples of the beautiful and the sublime.

The distinguishing character of such a personality as Mrs. Carter is a liberal, appreciative spirit, combined with an independence and positiveness of judgment which is always ready to defend itself by assigning a reason. Among such readers, a variety of poetry could find a welcome, and though the commonplace and the mediocre would often be liked, in the end only substantial thought in beautiful form would be read again and again, until it conquered its way to the place of highest honor.

But up to 1750 melancholy poetry though a favorite kind, had produced only one acknowledged masterpiece and that, too, met unfavorable criticism. The uneven workmanship of *The Seasons* was recognized even by its friends, and the poet Somerville had warned Thomson in a poetical *Epistle* that his Muse wanted "the reforming toilet's daily care."

> For kind and wise the parent who reproves
> The slightest blemish in the child he loves.
> Read Philips much, consider Milton more,
> But from their dross extract the purer ore,
> Let perspicuity o'er all preside.[48]

But though Thomson's revisions sometimes improved single lines or passages, the whole became less rather than more coherent and convincing. Young's "morals" were always admired and his style regarded as "original," and at times "sublime," but many passages were unfavorably criticized. Wherever poets, such as Blair and Young, had loved and imitated Shakespeare, they had gained something like eloquence, a greater sonority and freedom in the line, a more sincere accent. Wherever they had pored over Spenser and Milton's minor poetry, as had Thomson and the Wartons, they had gained in charm of atmosphere. But with the exception of Thomson, they were still far from atoning by exquisite phrasing and tone color for their abandonment of rhyme.

The tendency to self-analysis, so strong in Young, the personal note of the Wartons, and the whole melancholy tone were ignored by the best intellects of these first fifty years of the century, Swift, Addison, Pope. Their energy went to popularizing the "study of mankind," to satirizing vice, folly, and ignorance, to explaining and applying the laws of beauty in literature, and to upholding standards of

[48] *Epistle to Mr. Thomson, on the first edition of his "Seasons"* in Chalmers, *Works of the English Poets,* vol. XI.

morals and of art. Both for their own time and for modern readers, the advantages of skilful handling lay with them. If the poetry of the self was to become as much a power among men as were plays, satires, and poetical essays, it was in need of greater brevity, clarity, simplicity, and sincerity — most of all of organic unity.

CHAPTER VI

THE PERFECTION OF FORM; GRAY'S "ELEGY," 1751

WHETHER as a reaction against the excesses of descriptive poetry, or from causes more complex and less explicable, there is evident about this time, 1740–50, a synchronous and self-conscious effort on the part of several poets towards exquisite form in the melancholy *genre*. Success was cumulative, and was finally achieved by Gray through the ever finer application of methods learned from both antique and English "classical" authors, methods already tried with excellent results by Akenside, the Wartons, Hammond, Shenstone, and Collins.

In my fourth chapter I have tried to show how the two Wartons, largely in imitation of Milton's minor poems, restricted the single poem to the expression of a single feeling of a simple kind, instead of following Thomson's more miscellaneous and expansive method. The same principle — that on which the best lyric poetry has always been composed — governed the work of all the others here mentioned.

James Hammond, who died in 1742 at the age of thirty-two, left behind him certain *Love Elegies*, published for the first time anonymously in 1742. These were imitations of Tibullus, but expurgated to suit contemporary taste.[1] They instantly became popular, partly because they were tremendously sad and sentimental, partly because Hammond was prominent in the Prince of Wales's party. Thomson, in the 1744 edition of *The Seasons*, inserted a

[1] Some editions prefix the motto, *Virginibus puerisque canto*. Quotations from Chalmers, *English Poets*, vol. XI.

eulogy (*Winter*, 555–577) calling Hammond "the darling pride, the friend and lover of the tuneful throng," and leader of "youthful Patriots."

In the endeavor to reproduce the effect of the classical elegiac metre, which has hexameter lines alternating with pentameters, Hammond kept pentameter as the characteristic English line, but paired alternate lines by the use of rhyme. If the *Elegies* were, as the title page asserts, written in 1732, Hammond was the first of this period to use this quatrain for elegies; fourteen in all are in this metre, which Shenstone calls "Hammond's metre"[2] though it had been used several times before in English poetry.

The poems, as a whole, celebrate the poet's love for Delia, said to be a real person.[3] But whatever the particular circumstances, Hammond manages to give a pathetic turn to almost every poem. For instance, in *Elegy III* there is drawn the picture of a maiden faithful in love, who is contrasted with his unfaithful Delia. But the reward of faithfulness appears to be only that her friends shall mourn her loss, when she is dead (as in Tibullus II, 4).

And when the lamp of life shall burn no more,
When dead she seems as in a gentle sleep,
The pitying neighbour shall her loss deplore,
And round the bier assembled lovers weep:

With flow'ry garlands each revolving year
Shall strow the grave where Truth and Softness rest,
Then home returning drop the pious tear,
And bid the turf lie easy on her breast.

Elegy IX ends with a sort of epitaph on the poet himself, who imagines himself lying dead (as in Tibullus III, 2).

[2] For a full account of its use by Davenant, Dryden, Davies, Hobbes, Hammond, and Shenstone, see Alden, *English Verse*, pp. 72–74.

[3] Delia is the name of the beloved in Tibullus. The *Dict. Nat. Biog.* names Catherine, or Kitty, Dashwood as Hammond's love.

Here lies a youth borne down with love and care,
He could not long his Delia's loss abide;
Joy left his bosom with the parting fair, .
And when he durst no longer hope, he dy'd.

Elegy XIII (which bears a considerable resemblance to Tibullus I, 1) is in praise of a country life with Delia, but nevertheless has a tragic ending, unlike the ending of the Latin poem.

Let [friends], extended on the decent bier
Convey the corse in melancholy state,
Thro' all the village spread the tender tear,
While pitying maids our wondrous love relate.

William Shenstone, reading Hammond's *Elegies,* was struck by the success of the metrical effects and by the suitability of the Roman elegiac *genre* to express certain thoughts of his own. The whole subject of elegy as practised by the Roman poets interested Shenstone, and though his *Poems,* printed (for the amusement of his friends, as he says) at Oxford in 1737, contained nothing in the melancholy tone, he very soon after began to work upon some "Elegies in Hammond's metre, but upon *real* and natural subjects."[4]

Shenstone in his *Prefatory Essay on Elegy* considers

[4] *Works in Verse and Prose,* London, 1764–69, vol. III, p. 77. This letter indicates that some of the poems were written by February, 1743, though not in their final state. Some of them were published first in Dodsley's *Collection* in 1748. When, after Shenstone's death, Dodsley published an edition of his *Works in Prose and Verse* in two volumes, 1764, twenty-six elegies begin the book, together with a *Prefatory Essay on Elegy,* which, Dodsley's footnotes say, was written "almost twenty years ago." We may assume then, that Shenstone's *Elegies* were fairly complete, and his theory of the nature of elegy developed by 1744 or 1745. He must have been writing them in his thirtieth year, his choice of mood and subject being a mature choice, not the mere first impulse of youthful dejection.

elegy as a form appropriate to what he calls "tender and querulous ideas," which we may paraphrase as pathetic and melancholy themes. So long as this tender and pathetic character is maintained, the form may be used for a variety of subjects. "It throws its melancholy stole over pretty different objects; which like the dresses at a funeral procession, gives them all a solemn and uniform appearance." Thus, in his opinion, the elegy is not necessarily a lament over a person who is dead or, as with Tibullus, a complaint over unhappy love, though it may include these subjects.

Nor must the elegy evade the responsibility laid upon all poetry, namely, the encouragement of virtue. The epic, and the tragic drama inculcate public virtues; the elegy is suitable to illustrate and recommend private virtue. Hereupon, Shenstone, in accordance with Shaftesbury's theory so often reiterated by Thomson and others, enunciates the doctrine that "There is a truly virtuous pleasure connected with many pensive contemplations . . . [the elegy] by presenting suitable ideas, has discovered sweets in melancholy, which we could not find in mirth; and has led us with success to the dusty urn, when we could draw no pleasure from the sparkling bowl." Some of the subjects which elegy may treat with moral advantage to the reader, are the innocence and simplicity of rural life, the sweets of liberty and independence, the honest delights of love and friendship, the glory of a good name after death, the futility of pride in noble birth, the innocent amusements of letters, and in general the humane temper.

But, whatever the subject, it must be so treated as to "diffuse a pleasing melancholy"; the style must imitate the voice and language of grief; it must be simple and "flowing as a mourner's veil." The versification must, therefore, permit free and unconstrained expression, while remaining simple. On these grounds Shenstone chooses "heroic metre with alternate rhyme, " which he thinks will not become monotonous, provided each elegy is short. He alludes to its use in a collection of elegies, recently published by "a gentleman of the most exact taste, now untimely dead" (i.e., Hammond). The metre of *Lycidas* he rejects as too "dissolute" for a short poem, by which he means that the rhymes do not recur often enough to bind the lines together for the reader of only average sensitiveness. He does not think much of love elegies, which require little or no skill in reasoning or structure, though they do require "tenderness and perspicuity." Elegies of the other sort, which inculcate some sort of moral, require some reasoning power, some thought and order.

He then claims for his own *Elegies* the virtue of sincere feeling. "If he [the author] speaks of his humble shed, his flocks and his fleeces, he does not counterfeit the scene; who having . . . retired betimes to country solitude and sought his happiness in rural employments, has a right to consider himself a real shepherd." The reader feels, indeed, Shenstone's sincerity, though the emotions he expresses are of no great moment. His friends, too, recognized that Shenstone, as he himself says in several of his letters,[5] was naturally of a pensive or melancholy temperament. He was dissatisfied with his position in life, and frequently gave expression to that dissatisfaction in his letters, his essays, and his poetry; he did, however, love the country and the pleasures of retirement, though he would have liked them on a larger scale.

Shenstone feared that the public who, he said, had been accustomed to quicker measures (i.e., tetrameter, rhymed

[5] "Solitary life, limited circumstances, a phlegmatic habit, and disagreeable events, have given me a melancholy turn, that is hardly dissipated by the most serene sky; but in a northeast wind is quite intolerable." *Ibid.* p. 209. See also references below, note 8.

in pairs), might find his own metrical effects "heavy and languid." As a matter of fact, the repetition of the use of this particular measure for a series of elegies so soon after its skilful employment by Hammond caught popular favor, and was imitated almost immediately, though sporadically, by many minor poets up to the time that Gray made it peculiarly his own.

In their subjects, the elegies illustrate his own definition, that is to say, they treat of friendship, virtue, the charms of country life, the unsatisfactoriness of life in the great world, of ambition, and of riches. There are one or two laments over the death of friends and one (XVII) in which he indulges in melancholy merely for the pleasure of it.[6] Once or twice he strikes a note distinctly suggestive of parts of Gray's *Elegy*. For instance, in *Elegy III*, he mourns the obscure fate of a friend named Alcon, and describes his character in a stanza something like the Epitaph at the end of the *Elegy in a Country Churchyard*.

> He little knew to ward the secret wound;
>   He little knew that mortals cou'd ensnare;
> Virtue he knew; the noblest joy he found,
>   To sing her glories, and to paint her fair.
>
> He lov'd the muse; she taught him to complain;
>   He saw his tim'rous loves on her depend;
> He lov'd the muse, altho' she taught in vain;
>   He loved the muse, for she was virtue's friend.
>
> . . . .
> . . . .
>
> Piteous of woes, and hopeless to relieve,
>   The pensive prospect sadden'd all his strain.

Elegy VII contains the idea that the man ambitious of fame and power must necessarily incur guilt and stoop to

[6] As in his letter, *ibid.* p. 44.

flattery, envy, and falsehood — a thought similar to Gray's, that the lot of the poor

> nor circumscrib'd alone
> Their growing virtues, but their crimes confin'd.

In *Elegy IV* there are a few lines suggestive of Collins's *To Evening,* and of the description of evening in Gray's *Elegy. Elegies VI* and *VII* are pensive and picturesque, in a manner distantly recalling Milton's *Il Penseroso.*

It is worthy of note that a considerable number of elegies have a distinct reference to Shenstone's personal history, and may, therefore, be taken as subjective. *Elegy XI,* for instance, tells us that in his youth he was ambitious, but that in seven short years he had become discouraged with the possibility of making any headway in life. The disillusion is compared to going home, after a banquet.

> Where are the splendid forms, the rich perfumes,
> Where the gay tapers, where the spacious dome?
> Vanish'd the costly pearls, the crimson plumes,
> And we, delightless, left to wander home!

Such a view of his own position in life finds confirmation in more than one of Shenstone's letters.[7] In *Elegy XIII* he bewails, as he so often does in his letters, the separation of friends through the accidents of life. *Elegies XIX* and *XXIII* present precisely opposed views of his life in the country, and this contradiction is also found in his letters. The former poem, written in the spring of 1743, complains:

> Again the lab'ring hind inverts the soil;
> Again the merchant ploughs the tumid wave;
> Another spring renews the soldier's toil,
> And finds me vacant in the rural cave. . . .

while the latter gives only the pleasures of his situation at The Leasowes, his beloved country seat, where he is

[7] *Ibid.* pp. 44, 46, 49, 71, 79, 98, 116, 117, 229.

visited by his dear friends, Lyttelton, Thomson, and Pope.[8]

> Thro' these soft shades delighted let me stray,
> While o'er my head forgotten suns descend!
> Thro' these dear valleys bend my casual way,
> 'Till setting life a total shade extend.

The word "pensive" is very frequent throughout all the twenty-six elegies, and it is the right word rather than "sad" or "gloomy," to describe the mood of the entire group of poems.

Very characteristic of Shenstone's general attitude is the half satiric, half jocose little poem *Written at an Inn at Henley.*

> To thee, fair freedom! I retire,
> From flattery, feasting, dice and din;
> Nor art thou found in domes much higher
> Than the lone cot or humble Inn.
>
> . . . .
>
> Who e'er has travell'd life's dull round,
> Where'er his stages may have been,
> May sigh to think how oft he found
> The warmest welcome — at an Inn.

Shenstone's particular contribution to the development of melancholy poetry is, then, (1) the fixing of elegiac metre as "heroic metre with alternate rhyme," (2) the emphasis (with the Wartons, Collins, and Gray, of course) upon the short unit, instead of the long descriptive poem, for the expression of personal feeling, (3) the increased emphasis (with Young) on self-analysis, and self-expression, (4) the attainment of perfect intelligibility. His success in these improvements was undoubtedly self-conscious. He was a man who prided himself upon his taste in music, art, literature, and landscape-gardening, and who lived

[8] *Ibid.* pp. 46, 91, 159; 124, 138, 145.

chiefly to gratify these tastes. He constantly criticised minutely his own work, sent it to his friends for revision, and revised theirs.[9] He loved and often quoted Spenser, Shakespeare, and Milton, but found fault with them also.[10] He took pains to make even his letters *chef-d'oeuvres.*[11] In short, he practised his own preaching, "I believe it will appear upon examination, that works which cost most labour have generally been thought the *easiest* and pleased the *longest.*" [12] In all his labors he had an eye on "posthumous reputation," the idea of which, his second *Elegy* avers, excels the feeling of present joy.

A more exquisite taste, a truer ear, and a greater depth of feeling are evident in the poetry of William Collins, Shenstone's younger contemporary, about whose life and thoughts we know so little that we must infer his purposes largely from the internal evidence of his poems.

That Collins had some tendency to follow Thomson, is observable in those strange little poems, *Persian Eclogues,* later called *Oriental Eclogues,* first published in 1742, but written, Joseph Warton says,[13] at Winchester School when Collins was seventeen years old. The preface, added by another hand after Collins's death, says that the *Eclogues* are intended to give "a just view of the miseries and inconveniences, as well as the felicities that attend one of the finest countries of the East." Where Collins got his notions of the East we do not know, but the descriptions plainly have no reality but are made at second hand from Thomson.[14] The inconveniences suffered by Hassan, the camel driver (*Ecologue II*), are hunger and thirst and the

[9] *Ibid.* pp. 76–78, 134–135, 140, 207, 246, 247, 257, 314.

[10] *Ibid.* pp. 14, 23, 199, 219; 67; 93, 117.

[11] *Ibid.* p. 269.

[12] *Ibid.* p. 391.

[13] Dates, other facts, and quotations from *The Poems of William Collins,* ed. Bronson.

[14] *Ante,* p. 164.

usual hardships of the desert. He curses the love of gold, which tempts men to tread over such dangerous routes. This is a variation of the Complaint of Life. Collins uses "horror" effects when Hassan meditates upon the danger of death in the desert, ending his description of each horrible possibility, with the refrain:

Sad was the hour, and luckless was the day,
When first from Shiraz' walls I bent my way.

. . . .

What if the lion in his rage I meet! —
Oft in the dust I view his printed feet:
And (fearful) oft, when Day's declining light
Yields her pale empire to the mourner Night,
By hunger rous'd, he scours the groaning plain,
Gaunt wolves and sullen tygers in his train:
Before them Death with shrieks directs their way,
Fills the wild yell, and leads them to their prey.

(Refrain)

At that dead hour the silent asp shall creep,
If aught of rest I find, upon my sleep;
Or some swoln serpent twist his scales around,
And wake to anguish with a burning wound.
Thrice happy they, the wise contented poor,
From lust of wealth, and dread of death secure!
They tempt no desarts, and no griefs they find;
Peace rules the day, where reason rules the mind.

(Refrain)

Variants of the Retirement theme are found in *Eclogues III* and *IV*. In *Abra; or the Georgiana Sultana* (*III*), the scene is a forest, the time evening. Abbas, the emperor, loves and weds Abra, the shepherdess. After she is raised to power and high position, both often return to her rural home and lead the life of shepherds. *Agib and Lecander; or, The Fugitive* (*IV*) is a dialogue between two fugitives fleeing from the Tartars. The scene is a wild mountain side in Circassia; the time midnight. The two lament the ruin of their peaceful land by invasion. These *Oriental Eclogues* can scarcely be read to-day without a smile at their unreality and their sentimentality. Nevertheless, they have the charm of easy rhythm, pleasant phrasing, brevity, and clarity. Collins's *Ode on the Death of Mr. Thomson,* 1749, is permeated with a genuine love of the man's quality as a friend, and as the poet of all "whose heart in sorrow bleeds" and who love the "vales and wild woods" of England.

But Collins had other and better models in Shakespeare, Milton, and the Greeks. *A Song from Shakespeare's Cymbeline* is a very remarkable piece of sympathetic interpretation of the mood of a scene from Shakespeare. It is supposed to be sung by Guiderus and Arviragus over the tomb of Fidele. The second stanza uses with new charm the idea of wailing ghosts, the fourth stanza outdoes Thomson in its description of the robin redbreast, and the fifth gets a new *penseroso* effect out of evening meditation in a sheltered cell, while a storm howls outside. In *An Epistle Addressed to Sir Thomas Hanmer on his Edition of Shakespeare's Works,* 1743, Collins recalls charmingly certain favorite plays of Shakespeare. In the odes *To Beauty, To Fear, To Simplicity,* 1746, we have again the *penseroso* idea from Milton, with images and phrases often taken from Shakespeare. In *How Sleep the Brave,* 1746, the cadences are similar in effect to one of Ariel's songs in *The Tempest.* Something of Collins's mastery of lyric form is undoubtedly due to this loving imitation of Shakespeare, something also of his new and peculiar intensity, a certain heart-breaking quality, quiet as the pathos is.

From the classics, Collins learned to love the simple expression of natural beauty. In his *Ode to Simplicity* he implores her to assist his youth. However lovely the flowers of poetry, no garland can be made unless Simplicity weaves the wreath. Simplicity flourished in the virtuous days of the Roman republic, and lingered with the poets of the distinguished Age of Augustus, but then fled the world. The later Roman poets wasted their genius in excess. Only Simplicity can inspire poetry that shall elevate the soul. From the context and from Collins's other poems, we infer that by simplicity he does not mean mere clarity in expression, but a trait of character, namely, the spirit of sincerity in which poetry should be written, a high intention to write only under the promptings of nature and in accord with truth. In *The Manners: an Ode* he bids farewell to books as a source of inspiration and praises the observation of nature.

Collins's poems are in fact not at all "simple" in the modern sense. Their logic, though it will bear analysis, is often difficult. To read them with pleasure requires an active and a trained mind. But they entice to perusal by rhythm and phrasing so beautiful that we cannot rest till we have tracked down the meaning, and they satisfy Collins's own standard, the sincere expression of natural feeling in language strong and sweet. All Collins's poems have this compelling loveliness, and most of all the *Ode to Evening*.

This ode contains scarcely an idea or an image that had not been used again and again in the melancholy verse we have been describing at such length.[15] Its achievement is purely one of style; it says the old things better than they have ever been said before — or since. Its unrivaled musical effect is chiefly due to alliteration and tone color. For example, the sound of l occurs seventy-nine times in the fifty-two lines. In the eighth stanza, there is an average of nearly three l's to each line; in the fifth and the twelfth stanzas, an average of two l's to the line. There is sus-

[15] Joseph Warton's *Ode to Evening* was written earlier than Collins's, though published in the same month. *Ibid.* p. 111.

tained alliteration in several stanzas. The first is built up chiefly on the letter s, the second on w and b, while the third reënforces the effect of the first two by combining w, b, and s. This skilful use of tone color, combined with the smoothness of the rhythm, does away with the necessity for rhyme or stanzaic structure, although the poem is often printed in stanzas.

The design is of the utmost simplicity — a greeting to Evening in a strain as soft as her own returning footsteps, a wish to be absorbed in a mood harmonious with her still loveliness. The editor of the critical edition of Collins's poems, Walter C. Bronson, fails to understand why Collins introduces in the last stanza four allegorical personages, Fancy, Friendship, Science, and Health. He conjectures that Collins may have intended to suggest that the evening is the best time for reading poetry, entertaining friends, and studying.[16] This supposition is quite correct, for, as we have seen from the poems cited in this book, it is plain that these were the pensive pleasures, as enumerated by Milton, Thomson, Warton, and others. Health, also, was associated with country retirement, as opposed to the hectic pleasures of the city. It would have been very odd indeed, if Collins, in the middle of the eighteenth century, had omitted the enumeration of some such attendant spirits, and he might have added Virtue, as well as half a dozen others. That he selects only four, is evidence of his admirable restraint.

Much of the vocabulary of the ode *To Evening* is Miltonic, but in this appropriation of another poet's phrasing as well as in his restating of ideas and feelings generally current in the poetry of the time, Collins does as Chaucer, Shakespeare, and Milton unfailingly do. He touches nothing that he does not make his own, by enriching it with a new delight.

[16] *Ibid.* p. 114.

In his other *Odes on Several Descriptive and Allegoric Subjects,* published in December, 1746, with the imprint 1747, Collins treats with this new technical skill many of the old melancholy themes. He tries sometimes the true Pindaric, sometimes other forms of ode, always with marked success. In all, the perfect mastery of rhythm, the brevity, the selective power, the delicate restraint, the intensity gained by compression, constitute a new standard for poets to live up to, an example much needed at the time.

In the *Ode to Pity,* Euripides and Otway are cited as especially skilled in the art of arousing pity. The poet in imagination builds a temple to Pity.

> There let me oft, retir'd by day,
> In dreams of passion melt away,
>   Allow'd with thee to dwell:
> There waste the mournful lamp of night,
> Till, virgin, thou again delight
>   To hear a British shell!

In the *Ode to Fear* (a real Pindaric) the strophe is a vision of "frantic Fear," followed by her train of Danger, the Furies, and Vengeance. The epode (in the elegiac quatrain) praises the tragedies of Aeschylus and Sophocles. The antistrophe (remotely suggestive of Milton and of the fairy passages of Shakespeare) pictures the haunts of Fear, and expresses the hope that the poet may often read of Fear, but not know her in his own life.

> Thou who such weary lengths hast past,
> Where wilt thou rest, mad nymph, at last?
> Say, wilt thou shroud in haunted cell,
> Where gloomy Rape and Murder dwell?
>   Or in some hollow'd seat,
>   'Gainst which the big waves beat,
> Hear drowning seamen's cries in tempest brought?
> Ne'er be I found, by thee o'eraw'd,
> In that thrice-hallow'd eve abroad

When ghosts, as cottage maids believe,
Their pebbled beds permitted leave,
And goblins haunt, from fire, or fen,
Or mine, or flood, the walks of men.
O thou whose spirit most possest
The sacred seat of Shakespeare's breast,
. . . .
Hither again thy fury deal!
Teach me but once like him to feel,
His cypress wreath my meed decree,
And I, O Fear, will dwell with thee!

In the *Ode on the Poetical Character* (Pindaric) Collins again describes that retirement which is favorable to poetry, and expresses his admiration for Spenser and for Milton. The strophe laments the rarity of the true poetic vision. The antistrophe is a tribute to Milton.

High on some cliff, to heav'n up-pil'd
Of rude access, of prospect wild,
Where, tangled round the jealous steep,
Strange shades o'erbrow the valleys deep,
And holy genii guard the rock,
Its glooms embrown, its springs unlock,
. . . .
I view that oak, the fancied glades among,
By which as Milton lay, his ev'ning ear,
From many a cloud that dropp'd ethereal dew,
Nigh spher'd in heav'n its native strains could hear.
On which that ancient trump he reach'd was hung.

Thither, leaving Waller's myrtle shades, the poet pursues the guiding steps of Fancy, but in vain. To Milton alone has it been given to hear such heavenly music.

In *The Passions: an Ode for Music,* each Passion seizes the lyre and plays upon it, the metrical effects varying in accord with the feeling, as in Dryden's *Ode for St. Cecilia's Day.* One of these is Melancholy, evidently a mood of sublime rapture.

With eyes uprais'd, as one inspir'd,
Pale Melancholy sate retir'd,
And from her wild sequester'd seat,
In notes by distance made more sweet,
Pour'd thro' the mellow horn her pensive soul:
  And, dashing soft from rocks around,
  Bubbling runnels join'd the sound;
Thro' glades and glooms the mingled measure stole;
Or o'er some haunted stream with fond delay
  Round an holy calm diffusing,
  Love of peace and lonely musing,
In hollow murmurs died away.

Collins's contribution at this stage of the development of the melancholy lyric was a finer sense of beauty learned from reading the greatest poets, both classical and English, and an intense sincerity. He offers no new subjects, no wider range of feeling. He does not broaden the channel of melancholy poetry, but deepens it.

Both Collins and the Wartons may have been influenced by the lyric poetry of Akenside, the publication of whose *Odes,* discussed in Chapter V, preceded theirs by about a year, though it seems impossible to determine just when they were composed. His *Pleasures of Imagination,* having excited the approval of Pope and the disapproval of Gray,[17] had proved interesting enough to poets and critics to render important both his theory and his practice of poetry. Now Akenside had, for some years past, been pondering the nature of lyric as he had observed it in his reading of Greek, and had decided that "the perfection of lyric poetry depends . . . on the beauty of words and the gracefulness of numbers, in both which respects the ancients had infinite advantages above us." In his own odes, therefore, he wished to be "correct" and to attend to the best models.[18] He admired the simplicity of the Greeks,

[17] Dyce, *op. cit.*, pp. 17, 18 n. 1.

[18] *Advertisement* to the *Odes on Several Subjects,* 1745.

the refinement of Virgil's *Georgics,* and the ease of Horace.[19] He said of himself as poet "I tune to Attic themes the British lyre."[20] While granting the first place in poetry to Homer and Shakespeare, and delighting in the Spenserian stanza, he loved Milton best and imitated him oftenest.[21] Lyric poetry, he felt, should be refreshing.[22] He echoed Horace's wish to gather sweetness like the bee

in lowly sylvan scenes
And river-banks and fruitful greens.[23]

We may, I think, grant that he succeeded in making his lyric stanzas flow delightfully and that he occasionally attained the pure beauty he craved. *To the Evening Star*[24] is not unworthy of an honorable place among the evening poems of this decade. Lovelier far is the beginning of the *Hymn to the Naiads.*

To pay you homage due,
I leave the gates of sleep; nor shall my lyre
Too far into the splendid hours of morn
Engage your audience: my observant hand
Shall close the strain ere any sultry beam
Approach you. To your subterraneous haunts
Ye then may timely steal; to pace with care
The humid sands; to loosen from the soil
The bubbling sources; to direct the rills
To meet in wider channels; or beneath
Some grotto's dripping arch, at height of noon
To slumber, shelter'd from the burning heaven.[25]

[19] *The Design* prefacing *Pleasures of Imagination,* 1744.

[20] *Pleasures of Imagination,* 1744, bk. I, 604.

[21] *The Balance of Poets,* quoted in full in Bucke, *op. cit.,* pp. 93–103. *Ode VI, On the Absence of the Poetic Inclination.*

[22] *Ode X, On Lyric Poetry.*

[23] *Ode I, Allusion to Horace.*

[24] *Poetical Works of Mark Akenside,* Aldine ed. 1845, p. 247.

[25] *Ibid.* p. 296.

It remains to speak of Gray's own poetry before the publication in 1751 of his *Elegy Written in A Country Churchyard.*

Gray's analysis of his own temperament in his letter to West, May 27, 1742, is well known:

> Mine, you are to know, is a white Melancholy, or rather Leucho-choly for the most part; which, though it seldom laughs or dances, nor ever amounts to what one calls Joy or Pleasure, yet is a good easy sort of a state, and *ça ne laisse que de s'amuser.* The only fault of it is insipidity; which is apt now and then to give a sort of Ennui, which makes one form certain little wishes that signify nothing. But there is another sort, black indeed, which I have now and then felt, that has somewhat in it like Tertullian's rule of faith, *Credo quia impossibile est;* for it believes, nay, is sure of every thing that is unlikely, so it be but frightful; and, on the other hand, excludes and shuts its eyes to the most possible hopes, and every thing that is pleasurable; from this the Lord deliver us! for none but he and sunshiny weather can do it.[26]

This impression of his pensive temperament is confirmed by a letter to Wharton (Cambridge, March 8, 1758):

> It is indeed for want of spirits, as you suspect, that my studies lie among the Cathedrals, and the Tombs, and the Ruins. To think, though to little purpose, has been the chief amusement of my days; and when I would not, or cannot think, I dream.

It is the white melancholy, not the black, which appears in his poems.

In this same year, 1742,[27] Gray wrote his *Ode on the Spring, Sonnet on the Death of Richard West, Hymn to Adversity, Ode on a Distant Prospect of Eton College, Hymn to Ignorance,* and (probably) began the *Elegy,* all at his home in the quiet village of Stoke. All reflect variously the melancholy temper.

[26] *Correspondence of Gray, Walpole, West, and Ashton, 1734–1771,* ed. Toynbee, vol. II, pp. 42–43.

[27] Bradshaw, *Life,* in his (Aldine) ed. of *Poetical Works of Thomas Gray.* Quotations from *Works of Thomas Gray in Prose and Verse,* ed. Gosse.

In the ode *On the Spring,* 1748, that season which the Renaissance poets felt as the call to love, and which Thomson had described as the time of teeming life and passionate excitement, Gray seeks retirement (of course stretched at ease beneath a tree beside a stream) only in order to think

> How vain the ardour of the crowd,
> How low, how little are the proud,
> How indigent the great!

He sees, to be sure, the bright-colored swarms of insects, but

> To Contemplation's sober eye
> Such is the race of Man;
> And they that creep, and they that fly
> Shall end where they began.

Soon, either through accident or age,

> their airy dance
> They leave in dust to rest.

So, too, had Thomson written (*Summer* 342–351), but only as an incidental reflection occurring as one detail in a long description of the summer day, and he had applied the moral only to "luxurious men." But Gray turns the thought upon himself. He was but twenty-one, yet he already felt lonely and useless, like

> A solitary fly!
> Thy joys no glittering female meets,
> No hive hast thou of hoarded sweets,
> No painted plumage to display:
> On hasty wings thy youth is flown,
> Thy sun is set, thy spring is gone. . . .

The *Hymn to Adversity* addresses her as the daughter of Jove and nurse of Virtue. Wisdom and Melancholy are her attendants, together with Justice, Charity, and Pity, "dropping soft the sadly-pleasing tear." The poet begs her to turn towards him her milder not her more dreadful aspect, and thus to soften his heart, and, with the aid of her "philosophic Train,"

> Teach me to love and to forgive,
> Exact my own defects to scan,
> What others are, to feel, and know myself a man.

Here Gray, like Thomson, associates virtue and benevolent feeling with melancholy, but differs from Thomson in arriving at such a conclusion through sad personal experience.

The *Ode on a Distant Prospect of Eton College,* published in 1747, regards boyhood in a manner which seems singular unless we presuppose in the author the true elegiac temper. The sight of boys playing in a school yard causes in Gray only the reflection of the probably unhappy fate of every small youngster, as soon as he shall attain manhood. All around the little victims, wait the terrible throng of Black Misfortune, Angry Passions, Fear, Unhappy Love, Despair, Unkindess, Remorse, Madness, Poverty, Age, Disease, and Death. The only pleasure which he extracts from the scene, is the reflection "where ignorance is bliss, 't is folly to be wise." But humanity as a whole is under sentence:

> Condemn'd alike to groan,
> The tender for another's pain;
> Th' unfeeling for his own.

The "splenetic" fragment *To Ignorance,* beginning in the conventional "horrific" manner was never finished, nor was it published in Gray's lifetime. The *Sonnet on the death of Richard West* is a straightforward, but by no means noteworthy expression of personal sorrow.

The *Elegy,* begun in 1742, perhaps with the death of

West in Mind,[28] was resumed in 1749 at Cambridge after the death of Gray's aunt, Mary Antrobus, and finished at Stoke in 1750. Since its composition lasted over such a long period, it may be regarded as characteristic of Gray's habitual way of thinking, rather than as the expression of a single mood of grief caused by a single event. It is important, however, to remember that it was begun and ended in times of personal bereavement. Such recurrent sorrows cause in serious natures a review of experience as a whole and a sort of philosophic readjustment of the self to life. Gray's poem is evidently the ripened fruit of such thinking.

Its appeal to modern lovers of poetry, its constant place in modern anthologies, are due to this cardinal fact and to the plainly democratic note in some stanzas, but in its own time its appeal was even more certain and far stronger. For the reader of 1751, it was a marvelous synthesis of the thoughts and feelings of the melancholy poetry produced in the past fifty years, which had been so widely read and admired. Setting aside religious melancholy of a morbid tone, like Blair's or Young's, it yet avoided skepticism, atheism, or a cold deism, and preserved the flavor of a religious confidence in God, the Father and the Judge. Without rhapsody or excess, it was full of pensive feeling, lovely description, and a real philosophy, couched, for the most part, in the general terms to which the age was used, yet ending with a frank personal reference, interesting but in the best of taste. Greatest wonder of all, it reconciled with ease the conflicting ethical views that had arisen regarding the free indulgence of the melancholy mood. All this in phrasing which set up in the reader's mind long reverberations of passages from the

[28] Tovey thinks the Epitaph was the first portion composed. *Camb. Hist. of Eng. Lit.*, vol. X, p. 121.

best known poets, from earliest Greek times to the immediate moment.

In its essence, the poem combines the assertion of the right to individual tastes and feelings — to the choice of a way of life different from the prevailing one — with the benevolent attitude of Shaftesbury's school of philosophy. The upshot of its argument is that life may be well lived by a man of quiet tastes, "to fortune and to fame unknown," who has given to the poor only sympathy, and has confined his social activities to a very narrow circle. But all the first part of the poem up to the stanza where the gray-haired villager begins to describe the character of the young observer, is given up to the expression of "benevolent" sentiments. The poet thinks gently and pityingly of the humble, simple lives of the peasants buried in the country churchyard. If their experience has not been very wide, they have nevertheless been preserved from great crimes and great miseries. To be well spoken of after their death, is not an inadequate reward, for the most conspicuous life, like the most obscure, ends at last in an epitaph. And this is well because the excellence of life lies not in the outward deed, but in the character. Both the actual ideas of the poet, and his attitude towards his fellowmen are "humane," as that word was understood by his time. He has, furthermore, by representing his own life and character as obscure but not therefore despicable, identified himself with average humanity, after the manner of truly great poets.

In its treatment of natural scenery, we have again the combination of the conventional with fresh, true observation. This is an evening poem, a retirement poem, a graveyard poem; as in Collins's *Ode to Evening,* practically every detail of the description had appeared in poetry before. But Gray was actually in the habit, as his letters show, of walking about the country, visiting graveyards, ruins, and historical monuments. He, like Thomas Warton, had the antiquarian temper and his love of these things was genuine. Hence his descriptions ring true, and their familiarity strikes the reader not with a sense of triteness but of enriched meaning.[29]

In its choice metre,[30] in its length, unity, coherence. the *Elegy* follows classic tradition, as transmitted by Shenstone and Collins, rather than the expansiveness of Thomson and Young. In its self-portraiture, explicit morality, its mortuary atmosphere, it recalls Parnell, Blair, and Young, but refined by perfect taste into complete agreeableness. A few of the stanzas are surely deliberate imitations in the fashion of the day, from the poetry of his friends and contemporaries, Shenstone, the Wartons, Collins. Yet the poem is no mere literary exercise, but the ample and sincere expression of personal emo-

[29] In connection with this matter of the connotations of Gray's vocabulary, it should be remarked that probably the poet was unconscious of part of his immense debt to many of his immediate predecessors and to his contemporaries. When he is indebted to Shakespeare or to the classics, he seems aware of that fact, and gives credit in his notes to the source of his inspiration, yet he often does not add footnotes in cases where the resemblance is close, as many commentators have noticed, to passages in other pensive and melancholy poems. The likeness to Parnell's *Night Piece,* for instance, is quite marked, but Gray does not mention Parnell in any of his correspondence, except once, and then the reference is a contemptuous one, to Parnell's religious poetry published in 1748. We may, perhaps, find the explanation of Gray's failure to indicate all his sources, in something he says of his apparent borrowing from Matthew Green. "The thought on which my second Ode turns, is manifestly stolen from hence: — not that I knew it at the time, but, having seen this many years before, to be sure, it imprinted itself on my memory, and forgetting the author, I took it for my own."

[30] For a full account of the special reasons for the use of this metre, see Gosse, E. W., *Gray,* pp. 98–99. For an account of the circumstances of publication and its popularity, *ibid.* pp. 99–105.

tion, felt by a poet of special endowment. The result is the supreme melancholy lyric of the eighteenth century, as *Il Penseroso* was of the seventeenth.

But the eighteenth century poet wears his rue with a difference.

We recall that in *L'Allegro,* Milton, accepting the contemporary view of melancholy as an abnormal state, banished it to a desert cell, and gave the poem up to the happy description of the cures for melancholy enumerated by Burton—"mirth and music," jesting, dancing, exercise (especially walking, hunting, and playing games), attendance at shows, tourneys, marriage festivities, and the reading of books and the theatre.[31] In *Il Penseroso,* he rose higher than his sources and casting aside these superficial remedies, gave an original description of the *vita contempliva* recommended, as Burton too reminds us, by pagan and Christian sages. This Melancholy is a goddess, under whose influence the solitary walk becomes the appreciative contemplation of natural beauty, and the lonely study is peopled with the high companionship of philosophers, tragic and epic poets, and divines. "The pleasures of melancholy" are noble, but they are still the pleasures of a cloistered temperament.

We have seen, too, that after Milton, the poetry of melancholy took a variety of uncouth shapes, now reflecting the seventeenth century interest in Horace, Lucretius, and the *Georgics,* now warped by a decadent puritanism into hideous descriptions of disease, death, and the horrors of doomsday, now falling into argument over the origin of evil, the justification of suicide, or the reasonableness of the hope of immortality. In the early eighteenth century, the melancholy poets, breathing a new scientific and philosophic atmosphere, learned to look once more with pleasure

[31] *Ante,* pp. 19, 22 and ch. I, note 29.

on the world of nature and of men, and poured out their new enthusiasm in rhapsodic description. They justified the solitary life, not so much on the ground that it is a harmless self-indulgence, or that detachment from the world gives leisure for study, as on Shaftesbury's ethical system: namely, that the contemplation of nature is good for the soul, inducing actual virtue, love of God, and benevolence towards man.

Common sense presently criticised these poets as self-deceived, returning to Burton's position that melancholy is a mood dangerous to the individual, not to be safely indulged. Under the influence of one part of Shaftesbury's philosophy, the followers of Pope also declared it dangerous to society, an excessive manifestation of "self-love." They further objected to the diffuseness and incoherence of the literary forms in which "enthusiasts" chiefly expressed themselves.

In response to these criticisms, after renewed contact with classical sources, and also under the impulse of fresh interest in Shakespeare and Milton's minor poems, melancholy poetry again culminated in a wave-crest of pure beauty. Thus, Gray's *Elegy* is not only rich in unselfish feeling, touched with sympathy for "the near, the low, the common"; it is also exquisite in form. Milton had presented Melancholy as enlightened and noble; Gray pictures it as lovely and humane.

BIBLIOGRAPHY

LIST OF WORKS QUOTED OR MENTIONED

In addition to the books listed below, I am, of course, indebted to many works of general scope dealing with literary history or the culture of the period, such as the Cambridge History of English Literature and the works of Lecky, Hettner, and Courthope, as well as to studies of romanticism by Beers, Phelps, Babbitt and others. Where the obligation is specific, I have acknowledged it in the notes but without including the titles here, since they are well known to all students of the eighteenth century. I have omitted also the titles of the usual philological journals.

For the classical authors mentioned, I have used the texts with translations of the Loeb Classical Library, except in the case of Lucretius, for whom I have consulted the works listed below under his name.

COLLECTIONS

The works of the poets discussed may be found in one of the following collections, unless another source is given in a footnote.

Braithwaite, William Stanley, comp. The Book of Elizabethan Verse. . . Boston, 1907.

—— The Book of Georgian Verse. . . New York, 1909.

Chalmers, Alexander, comp. The Works of the English Poets, from Chaucer to Cowper. . . London, 1810. 21 vols.

Park, Thomas, comp. The Works of the British Poets. . . London, 1805–9. 48 vols.

Early Poetical Miscellanies

A Collection of Poems: viz. The Temple of Death. . . with Several Original Poems never before Printed. . . London, Printed for Brown and Tooke, 1701.

A Collection of the Best English Poetry. By Several Hands, viz. Lord Rochester, Mr. Dryden, Sir John Denham, Lord Roscommon, Earl of Mulgrave, Sir Robert Howard, Mr. Phillips, Bishop Spratt, Mr. Waller, Dr. Swift, Mr. Addison, Sir Richard Blackmore, Mr. Milton, etc. London, 1717. 2 vols.

Curll, Edmund, comp. Sacred Miscellanies; or, Divine Poems upon Several Subjects. . . London, 1713.

Dodsley, Robert, comp. A Collection of Poems. . . by Several Hands. 5th ed. London, 1758. 6 vols. [1st ed. London, 1748. 3 vols.]

Dryden, John, comp. [Dryden was both a compiler, with Tonson, of the following Miscellanies and a contributor to them. I have listed the titles of the first editions in each case from the Grolier Club Catalogue of an Exhibition of First and Other Editions of the Works of John Dryden, New York, 1900. For description of their contents, see the Cambridge ed. of Dryden's Poetical Works, and the Cambridge Hist. of Eng. Lit., vol. VIII, Bibliography of Ch. I. The editions I have seen are the so-called third, and the fourth listed below.]

—— Miscellany Poems. Containing a New Translation of Virgil's Eclogues, Ovid's Love Elegies, Odes of Horace, and Other Authours; with Several Original Poems. By the Most Eminent Hands. . . London, 1684. [Known as Dryden's First Miscellany.]

—— Sylvae; or, The Second Part of Poetical Miscellanies. . . London, 1685. [Known as Dryden's Second Miscellany.]

—— Examen Poeticum: Being the Third Part of Miscellany Poems. . . London, 1693. [Known as Dryden's Third Miscellany.]

—— The Annual Miscellany; for the Year 1694, Being the Fourth Part of Miscellany Poems. . . London, 1694. [Known as Dryden's Fourth Miscellany.]

—— Poetical Miscellanies; the Fifth Part. Containing a Collection of Original Poems with Several New Translations. By the Most Eminent Hands. London, 1704. [Known as Dryden's Fifth Miscellany, though published after his death.]

—— [and TONSON, JACOB, comp.] Poetical Miscellanies; the Sixth Part. Containing a Collection of Original Poems with Several New Translations. By the Most Eminent Hands. London, 1709. [The first issue of this contained no poem by Dryden. Known as Tonson's Miscellany.]

—— [and TONSON, JACOB, comp.] Miscellany Poems. Containing Variety of New Translations of the Ancient Poets: together with Several Original Poems. By the Most Eminent Hands. Pub. by Mr. Dryden. . . 4th ed. London, 1716. 6 vols.

GILDON, CHARLES, comp. A New Miscellany of Original Poems on Several Occasions. . . London, 1701.

LEWIS, DAVID, comp. Miscellaneous Poems by Several Hands. . . London, 1726. 2d series. London, 1730.

LINTOT, BERNARD, comp. Miscellaneous Poems and Translations. By Several Hands. . . London, 1712.

RALPH, JAMES, comp. Miscellaneous Poems, by Several Hands; Particularly the D—— of W——n, Sir Samuel Garth, Dean S——, Mr. John Hughes, Mr. Thomson, Mrs. C——r. . . London, 1729.

RAMSAY, ALLAN, comp. The Ever Green; A Collection of Scots Poems Wrote by the Ingenious before 1600. Repr. from the original ed. Glasgow, 1875. 2 vols. [1st ed. 1724.]

—— The Tea Table Miscellany; or, a Collection of Choice Songs, Scots and English. Repr. from the 14th ed. Glasgow, 1871. 2 vols. [1st ed. 1724.]

SAVAGE, RICHARD, comp. Miscellaneous Poems and Translations. By Several Hands. . . London, 1726.

STEELE, SIR RICHARD, comp. Poetical Miscellanies, Consisting of Original Poems and Translations. By the Best Hands. . . 2d ed. London, 1727. [1st ed. 1713.]

TATE, NAHUM, comp. Poems by Several Hands and on Several Occasions. London, 1685.

—— Miscellanea Sacra; or Poems on Divine and Moral Subjects. London, 1696.

ADDISON, JOSEPH. The Miscellaneous Works of Joseph Addison. Ed. A. C. Guthketch. London, 1914. 2 vols.

AKENSIDE, MARK. *See* Bucke, Dyce.

—— Odes on Several Subjects. London, printed for R. Dodsley.

at Tully's Head in Pall Mall and sold by M. Cooper in Paternoster-Row, 1745. (1st ed.)

—— The Pleasures of Imagination. A Poem. In Three Books. . . London, printed by R. Dodsley at Tully's Head in Pall-Mall, 1744. [1st ed.]

—— Poetical Works of Mark Akenside. [Aldine ed. with Life by Rev. Alexander Dyce, 1834.] London, 1845.

ALDEN, RAYMOND MACDONALD. The Rise of Formal Satire in England under Classical Influence. Philadelphia, 1899. (University of Pennsylvania, Publications. Series in Philology, Literature, and Archaeology.)

ALGAROTTI, CONTE FRANCESCO. *See* Carter, Elizabeth, tr.

ARBER, EDWARD, ed. The Term Catalogues, 1668–1709 A.D.; with a Number for Easter Term, 1711, A.D. . . Privately Printed. London, 1903–6. 3 vols.

AUBREY, JOHN. "Brief Lives." Chiefly of Contemporaries, set down by John Aubrey, between the years 1669 and 1696. Ed. A. Clark. Oxford, 1898. 2 vols.

—— Miscellanies upon Various Subjects. 4th ed. London, 1857. (Library of Old Authors.)

BAKER, HENRY. The Universe; a Poem. Intended to Restrain the Pride of Man. . . London, [1727.]

BALDENSPERGER, FERNAND. Young et ses Nuits en France. In his Etudes d'Histoire littéraire, Paris, 1907, pp. 55–109.

BAXTER, RICHARD. Poetical Fragments; Heart-Imployment with God and It Self. . . 3rd ed. London, 1699. Additions to the Poetical Fragments. . . London, 1700.

—— Reliquiae Baxterianae. . . Faithfully Publish'd from His Own Original Manuscript, by M. Sylvester. London, 1696.

BELJAME, ALEXANDRE. Le Public et les Hommes de Lettres en Angleterre au dix-huitième Siècle, 1660–1744. . . Paris, 1881.

BENSLEY, EDWARD. Robert Burton, John Barclay, and John Owen. In Cambridge Hist. of Eng. Lit., vol. IV, ch. XIII.

BERNBAUM, ERNEST, ed. English Poets of the Eighteenth Century. Selected and ed. with int. by E. Bernbaum New York, c 1918.

BESANT, SIR WALTER. The Athenian Oracle; a Selection. Ed. J. Underhill. . . London, 1892.

BLACKMORE, SIR RICHARD. King Arthur; An Heroick Poem in Twelve Books. . . London, 1697.

BLAIR, ROBERT. *See* Müller.

—— The Grave; a Poem. Illustrated by Twelve Etchings Executed by L. Schiavonetti from the Original Inventions of William Blake. New ed. New York, 1903.

BOLINGBROKE, HENRY ST. JOHN, First Viscount. *See* Collins, Hassall, Sichel.

—— The Works of Lord Bolingbroke. With a Life. . . Philadelphia, 1841. 4 vols.

BOWRING, SIR JOHN, ed. Specimens of the Polish Poets. . . . London, Printed for the Author, 1827.

BOYSE, SAMUEL. Retirement; a Poem Occasioned by Seeing the Palace and Park of Yester. . . Edinburgh, 1735.

BRADLEY, ANDREW CECIL. Shakespearean Tragedy. . . London, 1904.

BREWSTER, DOROTHY. Aaron Hill; Poet, Dramatist, Projector. New York, 1913. (Columbia University Studies in English and Comparative Literature.)

BRÜCKNER, ALEXANDER. Geschichte der polnischen Literatur. Leipzig, 1901.

BUCKE, CHARLES. On the Life, Writings, and Genius of Akenside, with Some Account of his Friends. London, 1832.

BURNET, GILBERT, Bishop of Salisbury. Bishop Burnet's History of His Own Times; with Notes by the Earls of Dartmouth and Hardwick, Speaker Onslow, and Dean Swift. . . 2d ed. enl. Oxford, 1833. 6 vols.

BURTON, ROBERT. *See* Bensley.

—— The Anatomy of Melancholy, What It Is, with All the Kinds, Causes, Symptoms, Prognostics and Several Cures of It. . . By Democritus Junior. . . New ed. by Democritus Minor. Boston, 1859. 3 vols.

CARTER, ELIZABETH. *See* Pennington.

—— Poems on Several Occasions. In Pennington, M., Memoirs of the Life of Mrs. Elizabeth Carter. . . 3rd ed. London, 1816.

—— tr. Sir Isaac Newton's Philosophy Explain'd for the Use of the Ladies. In Six Dialogues on Light and Colours. From the Italian of Sig. Algarotti. . . London, 1739.

—— [and Talbot, Catherine.] A Series of Letters. . . from the Year 1741 to 1770. . . London, 1809. 4 vols.

CHILD, FRANCIS JAMES, ed. The English and Scottish Popular Ballads. Boston [c. 1882–98.] 5 vols. in 10.

CHUDLEIGH, LADY MARY LEE. *See* Reynolds.

—— Essays upon Several Subjects in Prose and Verse. London, 1710.

—— Poems on Several Occasions. By the Lady Chudleigh. 3rd ed. corr. London, 1722.

COLLINS, JOHN CHURTON. Bolingbroke, an Historical Study; and, Voltaire in England. London, 1886.

COLLINS, WILLIAM. Poems. . . Ed. with int. and notes by Walter C. Bronson. Boston, [c. 1898.] (Athenaeum Press Series.)

COURTHOPE, WILLIAM JOHN. The Liberal Movement in English Literature. London, 1885.

COURTNEY, WILLIAM PRIDEAUX. A Bibliography of Samuel Johnson. Rev. . . by D. N. Smith. Oxford, 1915. (Oxford Historical and Literary Studies.)

COWLEY, ABRAHAM. Essays, Plays, and Sundry Verses. Ed. A. R. Waller. Cambridge, 1906.

—— Poems. . . Ed. A. R. Waller. Cambridge, 1905.

CUNNINGHAM, PETER. James Thomson and The Winter's Day. In Gentleman's Magazine, vol. XXXIX, pp. 368–9. (April, 1853.)

DEFOE, DANIEL. *See* Lee, Nicholson, Trent.

—— A True Relation of the Apparition of Mrs. Veal. In his Novels and Miscellaneous Works with. . . Memoir [by J. Ballantyne]. . . Oxford, 1840–41, vol. V.

DENNIS, JOHN. *See* Paul.

—— Select Works. . . London, 1718. 2 vols.

DICTIONARIES.

BLOUNT, T., comp. Glossographia; or, a Dictionary Interpreting All Such Hard Words. . . As Are Now Used in Our Refined English Tongue. . . London, 1670. New ed. London, 1707.

COLES, E., comp. An English Dictionary. . . Containing Many Thousand of Hard Works. . . together with The Etymological Derivation of Them. . . By E. Coles. . . London, 1717.

BAILEY, N., comp. Dictionarium Britannicum; or, A More Compleat Universal Etymological English Dictionary Than Any Extant. Coll. by Several Hands. Rev. . . by N. Bailey. London, 1730.

—— [and Scott, J. N., comp.] A New Universal Etymological English Dictionary. . . Originally Compiled by N. Bailey. Rev. and corr. by J. N. Scott. London, 1755.

JOHNSON, SAMUEL, comp. A Dictionary of the English Language. . . By Samuel Johnson. . . London, 1755. 2 vols.

MURRAY, J. A. H., comp. A New English Dictionary on Historical Principles. . . Oxford, 1888–1923.

DODSLEY, ROBERT. *See* Straus.

DONNE, JOHN. *See* Gosse, Ramsay, Spearing, Walton.

—— Devotions . . . with Two Sermons . . . To which is prefixed his Life by Izaak Walton. London, 1840.

—— Donne's Sermons: Selected Passages. With an Essay by Logan Pearsall Smith. Oxford, 1919.

—— The Poems of John Donne. Ed. from the old editions and numerous manuscripts with introductions and commentary by Herbert J. C. Grierson. . . Oxford, 1912. 2 vols.

DRELINCOURT, C. The Christian's Defence against the Fears of Death: with Directions How to Die Well. . . Abridged from the last French ed. by J. Milbank. . . To which is prefixed, an account of Mrs. Veal's apparition to Mrs. Bargrave. London, 1764.

DRUMMOND, WILLIAM. Poems of William Drummond. . . Ed. W. C. Ward. London, 1894. 2 vols.

DRYDEN, JOHN. Essays. . . selected and ed. by W. P. Ker. Oxford, 1900. 2 vols.

—— Poetical Works. . . Ed. G. R. Noyes. Cambridge ed. Boston, 1908.

—— Miscellany Poems. *See* EARLY POETICAL MISCELLANIES, Dryden, John, comp.

—— Works. . . With Notes. . . . and a Life of the Author by Sir Walter Scott. Ed. G. Saintsbury. Edinburgh, 1882–93. 18 vols.

DURHAM, WILLARD HIGLEY, ed. Critical Essays of the Eighteenth Century, 1700–1725. . . . New Haven, 1915.

DYCE, REV. ALEXANDER. Life of Akenside. In Akenside, Mark, Poetical Works. (Aldine ed.), London, 1845.

DYER, JOHN. *See* Greever.

ERASMUS, DESIDERIUS. Epistles. . . English translations by F. M. Nichols. London, 1901–1918. 3 vols.

FLATMAN, THOMAS. Poems and Songs. 3rd ed. . . London, 1682. 4th ed. London, 1686.

FLETCHER, JOHN. Nice Valour; a Comedy. In Works of Francis Beaumont and John Fletcher, ed., A. Glover and A. R. Waller, Cambridge, 1905–12, vol. X.

FONTENELLE, BERNARD LE BOVIER DE. A Week's Conversation on the Plurality of Worlds. . . 6th ed. tr. by Mrs. A. Behn, Mr. J. Glanvil, John Hughes, Esq., and William Gardner, Esq.

To which is added Mr. Addison's Defence on the New Philosophy. London, 1737.

Foster, Finley Melville Kendall. English Translations from the Greek; a Bibliographical Survey. New York, 1918. (Columbia University Studies in English and Comparative Literature.)

Fowler, Thomas. Shaftesbury and Hutcheson. New York, 1883. (English Philosophers.)

Gay, John. Poems on Several Occasions. . . London, 1720. 2 vols.

Good, John Walter. Studies in the Milton Tradition. . . Urbana, Ill., 1915. (University of Illinois Studies in Language and Literature.)

Gosse, Edmund William. Life and Letters of John Donne. . . New York, 1899. 2 vols.

—— Gray. New York, 1882. (English Men of Letters.)

Gray, Thomas. *See* Gosse, Northup, Toynbee, Tovey.

—— Letters. . . Including the Correspondence of Gray and Mason. Ed. D. C. Tovey. London, 1909–13. 3 vols. [Vol. 2 is the 2d ed. rev.]

—— Works . . in Prose and Verse. Ed. E. Gosse. London, 1884. 4 vols.

—— Walpole, Horace, and others. Correspondence of Gray, Walpole, West, and Ashton, 1734–1771. Ed. P. Toynbee. Oxford, 1915. 2 vols.

Green, Matthew. The Spleen; an Epistle. . . 3rd ed. corr. . . To Which Is Added Some Other Pieces by the Same Hand. . . London, 1738.

Greever, Garland. The Two Versions of Gronger Hill. In Jour. of Eng. and Ger. Philol., vol. XVI, 2, pp. 274–281. (April, 1917).

Hammond, James. Love Elegies. Written in the Year 1732. . . 5th ed. London, 1762.

Hassall, Arthur. Life of Viscount Bolingbroke. Oxford, 1915.

Havens, Raymond Dexter. The Influence of Milton on English Poetry. Cambridge, Mass., 1922.

—— The Literature of Melancholy. In Mod. Lang. Notes., vol. XXIV, pp. 226–7. (Nov., 1909.)

Hazeltine, Alice I. A Study of William Shenstone and of His Critics, with Fifteen of His Unpublished Poems, and Five of His Unpublished Latin Inscriptions. Menasha, Wis., 1918.

Hervey, James. Meditations and Contemplations. . . 20th ed. Edinburgh, 1767.

Hill, Aaron. *See* Brewster.
The Works of the Late Aaron Hill. . . 2nd ed. London, 1753. 4 vols.

Hutcheson, Francis. *See* Fowler, Scott, W. R.

—— System of Moral Philosophy. . . Pub. by his son, F. Hutcheson. . . [With] some account of the author by the Rev. W. Leechman. London, 1755. 2 vols. in 1.

Jacob, Giles. The Poetical Register; or, The Lives and Characters of All the English Poets. With an Account of Their Writings. London, 1723. 2 vols.

Johnson, Samuel. *See* Courtney.

—— Lives of the English Poets. . . . Ed. G. B. Hill. . . Oxford, 1905. 3 vols.

—— Works. . . Literary Club ed. Troy, N. Y. [1903]. 16 vols.

Kind, John Louis. Edward Young in Germany. New York, 1906.

King, Henry. The English Poems of Henry King, D.D. . . Ed. L. Mason. New Haven, 1914.

Krutch, Joseph Wood. Comedy and Conscience after the Restoration. (Not yet published. Columbia dissertation.)

Lee, William. Daniel Defoe: His Life and Recently Discovered Writings; Extending from 1716 to 1720. London, 1869. 3 vols.

Legg, L. G. Wickham. Matthew Prior: A Study of His Public Career and Correspondence. Cambridge, 1921.

Lucretius. *See* Martha, Masson.

—— De Rerum Natura libri sex. With notes and a translation by H. A. J. Munro. 3rd ed. Cambridge, 1873. 2 vols.

—— Lucretius on the Nature of Things. Tr. C. Bailey. Oxford, 1910.

Macaulay, George Campbell. James Thomson. London, 1907. (English Men of Letters.)

Martha, C. Le Poème de Lucrèce; Morale, Religion, Science. 4e éd. Paris, n. d.

Masson, John. Lucretius: Epicurean and Poet. New York, 1907–9. 2 vols.

Milton, John. *See* Good, Havens.

—— L'Allegro, Il Penseroso, Comus, and Lycidas. Ed. W. P. Trent. New York, 1898.

—— Poems upon Several Occasions, English, Italian, and Latin, with Translations by John Milton. . . With Notes Critical and Explanatory. . . by Thomas Warton. . . London, 1785.

—— Poetical Works. Milton, John. Ed. D. Masson. 2d ed. London, 1890. 3 vols.

Montalembert, Charles Forbes René de Tryon, Comte de. Monks of the West from St. Benedict to St. Bernard. . . [Tr. from the French.] London, 1861-69. 7 vols.

Moore, Cecil Albert. Shaftesbury and the Ethical Poets in England, 1700–1760. In Mod. Lang. Assn. of America, Publications, vol. XXXI, pp. 264–325. (New series, vol. XXIV, 1916).

More, Paul Elmer. With the Wits. Boston, 1919. (The Shelburne Essays, 10th series.)

Morel, Léon. James Thomson; Sa Vie et Ses Oeuvres. Paris, 1895.

Müller, Carl. Robert Blair's " Grave " und die Grabes- und Nachtdichtung. . . Weimar, 1909.

Neilson, William Allan. Essentials of Poetry. Lowell Lectures, 1911. . . Boston, 1912.

Nicholson, Watson. The Historical Sources of Defoe's Journal of the Plague Year. Illustrated by extracts from the original documents in the Burney Collection and Manuscript Room in the British Museum. Boston, 1919.

Norris, John. A Collection of Miscellanies. . . 4th ed. rev. by the author. London, 1706. 5th ed. London, 1710.

Northup, Clark Sutherland. A Bibliography of Thomas Gray. New Haven, 1917. (Cornell Studies in English.)

Oldham, John. Works of Mr. John Oldham, together with His Remains. . . London, 1722. 2 vols.

Palgrave, Francis Turner. Landscape in Poetry from Homer to Tennyson. . . London, 1897.

Parnell, Thomas. Poems on Several Occasions. . . Published by Mr. Pope. London. 1722. [With Life by Oliver Goldsmith, 1770.]

—— Poetical Works. Ed. J. Mitford. London, 1833.

—— Poetical Works. Ed. G. A. Aitken. London, 1894.

Paul, Harry Gilbert. John Dennis; His Life and Criticism. New York, 1911. (Columbia University Studies in English).

Pennington, Rev. Montagu. Memoirs of the Life of Mrs. Elizabeth

Carter, With a New Edition of Her Poems; to Which Are Added Some Miscellaneous Essays in Prose. . . 3rd ed. London, 1816. 2 vols.

POMFRET, JOHN. The Choice; a Poem by a Person of Quality. 2d ed. London, 1700.

POPE, ALEXANDER. *See* Vater, Warton, J.

—— Works, New ed. . . collected in part by. . . J. W. Croker. With int. and notes by the Rev. W. Elwin and W. J. Courthope. London, 1871–89. 10 vols.

PRIOR, MATTHEW. *See* Legg.

Poems on Several Occasions. . . London, 1718. Ed. A. R. Waller, Cambridge, 1905.

RALEIGH, SIR WALTER. Poems. . . Collected and Authenticated with Those of Sir Henry Wotton and Other Courtly Poets. . . 1540–1650. Ed. J. Hannah. London, 1892.

RALPH, JAMES. Miscellaneous Poems, viz.: Night. . . Zeuma, or the Love of Liberty. . . Clarinda, or, the Fair Libertine. . . The Muse's Address. . . London, 1729.

RAMSAY, MARY PATON. Les Doctrines Mediévales chez Donne, le Poète métaphysicien de l'Angleterre (1573–1631). London. . . 1917.

RAND, BENJAMIN. Life, Unpublished Letters, and Philosophical Regimen of Anthony, Earl of Shaftesbury. . . London, 1900.

REYNOLDS, MYRA. The Learned Lady in England 1650–1760. Boston. . . 1920. (Vassar Semi-Centennial Series.)

—— The Treatment of Nature in English Poetry between Pope and Wordsworth. [2d ed.] Chicago, 1909.

RICCALTOUN, ROBERT. A Winter's Day. Written by a Scotch Clergyman. Corr. by an Eminent Hand. In Gentleman's Magazine, vol. X. p. 256. (May, 1740.) *See* Cunningham.

RINAKER, CLARISSA. Thomas Warton; a Biographical and Critical Study. [Urbana, Ill., 1916.]

ROBERTSON, JOHN MACKINNON. Pioneer Humanists. London, 1907.

ROWE, MRS. ELIZABETH (SINGER). *See* Reynolds, Wolf.

—— Friendship in Death: in Twenty Letters from the Dead to the Living. To which are added, Letters Moral and Entertaining in Prose and Verse. 3 pts. New York, 1795.

—— The Miscellaneous Works in Prose and Verse. . . [Ed.] by Mr. Theophilus Rowe. To which are added, Poems on Several

Occasions by Mr. Thomas Rowe, and to the whole is prefixed, An Account of the Lives and Writings of the Authours. London, 1739. 2 vols.

SANDYS, SIR JOHN EDWIN. A History of Classical Scholarship. . . Cambridge, 1903–8. 3 vols.

SCOTT, JOHN. Critical Essays on Some of the Poems of Several English Poets. . . With an Account of the Life and Writings of the Author. By Mr. Hoole. London, 1785.

SCOTT, WILLIAM ROBERT. Francis Hutcheson; His Life, Teaching, and Position in the History of Philosophy. . . Cambridge, 1900.

SELLAR, WILLIAM YOUNG. The Roman Poets of the Republic. 3rd ed. Oxford, 1905.

SHAFTESBURY, ANTHONY ASHLEY COOPER, Third Earl of. *See* Fowler, Moorè, Rand, Robertson.

—— Characteristicks of Men, Manners, Opinions, Times. . . 5th ed. Birmingham, 1773. 3 vols.

—— Characteristicks of Men, Manners, Opinions, Times, etc. . . Ed. with int. and notes by John M. Robertson. London, 1900. 2 vols.

SHENSTONE, WILLIAM. *See* Hazeltine, Wells.

—— Works in Verse and Prose. . . London, 1764–9. 3 vols.

SHERLOCK, WILLIAM. Practical Discourse Concerning Death. . . 27th (?) ed. London, 1751.

SICHEL, WALTER. Bolingbroke and His Times. London, 1901–2. 2 vols.

SOBIESKI, or SARBIEWSKI, MATTHEW CASIMIR. *See* Bowring.

SPEARING, EVELYN M. Donne's Sermons, and Their Relation to his Poetry. In Modern Language Review, vol. VII, pp. 40–53. (Jan., 1912.)

STOLL, ELMAR EDGAR. Hamlet: An Historical and Comparative Study. Minneapolis, (1919). (Research Publications of the University of Minnesota. Studies in Language and Literature, no. 7.)

SPINGARN, JOEL ELIAS, ed. Critical Essays of the Seventeenth Century. . . Oxford, 1908–9. 3 vols.

STRAUS, RALPH. Robert Dodsley; Poet, Publisher, and Playwright. . . London, 1910.

SWIFT, JONATHAN. Correspondence. . . Ed. F. E. Ball. With int. by the very Rev. J. H. Bernard. London, 1910–14. 6 vols.

—— Poems. . . Ed. W. E. Browning. London, 1910. 2 vols.

—— Prose Works. . . Ed. T. Scott. With a biographical int. by W. E. H. Lecky. London, 1897–1908. 12 vols.

—— Unpublished Letters of Dean Swift. Ed. G. B. Hill. . . London, 1899.

TATE, NAHUM. Poems Written on Several Occasions. 2d ed. enl. London, 1684.

TEMPLE, SIR WILLIAM. Sir William Temple's Essays on Ancient and Modern Language and on Poetry. Ed. J. E. Spingarn. Oxford, 1909.

TEXTE, JOSEPH. Jean-Jacques Rousseau et les Origines du Cosmopolitisme littéraire. Paris, 1895.

THOMAS, WALTER. Le Poète Edward Young (1683–1765). Etude sur sa Vie et ses Oeuvres. Paris, 1901.

THOMSON, JAMES. *See* Cunningham, Macaulay, Morel, Riccaltoun.

—— Complete Poetical Works. . . Ed. with notes by J. Logie Robertson. London, 1908.

—— Thomson's "Seasons" Critical ed. . . . by O. Zippel. Berlin, 1908. (Palaestra LXVI).

TOVEY, DUNCAN C., ed. Gray and His Friends; Letters and Relics in Great Part Hitherto Unpublished. Ed. D. C. Tovey. Cambridge, 1890.

TRENT, WILLIAM PETERFIELD. Daniel Defoe; How to Know Him. . . Indianapolis, Ind., [c. 1916].

TUCKER, SAMUEL MARION. Verse-Satire in England before the Renaissance. New York, 1908. (Columbia University Studies in English.)

TUCKER, THOMAS GEORGE. The Foreign Debt of English Literature. . . London, 1907.

VATER, PAUL. . . Pope und Shaftesbury. Halle, 1897.

WALPOLE, HORACE, Fourth Earl of Orford. Letters. . . Chronologically arranged and ed. with notes and indices by P. Toynbee. . . Oxford, 1913–15. 16 vols. in 8. Supplement to the Letters. . . Ed with notes and indices by P. Toynbee. . . Oxford, 1918. 2 vols.

WARTON, JOSEPH. An Essay on the Writings and Genius of Pope. 5th ed. . . London, 1806. 2 vols.

WARTON, THOMAS. *See* Rinaker.

—— The Poetical Works of the Late Thomas Warton. . . 5th ed. corr. and enl. . . Together with Memoirs of his Life and Writings; and Notes, by Richard Mant. Oxford, 1802. 2 vols.

WATTS, ISAAC. Horae Lyricae. . . 3rd ed. . . London, 1715.

WELLS, JOHN EDWIN. The Dating of Shenstone's Letters. In Anglia, XXXV, 429–52. (Neue folge, bd. XXIII.)

WIGGLESWORTH, MICHAEL. The Day of Doom. In part in A Library of American Literature. . . Ed. Stedman and Hutchinson. New ed. vol. II, p. 9.

WINCHILSEA, ANNE FINCH, Countess of. Poems. . . Ed. with int. and notes by Myra Reynolds. . . Chicago, 1903. (University of Chicago Decennial Publications.)

WOLF, LOUISE. Elisabeth Rowe in Deutschland. Ein Beitrag zur Literaturgeschichte des 18. Jahrhunderts. Heidelberg, 1910. (Diss.)

WOTTON, SIR HENRY. Reliquiae Wottonianae: or, A Collection of Lives, Letters, Poems, with Characters of Sundry Personages. . . . 4th ed. London, 1685.

YOUNG, EDWARD. *See* Baldensperger, Kind, Texte, Thomas, Zippel.

—— The Works of the Author of the Night-Thoughts. . . Rev. and corr. by himself. New ed. London, 1792. 3 vols.

ZIPPEL, OTTO. Entstehungs- und Entwicklungsgeschichte von Thomson's "Winter". . . Berlin, 1907.

INDEX OF AUTHORS